Blue Ridge Folklife

Folklife in the South Series

Cajun Country
by Barry Jean Ancelet, Jay Edwards, and Glen Pitre

Kentucky Bluegrass Country
by R. Gerald Alvey

Upper Cumberland Country
by William Lynwood Montell

South Florida Folklife
by Tina Bucuvalas, Peggy Bulger, and Stetson Kennedy

Great Smoky Mountains Folklife
by Michael Ann Williams

Ozark Country
by W. K. McNeil

Carolina Piedmont Country
by John M. Coggeshall

Wiregrass Country
by Jerrilyn McGregory

William Lynwood Montell, General Editor, Folklife in the South Series

Blue Ridge Folklife

Ted Olson

Ted Olson

UNIVERSITY PRESS OF MISSISSIPPI *Jackson*

Copyright © 1998 by University Press of Mississippi

All rights reserved

Manufactured in the United States of America

01 00 99 98   4 3 2 1

The paper in this book meets the guidelines for
permanence and durability of the Committee on
Production Guidelines for Book Longevity of
the Council on Library Resources.

Library of Congress Cataloging-in-Publication Data

Olson, Ted.

    Blue Ridge folklife / Ted Olson.

       p.   cm. — (Folklife in the South series)

    Includes bibliographical references (p.   ) and index.

    ISBN 1-57806-022-2 (cloth : alk. paper). — ISBN 1-57806-023-0
(paper : alk. paper)

     1. Blue Ridge Mountains Region—Social life and customs.
2. Country life—Blue Ridge Mountains Region.   3. Folklore—Blue
Ridge Mountains Region. I. Title. II. Series.

F217.B6047   1998

975.5—dc21   97-27218
                                                          CIP

British Library Cataloging-in-Publication data available

C O N T E N T S

.

Folklife, a familiar concept in European scholarship for over a century, is the sum of a community's traditional forms of expression and behavior. It has claimed the attention of American folklorists since the 1950s. Each volume in the Folklife in the South Series focuses on the shared traditions that link people with their past and provide meaning and continuity for them in the present, and sets these traditions in the social contexts in which they flourish. Prepared by recognized scholars in various academic disciplines, these volumes are designed to be read separately. Each contains a vivid description of one region's traditional cultural elements—ethnic and mainstream, rural and urban—that, in concert with those of other recognizable southern regions, lend a unique interpretation to the complex social structure of the South.

The Blue Ridge region, which stretches along the Appalachian chain through portions of present day Georgia, North and South Carolina, Tennessee, Virginia, and West Virginia, was virtually forsaken during the nineteenth century's period of western expansion, by which time hardy colonists from the region had followed Daniel Boone, its most famous settler, into the frontier. Ted Olson provides keen insight into the folkways that developed in the wake of that migration. Olson's account discusses consequential political, social, economic, and environmental issues and identifies the Anglo-American, Celtic-American, German-American, African-American, and Cherokee influences on the culture of the region. His work provides a holistic approach to a region that has been documented in numerous books and articles but whose traditions have never been treated so comprehensively.

William Lynwood Montell
SERIES EDITOR

It is highly unlikely that I would have written this book without the encouragement of a number of people, and I would like to take this opportunity to acknowledge some of them. First, for supporting me in my various endeavors over the years, thanks to my mother, Claire Thomes Olson (a special acknowledgment is in order here, since she is the one who entrusted me with the family car when I was in high school so that I might explore the Blue Ridge on weekends), my siblings, Peter, Martha, Rick, and Libby, and my stepfather, Neil Clark. My late father, Kenneth G. Olson, who lived for a time in the Virginia Blue Ridge, was deeply interested in traditional cultures worldwide, and he often sent me fascinating books on such subjects.

I learned a lot about the Southern Appalachians while working at the Burgundy Center for Wildlife Studies in Hampshire County, West Virginia, and I would like to thank the directors, staff, students, and parents affiliated with that excellent educational program for allowing me to introduce a folklore/folklife curriculum. For their roles in the production of this book, I am grateful to Dr. William Lynwood Montell for originally bestowing upon me this assignment, to those associated with the University Press of Mississippi for their patience, to the many writers and scholars who charted the course for the study of Blue Ridge cultural history, and to the photographers who contributed to this book some profound and insightful images of the region. Finally, I would like to express my appreciation for the people I have met from the Blue Ridge, who have always been gracious hosts and friends.

Small portions of this book originally appeared, usually in somewhat different form, in several periodicals (*Appalachian Heritage, Appalachian Journal, Goldenseal, The Journal of the Appalachian Studies Association, Living Blues*, and *The State: Down Home in North Carolina*), and I would like to thank all the publishers and editors who facilitated their original publication.

The Blue Ridge often lives up to the name it was given several centuries ago by European mapmakers. On summer days the forests growing on Blue Ridge slopes emit huge quantities of hydrocarbons, which, when mixed with the region's characteristically humid air, distort the dense vegetation's green hue into a hazy, dreamy blue.

This book explores the folklife of most of the area geographers have called the Blue Ridge Mountain Province. Those geographers rightfully included the section of the Blue Ridge located in Pennsylvania and Maryland—a much less significant landmass than the Blue Ridge of the southern states—in their definition, while this book, more concerned with cultural than with geographical boundaries, rightfully omits that section, which is in part above the Mason-Dixon line and thus out of the scope, culturally and geographically, of the Folklife in the South Series. Duly noted, though, will be important aspects of traditional culture transported by settlers from Pennsylvania and Maryland into the Virginia and North Carolina Blue Ridge during the eighteenth century.

The section of the Blue Ridge explored here, which ranges from northern Virginia and the West Virginia panhandle to northeast Georgia and northwest South Carolina, is, cultural geographers might argue, technically not a "region," but rather a "subregion" of the Southern Appalachian "region." The term "subregion," though, seems inadequate for describing such a large geographical area, especially one which has fostered such a distinct cultural history. The term "province," from the aforementioned geographical term for the Blue Ridge, seems likewise inadequate for identifying a cultural area defined as much by unique historical, social, economic, political, and environmental circumstances as by geography. Thus, the Blue Ridge will be referred to as a region in this book. Indeed, this particular region deserves the dignity of that label, since it has figured so prominently in colonial and national history, and since its unique cultural history has been so influential in the evolution of other Appalachian regional cultures, as well as southern regional cultures (e.g., central Kentucky), midwestern regional cultures (e.g., the Ozarks), and mainstream American culture.

The Blue Ridge is one of the oldest ranges in the Appalachian chain, which in turn is one the oldest mountain chains in the world. Comprising

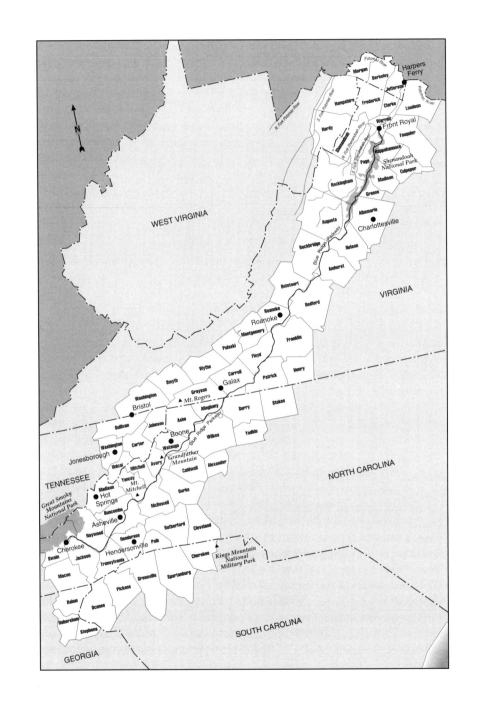

many separate mountain ranges located between Quebec's Gaspe Peninsula and Georgia and Alabama, the Appalachian chain is often divided by geographers into the "Northern" Appalachians (which includes all Appalachian ranges north of central Pennsylvania) and the "Southern" Appalachians (including the Blue Ridge, the Great Smokies, the Alleghenies, and other Appalachian ranges in the southeastern United States). Created by the collision of plates of the earth's crust, the Blue Ridge, before volcanic melting (in some areas) and constant weathering eroded the range to its present height, probably stood as high as the Himalayas stand today. Its rock (mostly metamorphic, with some igneous in its more southerly sections) dating back more than a billion years to the Precambrian era when simple aquatic plants were the only living creatures on Earth, the Blue Ridge offers no trace of the fossil record—and none of the coal deposits—so common in the sedimentary rock of the younger mountain ranges to its west.

The easternmost range in the Southern Appalachians, the Blue Ridge extends southwestward from Harrisburg, Pennsylvania, to northeast Georgia and northwest South Carolina. Along the way it passes through a slice of Maryland, the West Virginia panhandle, western Virginia, a small section of northeastern Tennessee, and western North Carolina. Although for the most part a continuous mountain mass, the Blue Ridge is interrupted in a few places by rivers—specifically, the Potomac and Shenandoah, the James, and the Roanoke. From its modest beginnings as a low escarpment in Pennsylvania and Maryland, the Blue Ridge rises south of Front Royal, Virginia, and takes on the appearance of a vegetated wall separating the Virginia piedmont to the east and the Great Valley of the Appalachians to the west. In the northern Virginia section of the Great Valley is the Shenandoah River, which flows northeastward in two forks around Massanutten Mountain (a long, low ridge paralleling the Blue Ridge); these forks converge near Front Royal, whereupon the Shenandoah River continues flowing northeastward, eventually emptying into the Potomac River at Harpers Ferry, West Virginia. The fertile Shenandoah River watershed and Massanutten Mountain and the low sedimentary ridges just to the west of that watershed may be quite different from the Blue Ridge in terms of geology, but their cultural history is interrelated.

From Front Royal to Roanoke, the Blue Ridge range is narrow and generally between 3,000 and 4,000 feet in height; high peaks in this section include Hawksbill Mountain in Shenandoah National Park (4,049 feet above sea level), Apple Orchard Mountain (4,225 feet), and Pleasant Mountain (4,054 feet). Nearby are two internationally renowned landmarks: Natural Bridge in Rockbridge County, once surveyed by George Washington and owned by Thomas Jefferson, and still heralded as one of the "seven natural wonders of the world"; and, in Charlottesville, Jefferson's architectural masterpiece, Monticello.

South of Roanoke the Blue Ridge is a broad and relatively low plateau (with few elevations above 3,000 feet); the most prominent peak in this section is Buffalo Mountain (3,971 feet). Near the Virginia-North Carolina border, just west of the Blue Ridge plateau on the other side of the New River, looms a separate, impressive complex of mountains (known locally as the Grayson Highlands) which features the highest peak in Virginia, Mt. Rogers (5,729 feet). Once in North Carolina, the Blue Ridge itself attains great height at Grandfather Mountain (5,964 feet). Situated to the east of the Blue Ridge throughout this section are various foothills, as well as separate clusters of low hills like the Brushy Mountains. To the west of the Blue Ridge, running parallel along the North Carolina-Tennessee border, are the majestic Unakas (composed of separately named ranges, including the Iron, the Unicoi, and the Great Smoky Mountains), featuring such high elevations as Roan Mountain (6,285 feet), Mt. Guyot (6,621 feet), and Clingman's Dome (6,643 feet). Southwest of Spruce Pine, North Carolina (the central town in an area of mineral mining), several spur ranges angle between the Blue Ridge and the Unakas, including the Black Mountains (one of which is the highest peak in the eastern United States: Mt. Mitchell, at 6,684 feet), the Great Craggies, and the Great Balsams. Divided by steep river valleys, these spur ranges combine with the Blue Ridge and the Unakas to form one of the most rugged landscapes in all of Southern Appalachia. South of Asheville, declining in height but not in width, the Blue Ridge continues into northeast Georgia and northwest South Carolina before petering out.

Despite its length and narrowness the Blue Ridge possesses a distinct natural history. The range's higher elevations harbor localized populations of many plants and animals native to the northern United States and Canada, a reminder of the fact that, over ten thousand years ago, glaciers covered much of what is now the northern United States, and northern species temporarily found refuge in the south. After a warming climate melted the glaciers, these species returned north and died out in what is now the southern United States, except in the highest peaks of the Southern Appalachians. Naturalists since colonial days have delighted in exploring (to quote from Marcus B. Simpson, Jr.) the Blue Ridge region's "biological archipelago of northern species surrounded by, and intermingled with, the flora and fauna of the Southeast."

Also distinct, because of unique circumstances of settlement, is the Blue Ridge region's cultural history. In the years preceding the founding of this nation, the Blue Ridge region was the frontier, a mountain wilderness in which hardy, independent settlers from several cultural backgrounds—

disaffected lower-class English people, Celtic people, and other Europeans who did not fit into Anglo-dominated colonial society—formed their own societies. In 1772, the Blue Ridge was the site of the Watauga Association, the first democratic, representative government ever formed in North America. In 1780, settlers from the region defeated Patrick Ferguson's army of British loyalists at the Battle of Kings Mountain, helping to win the Revolutionary War for the patriots. Shortly thereafter, settlers in the southernmost section of the Blue Ridge staged the nation's first gold rush, which sped up the forced eviction of the region's aboriginal residents, including the tragic displacement of the predominant native group, the Cherokee, during the Trail of Tears in the 1830s (a deeply ironic episode in American history, given the fact that settlers from the Old World had endured the difficulties of living in this rugged New World wilderness in large part because they had borrowed so heavily from regional Native American cultural traditions).

By the early nineteenth century, many settlers had followed the most famous Blue Ridge settler, Daniel Boone, in pushing the frontier westward. The large-scale abandonment of the Blue Ridge was a direct result of settlers having overpopulated the region and having exhausted its natural resources, especially wild game. Those who remained behind, however geographically isolated and politically and economically marginalized, created fulfilling lives for themselves by forging an effective and often sophisticated folklife, the earliest non-Native American traditional culture in Southern Appalachia. Some manifestations of this folklife still survive in the Blue Ridge, since the region was spared, by coincidence of geology and topography, from the more environmentally damaging embodiments of industrialization (coal mining and dam building) which so heavily affected traditional cultures in later-settled southern mountain ranges (such as the Great Smokies, the Alleghenies, and the Cumberlands).

The term folklore refers to an individualized use of some tradition, whether it be a particular element of traditional knowledge utilized by one person to conduct an everyday task, or a particular type of traditional communication employed by people interacting with others in a specific social situation, or a particular action performed in a traditional manner for a traditional purpose (i.e., not for money or status). Folklife is a composite term which encompasses all the folklore (whether thought, communicated verbally, or acted out) practiced in a given region. A region's folklife is, simply put, the everyday life of the people (individuals, families, and all the other groups) within that region. Each region possesses a different folklife, since the particular combination of historical, social, economic, political, environmental, and geographical factors influencing the evolution of such folklife is unique to that region. Folklife is learned traditionally—that is, people learn their region's folklife from those of the same or of a previous generation by means of informal and unself-conscious verbal instruction and/or demonstration, and not through more formal modes of teaching (like schools or workshops). Folklife tends to be rural and pre-industrial—it is not elite (i.e., official and institutional) culture or mass culture, but rather the culture of "folk" who live in a particular place and who observe the particular traditions associated with that place (as, in most cases, their ancestors did before them).

Blue Ridge Folklife traces the historical development of the traditional culture which evolved in the Blue Ridge region. Before surveying the various manifestations of folklife in the region, the book discusses numerous historical events which in some way contributed to the shaping of traditional Blue Ridge culture. Interesting in and of itself, this background information underscores the important role of the Blue Ridge in the history of this nation and illustrates the significant influence of the region's traditional culture on the emerging American culture. After two chapters of historical background, the book surveys, over three chapters, many characteristic, significant, and fascinating manifestations of the verbal, customary, and material folklife traditions found in the Blue Ridge. The book concludes with a look at the Blue Ridge today.

CHAPTER I

The Blue Ridge Region through 1800

Native Americans

The first human settlers in the Blue Ridge were aboriginal Native Americans, the descendants of people who had journeyed from Asia to North America across the Bering Strait land bridge as early as 50,000 years B.C. Exactly when these aborigines first arrived in the Southern Appalachians is unclear—climatic conditions in the southern mountains (e.g., extreme humidity and rainfall) were not conducive to the long-term survival of artifacts.

The oldest concrete evidence of aboriginal settlement near the Blue Ridge region (artifacts found in Russell Cave, Alabama) dates back at least to 8,000 B.C. This aboriginal group, termed Paleo-Indian by archaeologists, survived by hunting the large New World mammals, including mammoths, camels, and horses, which then roamed throughout the southeastern United States. Paleo-Indian culture declined between 9,000 and 8,000 B.C., after a period of glaciation led to the extinction of many larger New World mammal species.

As glaciers retreated northward from what is now the northeastern United States, a new aboriginal culture—the Archaic tradition—became dominant in what is now the southeastern United States. Most archaeologists conjecture that the Archaic tradition emerged as an evolutionary cultural progression of the Paleo-Indian tradition among the same group of aboriginal Native Americans. When investigating Russell Cave, archaeologists found Paleo-Indian artifacts underneath a deep layer of Archaic tradition artifacts. Evidence suggests that the people of the Archaic tradition adapted to the decline of large mammals by incorporating more diverse foods into their diet, including small game, fish, fruits, nuts, and vegetables. Because of the diversity of their diet and their limited reliance on roaming mammals, people of the Archaic tradition were less nomadic than people of the Paleo-Indian tradition, and their more sedentary existence necessitated their adapting to particular environments. Having developed more efficient survival skills, the people of the Archaic tradition found time to manufacture tools (such as needles and awls made out of animal bones), weapons (such as javelins and spears made out of stone and wood), and decorative objects (made out of polished stone). The Archaic tradition introduced two folklife practices which were to become important in later Native American cultures: ceremonial pipes (the people of the Archaic tradition smoked various native plants; tobacco, a South American plant, was introduced later) and burial ceremonies.

By the year 1,000 B.C. a new Native American culture, the Woodland tradition, had evolved out of the Archaic tradition. Although still reliant upon the hunting-gathering practices of their forebears, the people of the Woodland tradition improved upon their ancestors' food storage techniques (in part by producing pottery in which to store their food), which permitted them to establish permanent settlements and to exploit more effectively local food sources. The most remarkable activities in Woodland tradition, however, were small-scale agriculture and moundbuilding. The people of the Woodland tradition built two types of mounds: burial mounds, which marked the grave of a single body or several bodies and which usually contained numerous ceremonial objects such as pottery and pipes; and effigy mounds, which were constructed in the shape of such symbolic animals as eagles and snakes. Few of this people's signature earthen mounds are found near the Blue Ridge, suggesting rather sparse settlement in the region. The most important Woodland tradition site near the Blue Ridge was Tunacunnhee, in what is now the foothills of northwest Georgia. The Woodland tradition was certainly more prominent in the fertile Ohio River and Mississippi River valleys, where burial and effigy mounds reached spectacular size. Historian Charles Hudson provides an explanation for this group's infrequent settlement in the southern mountains: "It was during the Woodland tradition that the Indians first began to show a decided preference for living near the flood plains of rivers. It was in these flood plains that all of these native seed-bearing plants thrived. . . . Here, conditions were ideal for intensive seed-collecting to lead gradually to intentional cultivation—agriculture."

Beginning around 700 A.D., a new aboriginal culture emerged in the Mississippi Valley. This new culture, known as the Mississippian tradition, soon spread into what is now the southeastern United States. Mississippian tradition was substantially different from Woodland tradition. Although both cultures obtained food by a combination of hunting, gathering, and agriculture, Mississippian tradition employed a far more diverse agriculture which combined the propagation of native plants with those from Mesoamerica (plants like corn, beans, and squash, which may have been carried northward by Aztec traders). Also from Mesoamerican sources were the various symbols that the people of the Mississippian tradition engraved on pottery and shells (symbols representing war, conjuring, and fertility), and the practice of constructing temple mounds in the center of the fortified cities. Several non-Mesoamerican practices likewise distinguished the Mississippian tradition from earlier Native American cultures. People of the Mississippian tradition lived in large settlements fortified by ditches, canals, or palisades constructed out of logs placed vertically into the earth; these settlements featured specialized structures, such as earthen council houses. By 1,200 A.D., Mississippian tradition had fragmented into several regional variants, and the Blue Ridge essentially served as the divide between two of them: Middle Mississippian culture (which ranged from the Mississippi Valley eastward to the Blue Ridge) and South Appalachian Mississippian culture (found in parts of Georgia, South Carolina, and North Carolina). South Appalachian Mississippian culture was probably the result of a particular Woodland culture adopting certain cultural traits from the Middle Mississippian tradition. The people of this Woodland culture, in fierce competition for fertile river bottoms, obviously recognized that centralization would permit long-term settlement and a more peaceful coexistence between groups; they also realized that, by borrowing the new Mesoamerican crops of the Middle Mississippian tradition, they could dramatically improve their diet. The South Appalachian Mississippian culture was still intact when Europeans first entered the Blue Ridge region.

Early European Exploration

The earliest European expedition to venture into the Blue Ridge region was led by Spaniard Hernando de Soto. In 1539, Soto landed near Tampa Bay, Florida, with over six hundred soldiers and some additional men (mostly servants and slaves). Soto's expedition headed toward the Appalachian interior with two goals—to find adventure and to discover gold and other precious metals rumored to be in the region. Numerous Native American tribes (most of them Mississippian cultures) resisted the Spaniards' advance. In May of 1540, Soto's expedition crossed the Blue Ridge, probably guided by Native American scouts who knew of a well-established trail over the mountains. The expedition passed through the domain of the region's predominate tribe, the Cherokee, quickly and without difficulty (it is possible that the tribe had already been decimated by smallpox or another

European disease spread to the Cherokee from coastal tribes, which likely had contracted that disease from earlier European explorers).

The next Europeans to explore the Blue Ridge wilderness were two Englishmen, James Needham and Gabriel Arthur, who entered the Virginia Blue Ridge in 1673. Needham and Arthur eventually met the Cherokee, who still possessed material objects given them by Soto's party. Later, Arthur was captured by a tribe from Ohio; when released, he returned to Virginia through the mountain pass later called Cumberland Gap (named in 1750 by English explorer Dr. Thomas Walker, commemorating the Duke of Cumberland's conquest of the Scottish army at the Battle of Culloden). Arthur was the first Englishman, and probably the first European, to travel through a passageway which, one century later after Daniel Boone and colleagues opened Kentucky for settlement, would serve as the nation's main gate to the "West" (nearly half a million settlers would pass through Cumberland Gap in the eighteenth century).

Early exploration of the Appalachian wilderness by adventurers like Needham and Arthur established trade between Europeans and Native Americans, a situation which, however good it may have been for both parties initially, ultimately benefitted only the Europeans.

The English Effort to Control Trade with the Cherokee

By 1690, English colonists from Charleston, South Carolina, were venturing into the mountains to trade with Cherokees. Traders who desired both deerskins and Native American slaves offered the Cherokees a wide range of products manufactured in England, including weapons, cooking utensils, cloth, beads, and liquor. The Cherokee and other tribes became dependant upon these products, and by 1711 most male Native Americans were deeply in debt to the traders. This led to the Yamasee War (1715–17), in which Cherokee and Creek warriors joined the warriors of other tribes in revolting against the English traders. The war ended after the traders developed an alliance with the Cherokee, who turned against the Creeks. For the next few decades, English colonists maintained a duplicitous relationship with the Cherokee—on the one hand maintaining full trade with them, on the other hand facilitating the ongoing decline of the tribe's culture by encouraging intertribal warfare between the Cherokee and the Creeks and by supplying them with huge quantities of liquor. By 1750, English settlers were migrating into the southern part of the Blue Ridge region, a territory previously established by formal treaty as the property of the Cherokee.

During the French and Indian War (1756–63)—the struggle between

England and France for the political control of eastern North America—many English settlers avoided exposure to the fighting by moving from the North Carolina and Virginia piedmont onto Cherokee lands in the Carolinas. Upset at this infringement, the Cherokee staged a series of attacks on English settlements and fortifications, a situation which came to be known as the Cherokee War. The Cherokee won several of these contests, including one major victory, the capture of Fort Loudoun on the Little Tennessee River in 1760. In retaliation English soldiers under Major Hugh Waddell in 1761 stormed Cherokee towns along the Little Tennessee River; suffering many casualties, the Cherokee pled for peace. The English, recognizing that they could not fight the Cherokee and the French at the same time, forged a new alliance with the Cherokee. By 1763, this alliance had defeated the French and their Native American allies. English monarch King George III rewarded the Cherokee for their loyalty by issuing the Proclamation of 1763, which established a boundary line intended to prevent colonists from venturing onto Cherokee land. Colonists were forbidden from going westward past the Blue Ridge; those who had already crossed that boundary line were ordered to return eastward. Unfortunately for the Cherokee, the English military never enforced this edict, and settlers ignored it. Soon, new groups of settlers were establishing homesteads on Cherokee land.

Settlement of the Blue Ridge

In 1751, the English governor of the North Carolina colony, Gabriel Johnston, wrote: "Inhabitants flock in here daily, mostly from Pennsylvania and other parts of America. They commonly seat themselves toward the West and have got near the mountains." The English were not the only European people settling in the Blue Ridge frontier on the eve of the Revolutionary War: the backcountry of all the colonies from Pennsylvania to Georgia had been settled by a mixed population of English, Scots-Irish, Highland Scots, Welsh, Irish, Dutch, various German Protestants, and Protestant French Huguenots. (Common surnames in the Blue Ridge today bear witness to the diverse nationalities of early settlers: Smith is English, Shook is German, Patton is Irish, and Williams is Welsh, while the dozens of surnames beginning with Mc or Mac are Scots-Irish or Highland Scots.)

Each of these national groups had its own specific motivations for leaving Europe and settling in the New World, but all immigrants had in common a yearning for economic and religious freedom and a desire for self-determination. For instance, in the early eighteenth century more than a hundred thousand German Protestants escaped persecution at the hands of

The Oconaluftee Indian Village, a "living history" museum in Cherokee, North Carolina, offers a reconstruction of an eighteenth century Cherokee village, with demonstrations of traditional Cherokee crafts and other folkways. (Photo by Hugh Morton)

Roman Catholics in Germany by emigrating to Pennsylvania, attracted to William Penn's colony by its promise of religious tolerance; however, with land growing scarce in eastern and central Pennsylvania, many German immigrants had to choose between moving westward into a rugged territory (western Pennsylvania) still occupied by Indians or heading southward through Maryland into the fertile valley of the Shenandoah River in Virginia. Having been skillful farmers in Germany, most chose to farm in the Shenandoah Valley.

The most fertile land along the Shenandoah River, though, was quickly taken, which forced later-arriving settlers and subsequent generations to make new choices: to head eastward to settle on the crest of the Blue Ridge; to move southeastward over the Blue Ridge to settle on the western edge of the Virginia and North Carolina piedmont; or to move southwestward along the Great Valley of the Appalachians (which ran parallel to the Blue Ridge along its western edge) toward the North Carolina border and the heart of the Cherokee wilderness. Journeying through this mountainous terrain was slow and dangerous because of hostile Native Americans, wild animals, unsurveyed terrain, treacherous roads, and extreme weather changes. The place where settlers established their homesteads was often determined by uncontrollable factors like the breakdown of a settler's horse or wagon, a sudden injury or disease, and the availability of water and game.

The predominate group to settle in the Blue Ridge in the pre-Revolutionary period, the Scots-Irish, either repeated the settlement pattern of German settlers, or ventured into the Blue Ridge from the Virginia tidewater and the Carolina piedmont. Having faced political and religious oppression in the Old World at the hands of the English government (especially on the English plantations in northern Ireland), these Scots-Irish judged the southern mountains to be a refuge from the English-controlled governments of the various American colonies.

Before the Revolution, colonial governments tolerated backcountry settlers, believing that they served to buffer lowland settlements from attacks by Native Americans. People in the backcountry, on the other hand, were highly distrustful towards the various colonial governments, since governmental oppression in the Old World was a primary reason for many of these settlers' immigration. Nonetheless, the colonial governments' neglect of the backcountry increased, as did the anger of the backcountry people. This situation led to the rebellion of the Regulators. An antiestablishment protest movement, the Regulators terrorized the North Carolina and South Carolina backcountry during the 1760s, in an attempt to draw the attention of the governments of both colonies to the lack of political representation in the southern frontier. After being defeated at the Battle of Alamance (in the North Carolina piedmont) in 1771, many Regulators fled westward, into and beyond the Blue Ridge, to escape repercussion; there, unrepentant, some Regulators vented their hostility towards the colonial governments on the Cherokee.

The Regulators and other settlers pressed the tribe to surrender more land. In 1773, the Cherokee ceded much of its southern territory to England, including the southernmost foothills of the Blue Ridge. Settlers used some of this land for the raising of cattle—the rapidly expanding population of the southern colonies had created a large market for meat. An inexpensive yet profitable enterprise to operate on uncleared land, cattle raising required only a makeshift log cabin for a cattle herder and a crude cowpens (a corral to hold the cattle before they were taken to market). Cattle were allowed to feed freely in the woods; when they had grown fat on the fruits of the forest, a drover would transport the herd from the hills to merchants, who would then distribute the meat in nearby settlements. In the early nineteenth century some mountain cattlemen left the Blue Ridge for the West, taking with them this practice of open-range grazing, which proved extremely profitable on the plains of Texas.

The Watauga Association

By the 1760s, many new immigrants to the southern colonies were by-passing the eastern settlements to avoid direct confrontation with the tyr-anny of the English-dominated Carolinas; instead, they were heading west-ward to the western edge of the piedmont. The more adventurous among them were hurdling the Blue Ridge and settling on that range's western slope, which then was still colonial territory of North Carolina. Other set-tlers were migrating southward from Pennsylvania down the Great Valley of the Appalachians, and some of them settled in this same area.

By 1770, Scots-Irish settlers, believing they were living within the more politically tolerant colony of Virginia, were setting up homesteads in the valleys of the Watauga and Nolichucky Rivers. In 1771, these settlers dis-covered that they were actually residing within the boundaries of North Carolina, which meant the land on which they had settled had been de-clared Indian land by official treaty. These settlers could not obtain titles to the land on which they had built their homesteads. Accordingly, the North Carolina colonial government ordered the settlers to leave the Wa-tauga and Nolichucky Valleys.

The Cherokee, though, showed tolerance, offering the settlers a ten-year lease. Having obtained from the Cherokee a tenuous agreement for peaceful coexistence, these settlers on the western edge of the Blue Ridge region nonetheless faced a difficult predicament: literally and figuratively, they were cut off from the political representation and economic support of the colonial government. In May 1772, recognizing the need for a legal system and a formal government, the settlers along the Watauga River formed the Watauga Association, which was the first democratic, representative gov-ernment to be established in the New World. Designing their own constitu-tion—the first formally written and democratically drafted constitution in American history—the members of the Watauga Association established a democratic system of government featuring executive officers, a legislature, and courts. Signed by every member of the Watauga settlement, the associ-ation's constitution incorporated many of the laws of Virginia (and ignored the laws of North Carolina).

In the spring of 1774, the Watauga settlers, in appreciation for the Chero-kees' earlier generosity, invited nearby members of the tribe to attend a celebration they were staging not far from the present-day community of

In 1976, the Southern Highlands Attractions Association marked the nation's
bicentennial celebration by issuing an advertisement to commemorate historical
figures who played vital roles in the settlement of the Southern Appalachians. Used
in that advertisement was this photograph, in which actors portray, from left to
right, Chief Junaluska, Daniel Boone, George Washington, and Thomas Jefferson.
Boone and Jefferson were Blue Ridge residents, Chief Junaluska lived nearby, and
Washington knew the region well, having travelled there as a surveyor. (Photo by
Hugh Morton)

Jonesborough, Tennessee. Several tribe members attended the celebration,
which offered a number of festivities, including a footrace and a horse race.
Despite the settlers' good intentions, however, the celebration quickly became tragic. One of the settlers in attendance that day was Isaac Crabtree,
who lived not in the Watauga and Nolichucky settlements but in an adjoining settlement. Having earlier (in October 1773) witnessed a massacre of

settlers by a band of Indians in southwestern Virginia (one of the slain was Daniel Boone's son James), Crabtree retaliated, murdering a Cherokee brave. The other tribe members abruptly fled the celebration, with the Watauga settlers fearing certain reprisal. One of the leaders of the Watauga settlement, James Robertson, promptly met with the Cherokee chiefs in order to apologize publicly for the murder. His contriteness, along with his pledge to punish the perpetrator of the crime, convinced the Cherokee not to seek revenge on the Watauga settlers.

The Watauga Association endured for more than three years, up to the beginning of the Revolutionary War (1775–83). At this point, the Watauga Association dissolved its government and formed an alliance with the settlers who lived along the Nolichucky River. This was done for mutual survival, for the English, who were now at war with the colonists, had instituted a military strategy which severely threatened the security of the Watauga and Nolichucky settlers: the English again allied themselves with Native Americans, mostly Cherokee, with the goal of goading them into waging war with the mountain settlers, which the English hoped would threaten the security of all the southern states. Ultimately, however, the mountain alliance was too strong. Their recently constructed forts giving them a defensive advantage, the settlers withstood the Indian attacks, and, by the end of 1776, they had secured the new nation's western frontier, frustrating the English.

The Transforming of Virginia

By 1750, Virginia was already heavily settled—east of the Blue Ridge, that is. Yet, within a generation, the Blue Ridge wilderness would be subjugated. By the end of the Revolutionary War the demands of fighting a revolution and building a nation had transformed Virginia and Virginians, and the Virginia Blue Ridge was no longer considered the western frontier, but rather a geographical hurdle which slowed, but could not stop, westward expansion. According to historian Rhys Isaac:

Aspects of the reorganization of social action and social expectation can be discerned in the great movements of population that were taking place in the wake of the revolution. A radical redirection of cultural outlook was already apparent in the celebration of the shirtmen of '75. After the opening of the Kentucky land office in 1779 the westward orientation . . . grew more intense, and the steady flow of settlers over the mountains swelled to a prodigious flood. The region between the Chesapeake and the Blue Ridge had changed its relative position. From being on the transatlantic margin of the British maritime empire, it became part of the eastern seaboard of an expanding continental nation-state.

A Legendary Figure

Daniel Boone was in many respects an archetypal Blue Ridge character. Like many other Blue Ridge settlers of his generation, he was born in Pennsylvania, on October 22, 1734, in Exeter township (near what is now the town of Reading), Berks County, Pennsylvania. His father, Squire Boone, was an English immigrant who worked as a weaver, a farmer, and a blacksmith; his mother, Sarah Morgan, was of Welsh descent. Daniel received his first rifle, a gift from his father, when not quite a teenager, and he developed strong marksmanship skills during short hunting forays into nearby forestland. His parents tolerated his love for hunting because the young man proved to be a dedicated provider of food for the large Boone family (Squire and Sarah had eleven children to feed).

Both of Daniel's parents were practicing Quakers. However, in 1742, Squire Boone was seriously reprimanded by the local Friends community for permitting his oldest daughter, Sarah, to marry a "worldling" (in that day Quaker marital unions required approval from a committee of Friends). In 1748, that same group of Friends expelled Squire when he refused to apologize for allowing his oldest son, Israel, to marry another "worldling." Squire Boone felt hampered by the rigid social code in that Pennsylvania settlement, so in 1750 he moved his family to the frontier.

Several Boone relatives had already left Pennsylvania for the Shenandoah Valley in Virginia, and they had sent word of inexpensive real estate in western Virginia and North Carolina. Daniel, then fifteen, served as the guide for his family's expedition; joining the Boones was an apprentice in Squire's blacksmith business, Henry Miller, who was also Daniel's best friend. First, the family travelled in Conestoga wagons westward on the Allegheny Trail, then southwestward along the Virginia Road, which was the primary emigration route by which settlers journeyed through Pennsylvania toward the southern frontier. The Boones travelled this road alongside immigrants of several nationalities, including English, Scots-Irish, German, and Swiss. After fording the Potomac River near Williamsport, Maryland, and continuing southward through what is now Berkeley County, West Virginia, the Boones reached the Shenandoah Valley. After reuniting with their relatives, they established a camp beside Linnville Creek, near the present site of Harrisonburg, Virginia.

Anxious for further adventure, Daniel Boone soon embarked on his first "long hunt" (a prolonged hunting trip which frontier hunters co-opted from Native American tradition); Henry Miller joined him. In the field for several months, their search for game led them eastward over the Blue Ridge (they crossed at Roanoke Gap) toward the western piedmont near the North Carolina-Virginia border. In late fall of 1750, the young men rejoined the Boone family long enough to inform them that they were returning to Pennsylvania to sell the animal skins they had taken from the wilderness.

After selling the skins in Philadelphia, Boone immediately spent all his money, revealing by this act an aspect of his character which only grew stronger with the years: a personal philosophy of carpe diem, increasingly manifesting itself in his craving for constant adventure. Boone and Miller returned south, but while Miller settled down in Augusta County, Virginia, to establish himself as a successful businessman and landowner, his days of adventuring over, Boone eagerly headed toward the frontier of North Carolina to join his family—in late 1750 Squire Boone had purchased 640 acres on the western piedmont of North Carolina near the Yadkin River (in present-day Davie County).

According to a local legend, the Boones, upon arriving in North Carolina, moved into a cave beside the Yadkin River. Whether that story is based on fact or is apocryphal, records suggest that, by February 1752, the family had constructed some kind of dwelling on their plot of land. From these simple beginnings, the Boone family carved out of the wilderness a network of farms. Daniel Boone, though, disdained farming, preferring instead hunting game in the piedmont and Blue Ridge forests. For Boone, hunting was more of a vocation than an avocation; it allowed him to provide food and clothing for his parents and siblings, and, later, for his own large family. Nonetheless, he prided himself on his ability with a gun, and he never declined an opportunity to prove his skill in shooting competitions with other frontiersmen. Boone soon earned the reputation of being one of the most accomplished marksmen in North Carolina.

After a stint with the English army during the French and Indian War, during which time he assisted General Edward Braddock in a failed attack on the French Fort Duquesne (near the current site of Pittsburgh, Pennsylvania), Boone returned to his family's enclave by the Yadkin River. He soon began to court Rebecca Bryan, a young woman who lived near the Boones on her family's farm. Born in western Virginia in 1739, Rebecca, like Boone, was raised a Quaker. According to a family story, during their courtship, Boone, realizing that his wanderlust would place unusual demands on a wife, put Rebecca through a series of tests in order to discover her aptitude for frontier life. Rebecca passed every test, revealing herself to be a woman of great strength and patience. The two were married on August 14, 1756, and set up a homestead near what is now Farmington, North

Carolina. Nine months after their marriage, the couple's first child was born, to be followed by nine subsequent children over the next two decades (one of whom was alleged to have been illegitimate, conceived by Boone's brother Ned during one of his long absences; apparently, Daniel Boone forgave his wife and brother and accepted the child into the family without hesitation).

The early years of the Boones' marriage were particularly difficult. Boone quickly established a pattern of leaving for weeks at a time to go on hunting trips into the wilderness, leaving his wife behind to watch the children, keep house, tend the garden, even to hunt small game. Rebecca kept her family together against enormous odds; she was in many ways the archetypal frontier woman. Boone's absences from home grew longer and longer: the western piedmont was quickly filling up with settlers and was beset with unpredictable environmental conditions (droughts, stunted crops, and low game populations), and he had to travel further and further into the southern mountains to find game.

Making a living on the North Carolina frontier was not the Boones' only hardship. The rogue fringe of settler society often terrorized other settlers, making the frontier a truly dangerous place. During the early years of their marriage, the Boones had to contend with larger historical predicaments. These were the years of the French and Indian War, a time when Native Americans were attacking settlers in the North Carolina frontier; some of these warriors, such as the Shawnees of Ohio, were encouraged and armed by the French. At first the Cherokees had sided with the colonists, until 1759 when English soldiers and settlers instigated a rash of random terrorist attacks against the Cherokee. Reacting in part to these specific events and in part to the stress of steady displacement from their ancestral lands, the Cherokee began to lash out against the colonists at their farmsteads and fortresses. In 1759, with the Yadkin River settlements being besieged by Cherokee (part of a larger struggle known as the Cherokee War), the Boones fled to the relative safety of the central Virginia piedmont (in Culpeper County). His family secure for the time being, Boone, during the winter of 1760–61, embarked on his annual wintertime hunt.

During this hunting trip, in December 1760, Boone met a slave who, when herding cattle, had discovered a new hunting ground. Intrigued, Boone followed the slave up a buffalo trail to the crest of the Blue Ridge near the North Carolina-Virginia line; from there Boone traveled on alone northward into Virginia. By Whitetop Mountain (near Mt. Rogers), Boone headed west, entering for the first time the watershed of the Ohio River and the Gulf of Mexico.

Native Americans and other settlers had previously explored the wilderness to the west of the Blue Ridge, but as word spread about the wealth of game there, Boone came to be associated with the area. His skills as a professional guide and expert marksman much in demand, he led countless other piedmont men on hunting trips across the Blue Ridge. Boone often crossed the crest of the Blue Ridge on a trail that came to be known as Boone's Trace, a footpath still visible today from the Blue Ridge Parkway north of Boone, North Carolina.

With others witnessing his skills as guide and marksman, Boone developed a reputation for being the greatest hunter in the Blue Ridge, and his legendary status has endured. In the east Tennessee mountains during the nineteenth century, for instance, a master hunter was called a "Boone." Yet, though most of the stories told about his greatness were complimentary, he was occasionally portrayed as a ruthless Indian-killing frontiersman. This was far from fact: Boone was strictly a professional guide and game hunter. In a lifetime of explorations and expeditions through Indian lands he took the lives of three Native Americans, and these killings occurred in situations of self-defense. According to one of his contemporaries, "Boone had very little of the war spirit. He never liked to take life and always avoided it when he could." Boone had tremendous respect for the Cherokee and their woods-wise ways, and his own woodsmanship similarly impressed Cherokee warriors and hunters. Several times he was captured by Cherokee hunting parties, and, by appealing to their mutual belief in the code of the forest, each time he was able to negotiate his release.

After a brief sojourn in Florida in 1765, Boone moved his family up the Yadkin into the Brushy Mountains (not far from the present-day town of Wilkesboro, North Carolina). The Boones had left their former farmstead because of a significant increase in settlement near the Forks of the Yadkin—Boone was notorious for his disdain of crowded living conditions. Now in the foothills of the Blue Ridge, the Boones were again on the edge of European settlement. The family eventually located a suitable homesite beside the Yadkin River, and were soon joined by some kinfolk. After establishing a new farmstead for his family, Boone in the spring of 1769 once more embarked on an extended hunting trip. He would not see his family again for two years.

On this trip, Boone, thirty-four years old, would accomplish the feat that sealed his fame: the exploration of the region that came to be called Kentucky. This 1769 expedition was actually Boone's second trip into the Kentucky wilderness, but winter weather had curtailed his previous trip (in 1767) before his small hunting party had advanced very far into that new territory. Before Boone's 1769 expedition, French and British trappers had occasionally navigated their way down the Ohio River to trade with the Shawnees in central Kentucky, but the area had never been explored by Europeans. Reports about the Kentucky territory—about its ample popula-

Actor Fess Parker, who played Daniel Boone on television, visited Boone, North Carolina, one summer to attend the long-running seasonal historical drama *Horn in the West*, which depicts the famous frontiersman's adventures in the southern mountains. (Photo by Hugh Morton)

tions of game, for instance—had circulated among colonists for years, with many of these reports depicting the region quite romantically, as a kind of earthly paradise. Boone's own reasons for exploring Kentucky were both romantic and pragmatic. England had recently obtained possession of the Kentucky region from the Iroquois through the Treaty of Fort Stanwix, and Boone, with the same sense of duty that led him to enlist in the English army, was eager to be the first colonist to evaluate England's new acquisition. Also, the Blue Ridge foothills had proven to be a difficult place to raise a family: by exploring Kentucky, which was rumored to be fertile and well watered, Boone might find a good place to relocate his family, and thus might better their economic lot. Furthermore, though he wasn't overtly a supporter of the antiestablishment Regulator movement which was raging through the North Carolina backcountry at this time, Boone was certainly sympathetic with one of the Regulators' tenets, which was that the colonies were rapidly becoming overpopulated and life there bureaucratized. Thus, Boone was more than willing to undertake the difficult task of navigating safe passage over the entire Southern Appalachian mountain complex in order to find a new home in Kentucky.

On May 1, 1769, he and a group of five other explorers mounted their horses near Boone's farmstead and began their long ride toward Kentucky. This party followed Elk Creek upstream to its source, then continued uphill until they had reached the crest of the Blue Ridge; from there they wove their way northwest around Stone Mountain and Iron Mountain, then descended into the valley of the Holston River (in what is now Tennessee). From there the party followed an old Indian trail, the Great Warrior's Path, into Virginia, through the Cumberland Gap, and into Kentucky. Long used by Native Americans for passage across an otherwise impassible mountainous country, Cumberland Gap was the primary route by which settlers from the east would soon cross the Appalachians into the newly publicized settlements in Kentucky.

Boone's journey into Kentucky was not without danger. He and one of his fellow explorers were captured and held for a week by Shawnee warriors, who were angry at the colonists for the Treaty of Fort Stanwix, which the Shawnee felt had jeopardized their ancestral hunting grounds; these warriors were especially angry that they had had no say in the treaty and felt that the Iroquois had had no right to surrender the Kentucky territory to England. Boone and his colleague escaped unscathed, but trouble with the Shawnee would continue to frustrate his subsequent trips to Kentucky.

Upon his return to North Carolina in 1771, Boone found himself in legal trouble with creditors, and his Yadkin River landholdings in jeopardy. His personal debts led him to move his family temporarily to the other side of the Blue Ridge, into the valley of the Watauga River, until his financial situation was resolved. In the fall of 1772, Boone left for another sojourn into Kentucky, and his family moved back across the Blue Ridge. The following year Boone returned to his farmstead by the Yadkin River and informed his family that they were moving again—this time to Boone's land of opportunity, Kentucky.

Traveling with a string of pack horses, the Boones and a group of settlers made slow but steady progress toward Cumberland Gap; before the party had gotten far, Boone dispatched his oldest child—James, who was sixteen years old—to fetch additional supplies. On their way back to rejoin his father and the rest of the group, James and a small party of settlers (including Isaac Crabtree), while camped on the night of October 9, 1773, by Wallen's Creek in Virginia, were attacked by a band of Native Americans composed of warriors from several tribes who had gathered together for an intertribal conference. The warriors killed several in the exploration party, including James Boone. A grieving Daniel Boone, fearful for the safety of the rest of the settlers, canceled the expedition. The Boones returned to the safety of the settlements near the Clinch River in Virginia, where the family spent the winter. The first attempt by Europeans to establish a settlement in Kentucky had failed.

Boone's subsequent activities were those of a person playing an increasingly public role. No longer acting primarily in his own and his family's interest, he was now serving the needs of the colonial people, both the common folk and the ruling class. By this time, population pressures in the piedmont region were forcing widespread discussions about Kentucky as the logical next place of settlement for new immigrants and disgruntled colonists. As word of Boone's extensive experience in Kentucky spread through the colonies, the colonial ruling classes—especially government officials and land speculators—realized he might play a significant role in their chief political and economic goal, which, of course, was to open the West to settlement and to make it as profitable as possible.

In June 1774, Boone received orders from the governor of Virginia to travel to Kentucky to warn land surveyors about an imminent uprising by the Shawnees, who were reacting to the threat that European settlement in Kentucky would pose to their traditional hunting grounds. Searching far and wide, Boone was not able to locate any of the few surveyors then in Kentucky; nevertheless, his exemplary service was recognized by the military leaders of the Virginia frontier militia, and he was soon asked to organize and lead a company of soldiers to defend several fortresses in the Clinch Valley from Shawnee warriors. Boone's leadership was so effective that he was swiftly promoted to captain. This defensive campaign ended late in 1774, after the Treaty of Camp Charlotte (signed in desperation by the Shawnee after a division of the Virginia military had surrounded their villages near the Scioto River in present-day Ohio) ended the Shawnees' rights to hunt in Kentucky.

With Shawnee chiefs promising to keep their tribe on the north side of the Ohio River (a promise later broken), land speculators began to plot the settling of Kentucky. The planner and financial backer for one of the first settlement schemes was Richard Henderson, a North Carolina government official. To finance the construction of his proposed Kentucky settlement, "Transylvania," Henderson set up the Transylvania Company. As a court justice in North Carolina, Henderson had once attempted to arrest Daniel Boone for debt, but now he turned to Boone for help. Henderson intended to build a road leading from the Watauga settlements over the mountains and through Cumberland Gap into Kentucky, and he would now need the assistance of the only non-Indian who could handle this monumental task—Boone. Henderson himself negotiated with the Cherokees to obtain the deeds to the land on which his proposed road and settlements would be built, then hired Boone to coordinate the construction of the road and the establishment of settlements in Kentucky.

The road that Boone built in March 1775 with the help of more than fifty fellow frontiersmen was, of course, the famous Wilderness Road (sometimes called Boone's Old Trace). For much of the length of the Wilderness Road, Boone and his crew followed the Great Warrior's Path, though they also incorporated sections of animal trails. When the road builders entered the Kentucky territory, they faced renewed attacks by bands of Shawnee. Many of the terrified road builders threatened to flee back to the Virginia settlements, but Boone kept the group together. By late April, they had built a makeshift fort on a section of the bank of the Kentucky River which had been chosen as a good location for the capital of the first European settlement in Kentucky. The initiator of the new settlement, Henderson, recognizing that such a grandiose plan would never have been realized without stalwart leadership, named the capital Boonesborough.

However, Henderson's settlement venture, Transylvania, was no utopia. Victims of his unequal treatment, the investors in Henderson's scheme grew disgusted by his greed and nepotism. And Boone's Wilderness Road had opened the floodgates. Soon rival companies rushed into Kentucky to create their own settlements, challenging Henderson's claims to supremacy in the region. When the Revolutionary War erupted, politicians, recognizing the ideological benefits of western expansion, denounced as invalid Henderson's deeds to his Kentucky land—after all, they asserted, the Cherokee had had no right to cede Kentucky, for it was never their land in the first place. No sooner was it settled than the "promised land" to the west of the Southern Appalachians had become tainted by social and political unrest—an uncanny premonition of the opening of the American West less than a century later.

Boone disassociated himself from this squabbling—he had not come to Kentucky to govern others or to gain profit for himself. He had come for more personal reasons, including making what he deemed to be a better life for himself and his family. Boone returned to the Clinch Valley settlements to fetch his family, to escort them, on the path he himself had carved out of the wilderness, to their new Kentucky home.

With their emigration to Kentucky in September 1775, the Boone family reflected a larger trend: the gradual abandonment of the Blue Ridge region by settlers who only a generation before had seen the Blue Ridge as a fortification against the corruption of the colonies' political and social elite, but who now felt that the region was a prison impeding individual opportunity. The signing of the Declaration of Independence on July 4, 1776, forever altered the identities of all colonists, and the settlers in the Blue Ridge were no exception. With self-rule and self-determination came a new con-

These covered wagons, parked at an Appalachian State University stadium in Boone, North Carolina, after climbing the Blue Ridge from Yadkin County, North Carolina, were part of an organized celebration marking the anniversary of Daniel Boone's journey to Kentucky. (Photo by Hugh Morton)

sciousness of individuality—settlers no longer needed to define themselves according to ethnic, economic, or historical categories. The new nation, with its expanding frontier, permitted—and in many cases forced—settlers to reject the cultural boundaries of parents and ancestors, to evolve a dynamic set of cultural values which better reflected changed physical, social, and psychic needs.

During the last quarter of the eighteenth century many settlers abandoned the Blue Ridge region for the West, rejecting an isolated, hardscrabble life in the hills for the promise of material wealth and social mobility which people believed attainable in the fertile plain of central Kentucky. Many others, however, remained in the Blue Ridge, including several of Boone's relatives. Geographical place names in the North Carolina Blue Ridge bear witness to the former presence of Boones (Boone Fork, for instance, which flows westward from the crest of the Blue Ridge into the Watauga River, was named not for Daniel Boone but for his nephew Jesse Boone, who from 1810 to 1817 lived and farmed near the stream that today possesses his name). The explorer, who died on the Missouri frontier in September 1820, received posthumous commemoration from Blue Ridge residents in the middle of the nineteenth century when the name of the county seat of North Carolina's Watauga County was changed from Council's Store to Boone.

The New Nation's Political Visionary

Thomas Jefferson was born on April 17, 1743, at Shadwell, in Albemarle County. Then on the western edge of settlement in Virginia, Shadwell was near Charlottesville, the Blue Ridge town where Jefferson was to build his estate and where in 1819 he would found the University of Virginia. Jefferson's father, Peter (1708–57), an accomplished surveyor who drew the first accurate map of Virginia, encouraged his son's interest in Virginia's natural and cultural history. Thomas Jefferson's sole book, *Notes on the State of Virginia* (1787), was a sweeping treatise concerning the geographical, ecological, and social realities of his native state. Holding the scientific method in the highest esteem, Jefferson in his book attempted to classify geological, paleontological, botanical, and animal specimens found within the borders of Virginia.

As a product of the Enlightenment, Jefferson's knowledge was broad, yet he was far from being a dilettante. His wide-ranging reading (in 1815 Jefferson sold his collection of ten thousand books to the United States government to form the nucleus of the Library of Congress) complemented his practical skills as farmer (at one time he successfully farmed over ten thousand acres) and architect (he designed the Virginia statehouse, part of the University of Virginia, and, of course, his estate house Monticello).

In many respects, despite his diverse international roles, Jefferson embodied such frontier values as self-reliance, devotedness to life on the land, and an unflinching belief in democracy. Unlike the other founding fathers, who viewed any secession as a threat to the nation and who were thus unsympathetic towards the post-Revolution attempts of settlers in the Blue Ridge (i.e., the attempt to create the State of Franklin) and in Kentucky to separate themselves politically from North Carolina and Virginia, Jefferson accepted such movements as natural and necessary, if the United States was to fulfill its goal of being a democratic nation. It could be argued that Jefferson's ideal vision of a democratic society—a society made up of self-sufficient citizens farming small self-owned tracts of land—was nowhere better realized in the United States than in the region he knew best: the Blue Ridge.

The Battle of Kings Mountain

On September 26, 1780, over a thousand supporters of the new nation, residents of the western slopes of the Blue Ridge, departed on horseback from their encampment at Sycamore Shoals (near what is now the community of Elizabethton in Carter County, Tennessee) for their first Revolutionary War action. (All of the action in this description of the Battle of Kings Mountain, including the battle itself, took place in what was then the state of North Carolina; the site of the battlefield was later annexed to South Carolina.) These men, most of whom had only recently moved from the eastern to the western side of the Blue Ridge, were known as the Overmountain Men.

Having grown aggravated by the rise of pro-English Tory sentiment in communities near the Blue Ridge, and having been angered by Loyalist (English) military commander Colonel Patrick Ferguson, who had threatened to destroy the mountain patriots, the Overmountain Men had formed a democratically organized militia. Fearing that their treasured political and social independence was in jeopardy, they had decided to go on the offensive, rather than wait for Ferguson and the Loyalist army to attack them in their homes. Not equipped with conventional military uniforms, the Overmountain Men wore their frontier wardrobes: long fringed hunting shirts made of dressed deer hide, leather belts, leather or homespun wool pants, deerskin moccasins, and animal-skin caps or beaver-hide hats. Among the group were two future statesmen: John Sevier (the first governor of Tennessee), and Isaac Shelby (later, a governor of Kentucky).

On September 27, the Overmountain Men crossed the present-day boundary of North Carolina on the eastern knob of Roan Mountain, at an elevation of six thousand feet. At this point, two traitors, William Crawford and Samuel Chambers, stole off from the patriot army to inform Ferguson and the Loyalist army, who were encamped on the western edge of the Carolina piedmont in Gilbert Town (now Rutherfordton). English General Charles Cornwallis had ordered Ferguson to quell the Whig rebellion in the North Carolina mountains, a task which Ferguson was attempting to accomplish with the help of an army of just over one thousand Tory sympathizers, all of whom, with the exception of Ferguson himself, had been born in the New World.

On September 28, the patriots camped near what is now the community of Spruce Pine (in Mitchell County, North Carolina). The next day, they crossed the Blue Ridge at Gillespie Gap and looked down on the farms in the valley of the Catawba River, in the direction of Ferguson's army. Guessing that Ferguson, now forewarned by Crawford and Chambers, might be waiting in ambush, the patriots divided their army into two equal-sized groups, hoping that by such a strategy they might better locate Ferguson's army. One group of patriots, led by Colonel William Campbell, followed the crest of the Blue Ridge southwestward, then dropped off to the south into Turkey Cove, just six miles from the Catawba River. The other group, led by Colonel Charles McDowell, headed straight downhill from the crest of the Blue Ridge and followed North Cove Creek toward Quaker Meadows on the Catawba River, the site of a planned rendezvous with the other group of patriots.

On the 30th, the two groups reunited at Quaker Meadows, and were joined there by 350 additional patriots from the Blue Ridge foothills in Wilkes and Surry Counties. The North Carolina officers at this point decided to elect Colonel Campbell, who hailed from Virginia, as chief commanding officer of the patriot army. By now the alerted Ferguson had ordered his Loyalist troops to retreat toward Charlotte, where he hoped to receive reinforcements from Cornwallis (significantly, the two scouts Ferguson sent on September 30 to inform Cornwallis of the need for reinforcements did not find the general until October 7). Meanwhile, several groups of mounted patriots from the western piedmont—four hundred cavalry in all—were eighteen miles away at Flint Hill, waiting for Campbell and the patriot army to arrive for the impending attack on the Loyalist forces.

On October 4, an old man sympathetic with the patriot cause infiltrated a Loyalist encampment at Tate's Place by pretending to be a Tory; afterward, this man escaped under cover of darkness and the next day informed the patriots of Ferguson's proximity. That day, the leaders of the various groups of patriots met, whereupon Campbell decided to divide the fourteen hundred patriot soldiers into two groups. One group would confront the Loyalist army in battle, and the other would stand by as reinforcements. The cavalry that had been camped at Flint Hill was ordered to join a select force of Overmountain Men at Cowpens (near the present-day city of Spartanburg, South Carolina) before sunset on October 6.

Campbell's orders were carried out, and on the night of October 6 the patriot force at Cowpens found themselves hungry in the presence of cattle and corn. These were the property of a wealthy cattleman named Hiram Saunders, a Tory sympathizer whose cattle were kept in enclosures made of split-rail fences (cowpens). The patriots helped themselves to the food. Of this night's feasting, one soldier wrote: "A stirring bivouac at Cowpens—the English Tory's fifty acres of corn was eaten up in ten minutes." When they had finished feasting, the patriots accosted Saunders at his house, threatening him with injury or worse if he did not reveal Ferguson's whereabouts. Saunders pleaded ignorance; the patriots let him be, and left the Cowpens to search for Ferguson. One soldier later wrote: "We marched from the Cowpens that very same night. / Sometimes we were wrong, sometimes we were right. / Our hearts being run in true liberty's mould / We regarded not hunger, wet, weary nor cold."

On the morning of October 7, the patriots avoided Tate's Ford on the Broad River, which they feared was being guarded by Loyalist soldiers; instead, they crossed the Broad River two and a half miles downstream, at Cherokee Ford. Three miles from Cherokee Ford, at the exact spot where the Loyalist army had been camped only twenty-four hours before, the patriots stopped to eat breakfast. Allegedly at this time they learned of the Loyalist army's location from a girl informing a patriot spy that she had earlier that morning taken some chickens to General Ferguson and his army, who were camped at the top of a nearby ridge called Kings Mountain. Quickly marching eastward toward Kings Mountain (which measured roughly six hundred yards long and sixty to a hundred and twenty feet wide), the patriots intercepted a Tory spy on horseback carrying a written message, a desperate appeal from Ferguson to General Cornwallis for more troops and supplies. Under interrogation, this spy, John Ponder, confessed that Ferguson was on Kings Mountain—he was wearing a large checked overshirt.

With that knowledge, the patriots rushed for a strategic assault on the Loyalist army. When the patriots reached the base of Kings Mountain, they saw how difficult their mission would be—the Loyalist army had the high ground, the superior position. Yet the patriots had in their favor the element of surprise. They dismounted their horses, and the Battle of Kings Mountain began—it was three in the afternoon. Initially, the Loyalists charged with bayonets, and the patriots fell back; then from behind rocks and trees the patriots fired vollies of musket fire at the Loyalists, who retreated back up the ridge. The patriots drove back three Loyalist charges in all. Ferguson's soldiers tended to overshoot their targets in that difficult terrain, while the patriots—many of whom had become sharpshooters through hunting game in the Blue Ridge—made theirs.

The patriot army rushing up the ridge gained equal advantage by hiding behind trees and rocks. Because of the suddenness of the patriot attack, Ferguson had not ordered his army to construct field fortifications, which might have sheltered his men from the patriots' bullets. Nonetheless, from the perspective of the patriots, Ferguson was a valiant leader, riding to the front lines to encourage his troops, risking death. When it was clear the Loyalists were being routed, Ferguson refused surrender, choosing instead to attempt escape through a thin place in the patriots' line. Ferguson fell off his horse with eight bullet wounds, dead.

Second-in-command Abraham de Peyster surrendered the rest of the Loyalist army. The battle was over, an hour after it had begun, yet some patriots—recalling that English General Banastre Tarleton had massacred captured patriots the previous May—began firing on the Loyalists. Campbell quickly intervened, convincing the patriots that such actions amounted to murder. In all, the Loyalists sustained approximately two hundred dead, one hundred eighty wounded, and seven hundred imprisoned. The toll on the patriot forces was dramatically different: thirty dead and sixty wounded.

The victorious patriots returned to their Blue Ridge homes. Shortly thereafter, thirty Loyalists were tried at Gilbert Town; all were condemned to death, though only nine were actually hanged. Most of the other prisoners escaped, and no one chased after them.

For some years after the battle, many people avoided going near the battlefield—locals told ghost stories about Kings Mountain, believing it to be haunted. In 1878 the battlefield was consecrated as a national military park.

PATRICK FERGUSON, HERO FOR
RECONCILIATION

After the Loyalists surrendered, patriot soldiers lined up to gaze upon Patrick Ferguson's body; a few soldiers took possessions off the dead commander, mementos of the battle. These men from the Blue Ridge were curious about Ferguson in part because he was Scottish, having been born in Aberdeenshire, Scotland, in 1744; thus, his background resembled their own. Additionally, Ferguson embodied many of the attributes the patriots most valued: he was loyal and courageous, even in his final moments, and he possessed native intelligence and nobility of spirit. He was widely known to be the inventor of the breech-loading flintlock rifle, a weapon with a longer firing range than the conventional muzzle-loading rifle. Ferguson was also an acknowledged master trick shooter, rumored to be the best shot in the British Empire; as legend had it, "He could pull a pistol from its holster, toss it to a revolution in the air, grip it by the butt as it came down, whip it to an arm and knock from a branch a nearby bird." Patriots felt that Ferguson displayed great nobility when, at Chadd's Ford during the Revolutionary War's Battle of Brandywine (in eastern Pennsylvania on September 11, 1777), he had General George Washington in the sights of his rifle but refused to fire out of a sense of honor—it was, Ferguson later confessed in a letter, not right to fire at unsuspecting officers.

The victorious soldiers of the Battle of Kings Mountain were not the only ones to forgive Ferguson for his actions and threats against the patriots. For years, Americans of Scottish and Scots-Irish ancestry regarded Ferguson as a hero. In 1814, a survivor of the Battle of Kings Mountain, Dr. William McClean, erected a memorial marker which commemorated not only the patriots who died in that pivotal contest but also Ferguson. Just as Union regard for Confederate leader Robert E. Lee was to help the winners of the Civil War forgive the losers, respect for Ferguson among the winners of the Battle of Kings Mountain led to, on a smaller scale, a reconciliation with that battle's losers. In 1815, a reunion of soldiers from the Battle of Kings Mountain included both patriots and Loyalists.

In 1880, during the centennial celebration of the Battle of Kings Mountain, Major A. H. White of Rock Hill, South Carolina, placed two commemorative markers for Ferguson, one at the site of his death and the other by his grave. This grave marker, of considerable stature (seven feet high and two feet wide), recognized Ferguson for his "military distinction" and "honor," and proposed that he serve as a heroic figure to reconcile the people of the United States with the people of Great Britain. An inscription on the marker stated: "This memorial is from the citizens of the United States of America in token of their appreciation of the bonds of friendship and peace between them and the citizens of the British Empire." In 1930, at the sesquicentennial celebration of the Battle of Kings Mountain, another monument for Ferguson was erected on the battlefield.

White was the originator of a tradition which continued into the twentieth century: the setting of small stones on Ferguson's grave to create a cairn (a form of commemoration originally practiced by the Scottish), which eventually grew to be as large as the grave. The enduring sentiment for Ferguson led one twentieth century writer to comment: "Stones are not too hard for American hearts to enter, when left as symbols of respect and tokens of sympathy for an enemy who died like a Spartan."

THE IMPACT OF THE BATTLE

Before the Battle of Kings Mountain, the new American nation was tottering on the brink of collapse. Several events, including Benedict Arnold's treason and the defeat of patriot armies in South Carolina (at Charleston, Camden, and Fishing Creek), shook the confidence of the patriots. Fearing the breakdown of their new nation as a political unit, U. S. congressmen had in early 1780 considered a compromise with the English monarch, which likely would have involved giving some of the southern states back to Great Britain. The patriot victory at the Battle of Kings Mountain on October 7, 1780, was "the turning point in the Revolutionary War, and undoubtedly gained the freedom of the colonies and subsequently the establishment of the United States." The victory disrupted the progress of southern Tories and ended General Cornwallis's string of victories; furthermore, word of Kings Mountain spreading through the South convinced new recruits to fight for the patriot cause, leading to more victories, including the Battle of Cowpens, also fought in the Blue Ridge foothills (and, eventually, to a final victory)—all because of frontiersmen from the Blue Ridge, the Overmountain Men. According to Shepherd M. Dugger, a chronicler of the Battle of Kings Mountain: "[The Overmountain Men,] with no orders from Congress or the Continental Army, no uniforms, no provision wagons, no superior officer, no pay, no bayonets or sabers, no band of music, each with a rifle, a shot-pouch, his horse, and a poke of provisions, demon-eyed, vengeance-browed, just from his hornet's-nest in the Switzerland of America, broke the power of subjugation and held the states together."

Negotiations with the Cherokee

The English first formally exploited the Cherokee in 1721, when South Carolina's Governor Francis Nicholson, wanting to win the Indian fur trade from the French (then operating in the Mississippi Valley), convinced tribal leaders to sign a treaty ceding a fifty-square-mile tract of land to the English. In 1730, Sir Alexander Cuming coerced tribal leaders to swear loyalty to the English monarch. In 1731, to display his newly gained political prize, Cuming took seven Cherokee chiefs to London. These chiefs met many dignitaries, including King George II (who paid for their year-long visit). The Cherokee become the key player in two English schemes: the aforementioned control of the fur trade and, later, the containment of rebellious activity among the frontier settlers.

When the Overmountain Men were marching toward their confrontation with the Loyalist army at Kings Mountain, an English Indian agent convinced the Cherokee that it was a good time to organize an attack on the Watauga and Nolichucky settlements. Unfortunately for the Cherokee, the Overmountain Men, after swiftly locating and defeating the Loyalist army, did not remain near the site of their great victory; they returned promptly to their homes in the Blue Ridge. Tipped off by a Cherokee informant named Nancy Ward that an attack was imminent, John Sevier, fearing extensive damage to the settlements if nothing was done to prevent a Cherokee invasion, decided to go on the offensive. In December 1780, with two hundred of his fellow settlers, Sevier set off toward Cherokee territory.

On their second night out, the group first spied Cherokee warriors near the Nolichucky River, but no confrontation ensued. That night reinforcements arrived, amounting to another hundred troops. The next morning Sevier and the other settlers crossed the French Broad River at Big Island Ford and walked more deeply into Cherokee territory, soon recognizing signs of a massive encampment nearby. On their third night out, the settlers spent the night beside Boyd's Creek (in present-day Sevier County, Tennessee). The next morning, December 16, 1780, the settlers' advance scouts located the encampment three miles away—it was empty, though campfires were still burning. Sensing an ambush, Sevier ordered his troops to avoid the camp and devised instead a complicated strategy: first, to draw out the Cherokee from their hiding places, then to rotate troops in order to steadily encircle those warriors. Because of misinformation from English Indian agents who did not inform them that the settlers had returned victoriously from Kings Mountain, the Cherokee were unprepared for battle. While the Cherokee lost twenty-eight warriors (with many wounded) in the Battle of Boyd's Creek, the settlers lost no one (and only three wounded); afterwards, the settlers burned numerous Cherokee towns.

This was the first of John Sevier's thirty-five victories over the Cherokee, with no defeats. The English had promised the Cherokee that their alliance would be beneficial; English Indian agents had even promised that the Loyalist army would help the Cherokee evict the settlers from Cherokee land and force them to return eastward across the Blue Ridge. Now, in the Cherokees' time of need, the English were nowhere to be found. In the aftermath of the Battle of Kings Mountain, the Loyalists were concentrating all their attention on their tenuous position in the southern states. The English were losing their war against the patriots, and the Cherokee were proving less and less useful to the Loyalist cause. Yet, even after Cornwallis's surrender at Yorktown on October 19, 1781, the settlers continued to associate the Cherokee with the defeated English. Their anger toward the English, who soon left American soil, and toward the Loyalists, who were forced to assimilate into American life, was projected onto Native Americans, especially the Cherokee, whose decision to side with the English would continue to haunt them into the nineteenth century. President Andrew Jackson's harsh treatment of the Cherokee was no doubt influenced by his childhood memories of Indian attacks on mountain settlements during the early 1780s.

The State of Franklin

The federal government, impoverished by the Revolutionary War, sought to gain economic strength by acquiring landholdings from two land-rich states, Virginia and North Carolina. Settlers in the western sections of these two states, though, had other ideas. In 1784, these settlers undertook legal action which would lead, after many setbacks, to the creation of two new states, Kentucky and Tennessee. Before Tennessee ever existed, however, settlers on the western side of the Blue Ridge, in anger at ongoing nonrepresentation (these settlers, after all, had saved the state, and perhaps the nation, by winning the Battle of Kings Mountain), rebelled against the North Carolina government and established the Independent State of Franklin.

Named after the famed American statesman, the State of Franklin incorporated much of the same territory as the earlier Watauga Association. By the end of 1784, the proposed state's delegates had chosen a capitol, Jonesborough (now in eastern Tennessee), and a governor, John Sevier, and had drawn up a constitution modelled on the North Carolina state constitution (which Sevier had helped to draft in 1776). At first hesitant to be the leader of a separatist movement, Sevier gave the government of North Carolina every opportunity to satisfy the demands of the frontiersmen in order to avert secession; but, by the spring of 1785, it was clear to Sevier that North Carolina officials wished to suppress the movement toward the founding of the State of Franklin.

North Carolina never ceded lands to the new state or officially recognized it, so the government of Franklin began acting in its own interest. The Franklinites appointed one of their own constituents to Congress and negotiated two peace treaties with the Cherokee, which garnered new territory for the frontiersmen. Still, the government of North Carolina refused to budge.

The matter was not resolved until the national constitutional convention in 1787, when the new Constitution of the United States established guidelines for the formation of states. Essentially, the original states along the Atlantic coast were granted greater power in federal decision making than any proposed western states. The future of the State of Franklin now legally in the hands of North Carolina officials, the Franklinites became the recipients of considerable hostility. For instance, in 1788 a North Carolina governmental clerk named John Tipton confiscated John Sevier's slaves in an attempt to punish the Franklinites for establishing their own court system. Sevier and a hundred and fifty supporters surrounded Tipton's house, yet Tipton averted a skirmish by taking two of Sevier's sons as hostages. Agreeing not to fight, both sides released their prisoners, and Sevier and his men went home.

Not long after Sevier's term as governor of the State of Franklin expired in March 1788, the North Carolina government arrested him for treason, claiming that he had organized troops against the laws and government of North Carolina. After surrendering, Sevier was transported by Tipton over the Blue Ridge to the foothill town of Morganton, North Carolina, for a trial. No sooner had he arrived in Morganton, though, than some of Sevier's fellow Franklinites helped him escape, and he fled back across the Blue Ridge.

The North Carolina General Assembly pardoned Sevier for his activities on behalf of the proposed State of Franklin, though they barred him from future positions within the government of North Carolina. In 1789, the people to the west of the Blue Ridge, ignoring the legal constraints on Sevier, elected him to a succession of political appointments—he served as state senator, member of the federal Constitution ratification committee, and U. S. congressman for North Carolina's westernmost district (that portion of the state's population living to the west of the Blue Ridge). In each of these positions Sevier took the opportunity to champion the causes and the rights of Blue Ridge mountain people.

Congress soon ceded North Carolina's and Virginia's lands west of the Blue Ridge, but the State of Franklin was not ratified—that proposed state was considered too small, since the United States had acquired new lands to the west. The approved territory was officially termed "the Territory of the United States of America, South of the River Ohio," and was popularly called "the Southwest Territory." In 1792, a section of "the Southwest Territory" was established as the state of Kentucky, and, in 1795, another section, which included the original Franklin tract, became the state of Tennessee.

As the eighteenth century drew to a close, the balance of power within the United States was clearly shifting to the west. Many of the character traits which would empower Americans in establishing dominance in North America in the nineteenth century and around the world in the twentieth century first evolved in the eighteenth century, among frontiersmen living on the slopes of the Blue Ridge.

Not every eighteenth century Blue Ridge settler followed Daniel Boone westward. Those who remained in the Blue Ridge—whether by choice or by circumstance—were among the most culturally conservative settlers in the new nation. For them the Blue Ridge was not a prison, but rather a sacred space in which treasured traditional values were sheltered from the compromising, homogenizing forces of a rapidly changing nation. The traditional culture which evolved in the Blue Ridge, in its various local manifestations, is a syncretism of several distinctive Old World cultures which by necessity were tailored to a New World environment, with additional cultural information regarding wilderness survival borrowed from New World teachers, the Native Americans. By 1800, an intense period of exploration, settlement, and conflict (involving Native Americans and land claims) was ending within the region, and a distinctive Blue Ridge culture survived among those who remained behind.

CHAPTER 2

The Nineteenth and Twentieth Centuries

Gold

In 1799, twelve-year-old Conrad Reed, walking on his father's farm on the western edge of the North Carolina piedmont (in present-day Cabarrus County), spotted an unusual rock. According to local legend, Conrad brought the seventeen-pound rock to his father's cabin and used it as a door stop. Later, someone informed the Reeds that they had found an unusually large chunk of gold. Even larger gold nuggets were discovered on the Reed property. Word of the mother lode soon spread, and the rush was on.

Within a few years, prospectors from every walk of life and ethnic background had established mining operations in the Blue Ridge foothills. If a prospector was lucky he might find two dollars worth of gold each day—then a considerable amount of money—which he could sell to individual buyers (private investors or agents for foreign markets) or to the federal mint in Philadelphia (which by 1833 was purchasing nearly half a million dollars of North Carolina gold per year for the manufacture of gold coins). By the 1820s, North Carolina had earned the nickname "the Golden State" long before California was tagged with a similar moniker. Yet, since the foothills were inundated with prospectors—more than a thousand were active in Burke County alone—there were more unlucky ones than lucky.

Many European emigrants attempted to benefit from the North Carolina gold rush, including the Bechtler family from Germany; the Bechtlers, however, came to the Blue Ridge foothills to work as goldsmiths, not as prospectors. By 1830, the family had set up a shop near Rutherfordton where they produced various products made out of gold, including jewelry. What is of greater historic interest is that the Bechtlers established, also in

Rutherfordton, the new nation's first private mint. Recognizing that a lack of monetary currency had restricted the development of a trade network in the southern mountain region, the Bechtlers began to issue their own gold coins. Despite the fact that they bore no official national symbol, the Bechtler coins, with the blessing of the federal government, became valid currency even outside the southern mountain region. Many North Carolinians, upon leaving the state to improve their situations, carried with them Bechtler coins, which they used to purchase property and provisions in their new locations.

Border Disputes and Economic Struggles

The nineteenth century dawned in the Blue Ridge region with several states mired in political squabbling over territorial boundaries. By 1800, the border between North Carolina and Virginia had already been surveyed, but North Carolina's border with the new state of Tennessee was still in question. Although Tennessee was admitted to the nation in 1796, the process of surveying the Tennessee-North Carolina border did not begin until 1799, and disagreements regarding the exact position of the border were not resolved until 1821. There was also considerable debate over the exact boundaries between North Carolina and its neighboring states to the south, South Carolina and Georgia. Much of this confusion dated back to the years immediately after the Revolutionary War, when, in accordance with a treaty, the Cherokee moved westward out of the southernmost section of the Blue Ridge, clearing it for white settlement. One area in this section of the Blue Ridge, alleged to be part of South Carolina, was soon populated by Georgians, who successfully lobbied Congress to make it part of Georgia and who labelled it Walton County. Meanwhile, the government of North Carolina was granting land claims there to its own settlers, believing the area to be within its jurisdiction. Georgians openly squabbled with North Carolinians over the rights of settlement in Walton County. By 1808, with Congress refusing to resolve the problem, the two states agreed to conduct an official survey to determine the exact location of the 35th parallel, which formed the southern boundary of North Carolina in that part of the state. In the survey it was discovered that Walton County was actually well within North Carolina and thus could never have been part of South Carolina or Georgia. The Georgia settlers refused to accept the implications of this survey, leading North Carolina to commission a militia to control resisters; two separate skirmishes broke out, collectively called the Walton War. Much blood was shed and some lives were lost before the Georgia settlers withdrew. North Carolina held the field.

As their borders were established, these states proceeded to readjust their county boundaries, and in the mountains this was not a one-time process (the boundary lines of Ashe County, for instance, originally established in the northwesternmost corner of North Carolina in 1799, were redrawn twenty-three times). These readjustments were partly the result of a sudden population increase to the west of the Blue Ridge after 1819, when an 1803 treaty with the Cherokee (which had limited the westward settlement of whites onto Cherokee land) was repealed. Between the years 1800 and 1861 fifteen new counties were established in western North Carolina from former Cherokee territory or from portions of already-existent counties: Caldwell County (named after influential state educator Dr. Joseph Caldwell) in 1841; McDowell County (named after Major Joseph McDowell, a hero of the Battle of Kings Mountain) in 1842; Watauga County (which included land formerly included in the Watauga settlements) in 1849; Madison County (which bears the name of former President James Madison) in 1851; and Mitchell County (named after Dr. Elisha Mitchell, the University of North Carolina professor who died in 1857 while measuring the peak named after him, Mt. Mitchell) in 1861. Requests to rearrange the boundaries of mountain counties often came from the residents themselves, who hoped that their communities would receive better representation through more functional boundaries. Ironically, the frequent revision of county lines in the North Carolina Blue Ridge had the ultimate effect of slowing the development of stable and productive county governments. The limited state monies allocated to mountain counties were often rendered ineffective by a lack of competent administration within the counties.

For decades after the Revolutionary War, counties in the Blue Ridge region not only were generally underrepresented in state politics, but also received little benefit from the federal government. Much of the western North Carolina landscape had been decimated by the Revolutionary War, yet the state government of North Carolina put little effort toward boosting the region's economy. This was in part because the state's economy was sluggish, the result of many factors: a lack of harbors, the absence of an effective road system by which to conduct trade within the state, high transportation tariffs, and an over-dependence on agriculture. Given the state's predicament, it is little wonder that, after a second war against England (the War of 1812) ended in an American victory, North Carolina was not in a position to benefit from the postwar economic boom. The state remained economically constrained well into the nineteenth century, with the mountain counties being the state's hardest-hit section.

The institution of slavery boosted the dormant economy of North Carolina by increasing the state's agricultural production, but, while slavery was practiced throughout the eastern and central sections of North Carolina, it was less common in the Blue Ridge region. A similar pattern unfolded in Virginia. Most mountain farms were too small, and most people were too poor, to sustain slaves. Furthermore, the egalitarian nature of rural Blue Ridge society rendered slavery an alien concept to many residents. Nonetheless, slaves were held on some of the region's larger farms, particularly on those located in foothill counties on the eastern slope of the Blue Ridge, and near larger communities like Asheville (on his two Buncombe County farms, for instance, James McConnel Smith kept over 150 slaves). Slaves also toiled on farms in Virginia's Shenandoah Valley.

Agriculture remained small scale in most parts of the Blue Ridge, and there was little industry to boost the region's economy. In North Carolina, the state government—continuing the disparate treatment of eastern and western counties begun during colonial times (a situation which had spawned the Regulator movement)—blatantly ignored the needs of the state's western residents. To maintain control of state government during the early nineteenth century, easterners divided their counties into smaller units, thus increasing their representation in the state legislature.

C. H. King, a resident of the Virginia Blue Ridge, participating in a traditional agricultural activity: haymaking. (Courtesy of the Blue Ridge Parkway Photo Library)

Even if it had been less affected by corruption, that state's government had little to offer the people of the Blue Ridge—North Carolina was beset with problems. It was one of the poorest states in the union, with the highest rate of illiteracy (one-third of the state's adults). Additionally, the people of North Carolina had since colonial times avoided paying taxes, which meant that state coffers were always low. All told, the state was deeply troubled, and a significant number of Blue Ridge residents expressed their dissatisfaction by leaving North Carolina for the western frontier, echoing the actions of the earlier expatriates who followed Daniel Boone.

Political Representation

In 1812, a new legislator was elected to the North Carolina General Assembly, one who chose to stand up for the people of the Blue Ridge. By 1819 this man, piedmont lawyer Archibald DeBow Murphey, had conducted a thorough survey of the state's geography and its economic conditions. Based on his findings, Murphey proposed to improve the state's economy through the implementation of a superior transportation system, which would include the construction of a major road between the western mountains and central and eastern North Carolina. Murphey made two other proposals which he felt would improve the quality of life in the mountains: an up-to-date map of the entire state and a state-supported school system. The state legislature, predisposed as it was to uphold the needs of the eastern establishment at the expense of the state's western residents, killed Murphey's reforms when they were presented before the general assembly. In response, Murphey took the radical, ultimately unsuccessful step of proposing the overhaul of the North Carolina state constitution. In this, he was prophetic: though he did not live to see the enforcement of his proposed changes, subsequent legislators from the western counties, inspired by Murphey's example, began to reform North Carolina politics. David Lowry Swain, a lawyer from Buncombe County with a strongly reconciliatory personality, convinced politicians from the eastern establishment that political reform was in the best interest of all North Carolinians. When the newly formed Whig Party (composed largely of people from the western counties) elected him governor in 1832, Swain put forward a proposition, enacted into law in 1834, which submitted to the voting public the possibility of a constitutional convention. A majority of voters decided that the constitution should indeed be revised, a process which was completed by 1835. The revised constitution essentially rendered the government of the state of North Carolina a more democratic institution, one which served all sections of the state (if not all the people residing within the state—women, African Americans, and Native Americans being noticeably excluded from this era's definition of "democracy").

Unfortunately, while the North Carolina Blue Ridge was gaining representation within the state legislature, the region's social and economic gains were being threatened by national politics. In 1828, Blue Ridge voters helped to elect Andrew Jackson to the presidency, undoubtedly believing that Jackson, who was born in the Blue Ridge foothills near the North Carolina-South Carolina border, would represent their interests in national policy making. Jackson, however, assumed a political stance which freed the federal government from responsibility for local or regional concerns; according to Jackson, social and economic reforms were the responsibility of state governments, not the federal one. This meant that the North Carolina General Assembly, run by the eastern establishment, maintained political control over mountain counties, and that the people of the Blue Ridge remained economically disadvantaged.

The Displacement of the Cherokee

Jackson's lack of concern for regional groups was tragically expressed in his betrayal of the Cherokee. During the War of 1812, the Cherokee had demonstrated to Jackson, then general of the U.S. Army, their acceptance of the new nation, despite having lost so much ancestral territory. When Tecumseh, the powerful chief of the Shawnee, tried to coax the Cherokee to participate in a multitribal uprising against mountain settlers, the Cherokees' principal chief, Junaluska, refused to cooperate. Recognizing that the white people's occupation of the Cherokees' ancestral lands was probably irreversible, Junaluska and other Cherokee elders surmised that an uprising would refuel the futile violence of earlier Indian-white conflicts. The Cherokees' foes, the Creeks, though, did not share Junaluska's desire for compromise. In 1813, they attacked a federal outpost, Fort Mims, in the territory to the west of Georgia (later, southwestern Alabama), slaughtering five hundred settlers. Intent on retaliation, the U.S. Army led by General Jackson pursued the Creeks through a swampy wilderness. Jackson's task was made much easier through the help of numerous Cherokee warriors, including Junaluska. On March 27, 1814, the army and Cherokee assistants conquered the Creeks at the Battle of Horseshoe Bend (in present-day east-central Alabama). After the U.S. Army trapped the Creeks on a peninsula in the Tallapoosa River (at Horseshoe Bend), the Cherokee warriors dealt the Creeks the final blow by secretly stealing their boats, which the army used to cross the river and gain access to the Creeks' fortification. A legendary anecdote describes how, immediately before the battle, Junaluska witnessed a Creek warrior on the verge of attacking Jackson; interceding at the last moment, Junaluska killed the warrior, thus saving the general's life.

In the immediate aftermath of Horseshoe Bend, the Cherokee were valorized as heroes, with Jackson publicly declaring the nation's and his own personal appreciation. By this time Cherokee territory was drastically reduced, not only in the Blue Ridge but also in ancestral lands to the west. Yet, for the present, the tribe's future was not completely bleak. Throughout the 1820s, the Cherokee nation was politically organized, with a written constitution; most tribe members lived quietly and self-sufficiently on small farms. The Cherokee were celebrating a cultural renaissance. In 1821, a half-breed named Sequoyah introduced the syllabic alphabet he had been developing for twelve years, which was based on spoken Cherokee and had a distinct symbol representing each individual sound. Within a few years the tribe adopted this alphabet, making it the only written language in the history of the world devised single-handedly by an individual. After Sequoyah's alphabet system found a receptive audience with the Cherokee, a Cherokee-language version of the New Testament appeared (many tribe members had by this time converted to Christianity), as did a newspaper written in both Cherokee and English.

This period of peaceful coexistence, though, was to be short-lived, as rumors of gold on Cherokee lands in north Georgia spread across the country. With white Georgians coveting this gold, politicians made life miserable for the Cherokee living in that state, declaring their tribal nation invalid and enacting laws which forbade the Cherokee from owning property. Georgia officials staged a lottery to redistribute Cherokee territory to new white owners, and the Cherokee were ordered to leave Georgia by June 1, 1830, before which time the tribe was not permitted to meet. As a precaution, state officials arrested and detained in jail several tribal leaders. Alarmed at this mistreatment, the Cherokee sought legal defense from the federal government. The U.S. Supreme Court did in fact decree that Georgia had no right to evict tribe members from their property, that only the federal government could negotiate such a transaction. Georgia immediately ignored the Supreme Court's ruling. When the Cherokee pleaded with President Jackson for his intervention on their behalf, the former general, whose life had been saved fifteen years before by the great Cherokee leader Junaluska, retorted, "[Chief Justice] John Marshall has rendered his decision; now let him enforce it."

The tribe's future in Georgia now in doubt, a faction within their leadership attempted to resolve the conflict by negotiating with the U.S. government a treaty mandating the Cherokee to sell all that remained of their ancestral lands and emigrate west to the Indian Territory (present-day

Oklahoma). Recognizing that this faction's actions did not represent the interests of the tribe as a whole, the Georgia government put in prison the tribe's charismatic leader John Ross, who detested the idea of removal. Fraudulent by design, the treaty was signed by a small contingent of the tribe at the tribal capital, New Echota, Georgia, on December 29, 1835. The federal government promptly passed the treaty into law, and the tribe's subsequent appeals were ignored. The Cherokee were commanded to vacate their ancestral homeland by the spring of 1838. When that time arrived, most of the tribe had not left their farms, so the federal government instigated a more aggressive eviction plan. Seven thousand army troops under General Winfield Scott rounded up as many Cherokee as could be located and placed them in stockades. A thousand tribe members, eluding the army's grasp, went into hiding in the Great Smoky Mountains.

Leaving in two separate groups (one in June 1838, the other in October 1839), the stockaded Cherokee embarked on the thousand-mile forced march westward to Indian Territory, the torturous Trail of Tears. Tragically, one-third of the approximately seventeen thousand tribe members who began the march died along the way. Those who survived the Trail of Tears settled in the west, while those who had hidden in the Great Smoky Mountains were eventually permitted to remain in the east. Now landless, the Eastern Band of the Cherokee (as this group came to be known) benefitted from the assistance of a sympathetic white businessman, William Holland Thomas, who when orphaned as a child had been adopted by the tribe. Thomas obtained promised treaty monies from a resistant federal government, which the Eastern Band used toward the purchase of two large parcels of land near the Smokies, on which many of the descendants of the Eastern Band's original members still reside. The Cherokees' choice of Thomas as chief of the Eastern Band was an act of expedience; it was also ironic—the tribe had entrusted their most important political role to a white man.

Improvements in Transportation

One early sign of Archibald DeBow Murphey's growing influence within the North Carolina General Assembly was the 1823 allocation of state funds for a transmountain road, the Buncombe Turnpike. Completed in 1827, this road linked South Carolina with Tennessee, allowing safe wagon transport from Greenville, South Carolina, over the North Carolina Blue Ridge, then through the valley of the French Broad River to Greeneville, Tennessee. A toll road, the Buncombe Turnpike profoundly affected the Blue Ridge communities through which it passed, providing economic relief to an impoverished region. Inns, supply outlets, and wagon-repair shops sprang up in a number of places along the turnpike. Owing to its strategic location along the turnpike, Asheville, North Carolina, grew quickly as a supply center for travellers. An important tourist attraction also emerged along the turnpike: Warm Springs, later called Hot Springs. The Buncombe Turnpike not only benefitted the communities through which it was routed, but also served the nation by providing eastern markets with a steady supply of agricultural products, poultry, and livestock raised to the west of the Blue Ridge. The animal most commonly transported along the turnpike was the hog (one fall, over 150,000 hogs were recorded as having passed through Asheville). Drovers—either the owners of the animals or hired substitutes—guided these animals, which were followed by assistants, usually boys or young men who kept the animals together by cracking whips and crying out signature calls. By nightfall the drovers would stop to eat and rest at inns located along the turnpike; these inns featured special pens in which to keep the animals. In exchange for a night's rest, drovers would pay the innkeepers in money or animals (the latter would be fed to subsequent drovers). Also benefitting from the turnpike were local farmers, who profited by providing innkeepers with ample supplies of grain for animal feed.

Another important drover route was Daniel Boone's Wilderness Road. Along this road, drovers would guide Tennessee- and Kentucky-raised livestock and poultry eastward to the present-day site of Boone, North Carolina, where they would sell them to a middleman, Jordan Council. Council's own hired drovers would then transport the animals further eastward for sale in the piedmont. As other roads in the Blue Ridge were improved, they, too, were used by drovers. All the drover roads helped to increase the economies of the areas through which they coursed; areas not adjacent to the roads, however, were unaffected, a situation which led to increasing economic disparity between people living in river valleys (the usual route of a drover road) and those dwelling on remote hillsides.

The Emergence of Public Education

The establishment of public schools in the Blue Ridge region owed as much to federal as to state or local support. In the mid 1830s, the U. S. government, having recently amassed surplus funds through the sale of western lands, decided to allocate a portion of these funds to each state, with the provision that it spend the money on its own economic and social betterment. North Carolina's then-dominant political party, the Whigs, recently risen to power and sympathetic to the cause of improving mountain

In the early days of settlement in the Blue Ridge, circuit riders (preachers on horseback) brought religious counsel, somewhat irregularly, to remote communities. More recently, Reverend Robert Harris of Asheville drew enthusiastic responses when he revived the circuit rider persona. (Photo by Hugh Morton)

life (in the spirit of Murphey), earmarked most of the funds toward the establishment of a statewide public school system. In 1839, the state's general assembly created the Public School Law, which offered to support any county willing to pay with local taxes a portion of a school's operating expenses. Although a number of private schools had been in operation in the region since the early days of settlement, the first public schools appeared in the North Carolina Blue Ridge during the 1840s. These schools—usually crude one-room cabins—were often received with relative indifference: students were required to attend classes only a few months per year (usually in the dead of winter, for parents needed their children's labor the rest of the time), and the teachers were considerably underpaid, as well as often being ill prepared for their roles as educators. Officials of many Blue Ridge counties took advantage of legal loopholes in order to reduce local support of schools.

Resistance to the introduction of public education among the people of the Blue Ridge has been explained from two radically different perspectives. According to one position, the southern mountain people in general were cultural deviants; this perspective, widely promulgated for over a century, found succinct expression via prominent English historian Arnold J. Toynbee, who in 1935 wrote: "The 'Mountain People' of Appalachia are *ci-deviant* heirs of the Western Civilization who have relapsed into barbarism." According to the second, more empathetic position, the Blue Ridge people's resistance to public schools might be interpreted as the instinctive reaction of a traditional, largely rural subculture to the modern values of the American cultural elite.

The Beginnings of Tourism

The completion of the Buncombe Turnpike in the 1820s may have opened one area to settlement and tourism, but, by 1850, the Blue Ridge was still largely rural; the North Carolina Blue Ridge, for instance, possessed only two incorporated towns: Asheville, with a population of 800, and the foothill village of Rutherfordton, with 484 residents. By the 1850s, tourism, which would later have considerable economic impact on the region, was just beginning to make its presence felt. In those days visitors to the North Carolina Blue Ridge were generally wealthy South Carolinians (usually Charlestonians) seeking temporary escape from the lowland heat. Prewar tourists, desiring summer quarters which stylistically replicated their home environment, flocked to such plush accommodations as the Warm Springs Hotel (opened in 1831, it stood in the present-day town of Hot Springs, North Carolina) and the Farmer Inn (in Flat Rock, North Carolina). The lifestyles of these part-year residents contrasted radically with those of the local populace. While most people in the Blue Ridge worked year-round on small, self-sufficient farms, lowlanders passed summer days enjoying the leisurely activities allowed by their social and economic station—strolling or riding in carriages down country lanes through heavily landscaped resort grounds, for instance.

Some of those tourists purchased land in the Blue Ridge. South Carolinians were buying property in the North Carolina Blue Ridge as early as the late 1820s, especially near Flat Rock; a few even built homes there, anticipating the trend toward second-home ownership which eventually altered the Blue Ridge landscape. Two of the more grandiose mansions in the Blue Ridge, both built toward the end of the nineteenth century, are still regional landmarks: the opulent, French-chateau style Biltmore House near Asheville (surrounded by extravagant estate grounds designed by famed landscape architect Frederick Law Olmsted, George Washington Vanderbilt's house and estate are today a major tourist attraction) and the more modest mansion of denim manufacturer Moses H. Cone, Flat Top Manor House near Blowing Rock, North Carolina (now located along the Blue Ridge Parkway, this house serves as an outlet for the Southern Highland Handicraft Guild).

Accelerating the spread of second homes across the Blue Ridge were new roads which provided outsiders with easier access to more areas. Some of these roads, like the Hickory Nut Turnpike connecting Rutherfordton and Asheville, appeared as early as the 1850s. And by 1860 a new mode of transportation—the railroad—was fast approaching the Blue Ridge from the North Carolina piedmont. It would be some years, however, before railroads reached the crest of the Blue Ridge; the Civil War forced railroad companies to redirect materials and manpower toward the war effort.

The Coming of War

The Blue Ridge region in general, and the Virginia Blue Ridge in particular, served as the setting for considerable Civil War action. One of the more notorious causes of the war occurred at the northern end of the Blue Ridge, in Harpers Ferry, Virginia (by 1863 the town was part of the new state of West Virginia, formed by the pro-Union citizens of what had been western Virginia). On October 16, 1859, abolitionist John Brown and a small band of supporters invaded Harpers Ferry and seized the town's federal arsenal and armory. With stolen armaments, Brown and his supporters intended to head southward along the Blue Ridge, sparking a slave revolt as they went. Some northern abolitionists had supported Brown's antislavery activities for years, though they had also begun to question his soundness of mind, since by the late 1850s he had developed a reputation as an extremist prone to acts of violence. But while some saw Brown as a madman, others thought of him as a martyr who dared question a nation which tolerated the institution of slavery. One thing was clear: he was no military leader. Embarking on this raid with virtually no planning—few provisions, no escape route out of Harpers Ferry, and only a handful of recruits (just over twenty men total)—Brown seemed less concerned with the immediate success of his raid than with the long-term repercussions of his actions. Soon apprehended by federal authorities, Brown was rapidly tried, convicted for three crimes (murder, treason, and inciting insurrection), and hanged in Charles Town, Virginia (later West Virginia) on December 2, 1859.

Brown's actions spawned dramatic responses: many southern whites feared that he would incite subsequent slave revolts (this did not happen), while many northerners viewed him as a martyr who had acted, however unconventionally and ineffectively, out of sincere concern for the rights of the slaves. Brown's final court statement included this powerful indictment of the American legal system and its hypocrisy regarding slavery: "I deny everything but what I have all along admitted: of a design on my part to free slaves. . . . Had I interfered in the manner which I admit . . . in behalf of the rich, the powerful, the intelligent, the so-called great[,] . . . every man in this Court would have deemed it an act worthy of reward rather than punishment." Whether madman or martyr (or both), he was indeed, as novelist Herman Melville asserted, "the meteor of the War."

After the South instigated the Civil War in April 1861, the Union received some of its staunchest support from people living in the southern mountains. The people of the Southern Appalachians, after all, were descended from patriots who had shunned sectionalism during the struggle for American independence from the English. Also, since their farms were generally too small to support slavery, many mountain people saw little need to defend the institution. Furthermore, these people had long resented the wealthy slaveholders of the lowlands who, as the primary legislators of the southern states, had created laws which historically had furthered their own interests at the expense of those who dwelt in the mountains.

Yet, despite the pro-Union sympathies of many of the region's residents, the Blue Ridge held great strategic importance to the Confederacy. In the spring of 1862, for instance, Robert E. Lee—who at this stage of the war was a military adviser to Jefferson Davis, the president of the Confederacy—realized that Richmond might fall quickly to a united Union army, but that the rebels might save their capital if they fragmented the Union army; to accomplish this, Lee sent General Thomas J. "Stonewall" Jackson and his troops up the Shenandoah Valley, which led President Abraham Lincoln, fearing for the safety of the Union capital, to move General Irvin McDowell's thirty-five thousand soldiers closer to Washington. The ploy worked. Believing that a sizeable Confederate force was hiding behind the Blue Ridge ready to spring on Washington, Lincoln did not reinforce the hundred thousand troops in General George McClellan's Army of the Potomac, then positioned just outside Richmond.

The two armies had many close confrontations in the Shenandoah Valley (and in the parallel Luray Valley) during the war, and strategically important valley locations (such as Winchester, Virginia) changed hands many times. Despite superior leadership and a better knowledge of the region's terrain, the Confederates did not win every contest. In March 1862, at Kernstown, Virginia, "Stonewall" Jackson's force of forty-two hundred soldiers was defeated by a larger Union force of nine thousand men under General Nathaniel Banks. Nonetheless, the Shenandoah Valley was the site of Jackson's remarkable campaign of May and June 1862. According to historian James M. McPherson, "Jackson's [Shenandoah] Valley campaign won renown and is still studied in military schools as an example of how speed and use of terrain can compensate for inferiority of numbers." During this campaign, though his army was outmanned two to one (seventeen thousand rebels had to contend with thirty-three thousand Union soldiers), Jackson outmaneuvered three Union generals, and the Confederate army won five successive battles: at McDowell, Front Royal, Winchester, Cross Keys, and Port Republic. Displaying diligence, deception, and an effective use of terrain, Jackson saved Richmond and the Confederacy from an early fall.

In June 1863, the Virginia Blue Ridge served to screen the movements of the Army of Northern Virginia (led by General Lee) on its fateful invasion of Pennsylvania. One year later, the Shenandoah Valley was again a factor in the war, this time with dire consequences for the Confederacy. After Confederate General Jubal Early's July 1864 raid on Washington, Union General Ulysses S. Grant put General Philip Sheridan in charge of the Union's Army of the Shenandoah, with orders to march into the Shenandoah Valley to capture Early. On September 19, 1864, Sheridan's army, some thirty-seven thousand strong, attacked Early's fifteen thousand soldiers at Winchester. One-fourth of the Confederates were killed or taken prisoner, and Early and the remaining rebels fled southward to Fisher's Hill. On September 22, Sheridan's army chased Early and his soldiers from their defensive position, whereupon the rebels escaped into the Blue Ridge. To scare them out, Sheridan proceeded to destroy crops and property throughout the Shenandoah Valley. General Grant had commanded Sheridan to do so, reasoning that, since the region had been strategically beneficial to the Confederate army, the valley should be decimated.

On October 19, Early's soldiers, well rested and strengthened by the addition of new troops, attacked the Union encampment at Cedar Creek. The Union troops were caught by surprise, as Sheridan was absent, having travelled to Washington for a military briefing. The rebels captured over a thousand prisoners, and the rest of the Union army retreated northward. The Confederates, though, claimed victory prematurely, for Sheridan was just then journeying back to Cedar Creek from Washington by way of Winchester. Resolved to turn the tide of the day's events, Sheridan led the Union soldiers in a sweeping counterattack against a surprised Confederate army. In this phase of the Battle of Cedar Creek, the rebels were routed. At the end of the day the Union had not only regained the field but had also ended the threat that had been Early's army. The Confederate loss at Cedar

Creek was one of two events in 1864 which signaled the South's inevitable loss of the war (the other being the fall of Atlanta in September).

No major Civil War battles took place in the North Carolina Blue Ridge; however, because political loyalties within the region were sharply divided, countless skirmishes occurred there. These conflicts were particularly frequent after July 1863, when the Confederate congress elected to position militia throughout the South in an attempt to capture draft evaders, return deserters to their commands, and control marauders who were opportunistically exploiting undermanned southern farms and villages. Confederate soldiers were soon present in the Blue Ridge, causing conflict wherever they encountered Union sympathizers.

In 1864, fearing the destruction of North Carolina railroads by Federal cavalry raiders out of Tennessee (eastern Tennessee had been a bastion of Unionism from early in the war), Confederate leaders stationed additional troops in the North Carolina Blue Ridge. These troops were made up largely of citizen-soldiers who proved incapable of keeping the Yankee raiders at bay. In June 1864, one Unionist from east Tennessee, Colonel George W. Kirk, with a band of 130 men, invaded Confederate territory. Crossing the Blue Ridge, Kirk and his men attacked an unprepared Confederate camp in the foothill town of Morganton (in Burke County, North Carolina). After taking over a hundred prisoners, the invaders burned the camp's buildings (sparing the hospital) and destroyed Morganton's railroad depot, then headed back towards Tennessee, with Confederate soldiers pursuing in vain.

News of Kirk's prowess as a military leader spread quickly through the Blue Ridge, and those sympathetic with the Confederacy grew terrified. One period anecdote illustrates the discrepancy between rumor and truth during that turbulent time. On his return to Tennessee after destroying the Confederate camp at Morganton, Kirk allegedly stopped at a house near Pineola, North Carolina, and conversed with its occupant, John Franklin, who did not recognize him—the colonel was wearing no discernable uniform. At one point in the conversation, Franklin revealed his Confederate sympathies, negatively referring to Kirk (in the third person, of course), stating that he had heard that Kirk was mean, and asserting that he would kill the man if he ever had the opportunity. Kirk immediately drew a pistol and snapped, "Damn you, I am George Kirk." Franklin's wife apparently sank to her knees and begged for mercy for her husband, while Franklin meekly acknowledged that Kirk's bad reputation may have had little relation to the truth. Accordingly, Kirk spared Franklin's life and quickly departed for Tennessee. Franklin, remembering the Colonel's mercy, named his next son George Kirkland Franklin.

Kirk's successful invasion into Confederate territory persuaded Union sympathizers throughout the Blue Ridge that the Confederate presence in the region was a token force at best. Many who before had feigned support for the Confederate cause to escape persecution now felt safe to confess their allegiance to the Union. Early in the war, two Union sympathizers, W. M. Blalock and his wife, Malinda, who lived near Grandfather Mountain, both volunteered for the Confederate army (she in the guise of a young man) to avoid the harsher treatment soldiers received through conscription. Their ultimate goal was to desert their Confederate unit when it ventured near the Mason-Dixon line; the Blalocks, however, were never positioned close to Union territory. To escape their predicament, the Blalocks feigned illnesses. After they were released from their service, the Confederate officials realized they had been duped. The Blalocks eluded capture, however, and escaped into Union territory in Tennessee. Until the end of the war, W. M. Blalock travelled in the Blue Ridge as a Union spy.

Blalock was far from the only Blue Ridge resident to act against the Confederacy. Union sympathizers throughout the region established a network of "underground railroads" to ensure the safety of Union soldiers and other fugitive Unionists, including escaped slaves—even deserters from the Confederate army. Guides like Blalock provided safe passage for Unionists from the piedmont across the Blue Ridge to the Union lines in eastern Tennessee. By 1864, many Confederate citizen-soldiers in the region were covertly supporting the Union cause by overlooking pro-Union activities occurring around them.

One sign the Confederacy was losing its grip in the Blue Ridge was the rise of terrorism by "bushwhackers." Ostensively serving the interests of the Union, these people in fact often acted more out of self-interest. Toward the end of 1864, the bushwhackers' violent behavior was threatening all Blue Ridge residents, whether pro-Union or pro-Confederacy; vandalism against personal and public property was common, and random murders occurred with frightening frequency.

Confederate troops stationed in the Blue Ridge posed a major threat; among other transgressions, these soldiers often helped themselves to the possessions of residents. Observing just such an episode, in which drunken soldiers ransacked the town of Boone, Confederate officer J. C. Wills on April 29, 1864, wrote North Carolina's governor, Zebulon B. Vance:

> In crossing the Blue Ridge, on my way here . . . I met Gen. V. [Confederate General J. C. Vaughn] and two or three other officers (of his staff I presume). Half a mile behind him I met some half doz. of his soldiers, and I continued to meet them in squads, of from two to twenty, all the way to this place [Boone]—stragling [*sic*] along without the shadow of organization or discipline. In this manner, they continued to come through for ten days. The

whole command (some seventeen or eighteen hundred men) just disbanded, and turned loose, to pillage the inhabitants, and thoroughly did they perform their work. It was not merely stealing but open and above board highway robery [*sic*]. They would enter houses violently breaking open every door, and helping themselves to what suited their various fancies—not provisions only, but everything, from horses down to ladies['] breast pins.

One of the most effective Union raids of the South took place in both the North Carolina and the Virginia Blue Ridge. Occurring at the same time as General William Tecumseh Sherman's march through the South, the raid led by Major General George H. Stoneman received comparatively little attention, yet it was a crucial event in the final crushing of the Confederacy. By the beginning of 1865, the Union had considerably weakened the southern rebellion; the western and Gulf Coast sections of the Confederacy had fallen into Union hands, a situation which increased the importance of North Carolina as the Confederacy's safety zone for the resupplying of Richmond and Lee's army in Virginia. The Union wanted to debilitate the southern military infrastructure in the Blue Ridge and the western piedmont, in order to prevent the Confederate army and government from escaping southwestward out of central Virginia. On March 24, 1865, Stoneman and his command embarked from Morristown, Tennessee, to fulfill this mission. Early in the raid Stoneman's army divided itself and crisscrossed the Blue Ridge and the western piedmont, destroying three Confederate railroads and burning jails and factories from Boone, North Carolina, to Christiansburg, Virginia. Stoneman's raiders continued to demolish Confederate munitions in the North Carolina piedmont, even after Lee surrendered to the Union at Appomattox Courthouse on April 9, 1865. Compared to Sherman's invasion, which caused extensive destruction to the southern landscape, Stoneman's raid was benign (though it fulfilled its strategic goal). The citizens of the region remembered Stoneman for his restraint as a commander—little private property was destroyed during the raid, and Stoneman's troops for the most part acted in an orderly, respectful manner.

Recovery from the War

The cessation of the war in 1865 alleviated a major source of political and social turmoil in the Blue Ridge region, but the wounds of economic deprivation continued to fester. The war had had a profound impact on the region (it is not surprising that, after the war, many people, disgusted at their ruined environment and disillusioned with their political representation, left for the western frontier—echoing an earlier pattern of rejecting the limitations of Blue Ridge life). First and foremost, countless men, casualties of the war, never returned to their mountain farms, resulting in broken hearts and labor shortages there; others did make it home, only to find their families suffering from deprivation and their houses and farms destroyed. The returning soldiers' wartime affiliations often came back to haunt them, in the form of retaliation from those on the opposing side. Additionally, the now-dead Confederacy had exhausted the already-weak economies of Blue Ridge states, bequeathing only inflation and then economic depression. With little available currency and few opportunities for employment, the standard of living of many Blue Ridge people was reduced to a subsistence level, or worse; roads lay in ruin and schools stood in poor repair.

Economic recovery was slow in coming, owing to chaotic social and political conditions during Reconstruction. The termination of slavery had led to increased competition for jobs throughout the South. Although relatively few slaves had worked in the Blue Ridge before the war, after it was over numerous freed African Americans migrated to the mountains for work, a situation which gave rise to Ku Klux Klan activity in the region (for instance, two foothill counties in North Carolina, Rutherford and Polk, experienced considerable Klan activity during the postwar period).

The political representation of the Blue Ridge people during Reconstruction was marked by corruption. The military governments implanted throughout the South by the federal government, generally consisting of pronorthern carpetbaggers, impeded the governments of Blue Ridge states from passing legislation which would improve their rural infrastructure—and, as usual, the mountain counties of those states received the least share of what funds were available. Numerous scandals caused by self-interested carpetbaggers left state coffers empty. Having huge debts to pay off and little available tax money to work with, those states overlooked a substantial number of problems in their mountain districts. Only after Reconstruction ended in the mid-1870s did state governments reorganize and actively participate in the economic development of the Blue Ridge. The scheme chosen for improving conditions in the region involved unleashing the forces of industrialization, a decision which would lead to the exploitation of many within the Blue Ridge.

On the Brink of Industrialization

Federal and state governments had only marginal interest in the Blue Ridge before the Civil War, but after Reconstruction they sought much

Some Blue Ridge residents continued to transport heavy loads in handmade wagons drawn by teams of oxen well into the twentieth century. This photograph was taken in 1936 near Rock Castle Gorge, in the Virginia Blue Ridge. (Courtesy of the Blue Ridge Parkway Photo Library)

more, including taxes and a share of the region's natural resources. The federal government, for instance, had by this time begun to tax Americans for the liquor they produced (which had not been done since George Washington's presidency). This infuriated the Blue Ridge people, who refused to pay the demanded excise taxes. Federal revenue officers were sent into the mountains to force compliance with the liquor laws, and much violence ensued. The liquor makers ("moonshiners"), determined to protect what they saw as their cultural birthright, learned to hide their stills more effectively.

At the war's end, the effort to construct railroads into the North Carolina Blue Ridge was renewed. One of the first to negotiate the Blue Ridge's steep rise was the Western North Carolina Railroad, which extended an already-existing line out from Morganton. By connecting the western piedmont with Asheville, the Western North Carolina Railroad served to increase trade within the Blue Ridge; it was, however, a long time in coming, its completion delayed by political corruption, a lack of funds, and the difficult terrain. Although only four miles separated the westernmost foothill town, Old Fort, and the crest of the Blue Ridge, the Western North Carolina Railroad, winding circuitously up the Blue Ridge's eastern slope, required twelve miles of track. Constructing this section of track was especially difficult because of the need to blast away large quantities of rock, either through the use of unpredictable explosives (one crude technique involved hand drilling holes into rock and then stuffing them with a paste consisting of nitroglycerine, sawdust, and cornmeal) or through hydraulic manipulation (breaking rocks by heating them, then spraying them with cold water). Particularly dangerous was the carving out of tunnels—cave-ins were common. The lyric of a Blue Ridge folk song records one such incident, an accident which occurred at the longest of these tunnels, the Swannanoa Tunnel: "Asheville Junction, / Swannanoa Tunnel, / All caved in, babe, / All caved in." The primary victims of such accidents were convict laborers assigned by the state to this risky work; accidents along this stretch of the Western North Carolina Railroad took the lives of approximately 125 laborers. In 1880, after fifteen years of construction, the first train climbed up the Blue Ridge from Old Fort to Asheville.

Having mounted the Blue Ridge, the Western North Carolina Railroad was then extended in two routes toward the Tennessee border—one stretch following the valley of the French Broad River (completed in 1882), and another section coursing toward Murphy, North Carolina (completed in 1891). Another company was simultaneously constructing a railroad into the North Carolina Blue Ridge from the south—the Spartanburg-Asheville section of the French Broad Railroad, completed in 1886. By the early 1890s, these railroads were radically changing the rhythms of everyday life within the Blue Ridge; they were also providing easy access into the region for those on the outside, some of whom were attracted by the place's great beauty, and some of whom were more interested in its abundant natural resources.

Logging

Toward the end of the nineteenth century, much of the Blue Ridge was heavily forested despite nearly two centuries of settlement. For instance, Madison, Mitchell, Polk, Rutherford, and Surry Counties in North Carolina were at least 75 percent forestland. The construction of railroads into the Blue Ridge rendered the region more accessible, attracting the attention of national logging companies. By the 1880s, these companies had depleted much of the forestland in northern states and were looking to the Southern Appalachians for new sources of timber. The logging operations established in the Blue Ridge (some of these were large, but most were small) provided employment for many, though the work was difficult, since trees in the region—whether prized hardwoods like oaks, hickories, and walnuts, or less commercially profitable conifers like pines and hemlocks— were often enormous. Trees were dangerous when falling, and, once on the ground, they had to be transported to the mill over rough terrain. Companies often built splash dams across valley streams, which would back water up the valley and allow for the floating of logs downstream to the mill. Effective for accomplishing their intended purpose, splash dams were also environmentally destructive. Historically, trees were cut in traditional water-powered sawmills, but in later years more efficient steam-powered mills were utilized. Despite offering short-term economic relief to many rural residents of the region, logging led to long-term environmental degradation.

In the Blue Ridge, there was one beneficial consequence of this otherwise lamentable devastation: the introduction of a more environmentally concerned approach to logging. Based on scientific evidence and long-range management practices, this approach was unknown in the New World, though it had proven successful in Europe. In the 1880s, George Washington Vanderbilt, spending his inheritance from his grandfather Cornelius Vanderbilt's railroad fortune, purchased numerous farms and homesites outside of Asheville, some of which had been seriously denuded by extensive logging. After hiring architect Richard Morris Hunt to design and oversee the construction of his estate house (later called Biltmore House), as well as the country's premier landscaper, Frederick Law Olmsted, to build his estate grounds, G. W. Vanderbilt employed forester Gifford Pinchot to try to rehabilitate his damaged landholdings. Pinchot had just returned from France, where he had received formal training in scientific forest management. Pinchot saw his work on Vanderbilt's Blue Ridge estate as offering the United States a model logging practice, one which was profitable yet environmentally sound. As the forester announced in a brochure accompanying an exhibit on the Biltmore Estate at the 1893 World's Fair in Chicago: "The attempt to treat Biltmore Forest systematically derives a certain interest from the fact that it is the first practical application of forest management in the United States."

Shortly after Pinchot's arrival at the Biltmore Estate, Vanderbilt acquired an enormous (more than a hundred thousand acres), densely wooded tract of land to the southwest of Asheville, wanting it to serve as a wildlife preserve; his goal was to reintroduce and/or manage native animals and to permit the carefully monitored hunting of a few game species. Additionally, Vanderbilt intended for Pinchot to demonstrate on this parcel the effectiveness of scientific forest management; but, in 1895, before he had

had time to test his theories on the Biltmore Forest, Pinchot resigned, deciding to work as a freelance forestry consultant.

Replacing Pinchot on the Biltmore Estate was Carl Alwin Schenck, a respected German forester. Utilizing his European knowledge of forestry, Schenck advocated the selective cutting of trees over the predominant American approach of that era, clear-cutting; the selective method, he maintained, would provide steady timber yields without the environmental destruction of clear-cutting. He was only partially successful in applying European management techniques to New World circumstances; nevertheless, his nearly fifteen years of service for Vanderbilt was highly influential, in that Schenck established on the Biltmore Estate the first forestry school in the United States. Without a significant source of funding, Schenck's school, offering a one-year program, taught modern forest management to many of the first generation of professional American foresters (approximately three hundred in all).

Logging companies soon recognized the economic value of Schenck's work—as did a number of American universities, which developed their own, better-funded forestry schools. In 1909, Vanderbilt curtailed the Biltmore Estate's forestry program, forcing Schenck to relocate his school; thereafter it was based out of a nearby lumber camp owned by a commercial logging company. The school, though, began to emphasize field study in different forest ecosystems around the country and in Europe. Eventually, a combination of budgetary problems and World War I forced the forester to discontinue his school and move back to Europe. Today, the Pisgah National Forest maintains at the former site of Schenck's influential forestry school an exhibit commemorating "The Cradle of Forestry in America."

National Forests

After George Vanderbilt died in 1914, the Biltmore House was sold to a private buyer, and much of the Biltmore Estate's forested acreage was sold to the federal government to form the nucleus of the Pisgah National Forest (later, a small strip of this same land was ceded to the National Park Service for the construction of a section of the Blue Ridge Parkway). Officially established in 1916, the Pisgah National Forest was the first national forest unit east of the Mississippi River. Gifford Pinchot, who now served as the head of the United States Forest Service, and other foresters, in leading the movement for national forests in the Southern Appalachians, had recognized the importance of public forest land in safeguarding both the natural environment and public health. Widespread clear-cutting in the southern mountains during the first years of the twentieth century had caused extensive erosion, rampant wildfires, and, at times, destructive flooding (such as the devastating flood of 1916). By the time the federal government decided to take action against these problems, the mountain landscape was largely denuded.

With funds appropriated for the purpose, the government began to purchase parcels with which to establish national forests in the southern mountains. Accordingly, significant portions of the Blue Ridge region were set aside in George Washington National Forest and Jefferson National Forest in Virginia, Pisgah National Forest and Nantahala National Forest in North Carolina, Cherokee National Forest in Tennessee, Chattahoochee National Forest in Georgia, and Sumter National Forest in South Carolina. These forests have been managed according to the U. S. Forest Service's "multiple-use" management philosophy, which espouses several concurrent—and, according to some, mutually exclusive—missions, including timber harvesting, environmental restoration, game management, and recreation. In recent years a few areas within these Blue Ridge national forests, generally selected because they offer compelling natural features and because they are inaccessible, have been officially declared "wilderness areas" (examples are St. Mary's Wilderness Area in Virginia, Linville Gorge Wilderness Area in North Carolina, and Ellicott's Rock Wilderness Area on the Georgia-South Carolina border). Legally protected from future tampering (e. g., logging, mining, and road building), these wilderness areas offer a sense of what the Blue Ridge landscape might have looked like to Native American scouts, to European explorers like Hernando de Soto, to early naturalists like William Bartram, and to colonists like Daniel Boone.

Shenandoah National Park

In addition to setting aside portions of the region in national forests, the federal government undertook two other major conservation projects in the Blue Ridge: Shenandoah National Park and the Blue Ridge Parkway. When Shenandoah National Park and its sister park in the southern mountains, Great Smoky Mountains National Park, were jointly authorized in 1926, only one other national park had been established east of the Mississippi, and that one, tiny Acadia National Park in Maine, had been created under the most favorable circumstances imaginable (philanthropist John D. Rockefeller, Jr., had donated it to the government).

The founding of two parks near the population centers of the eastern United States presented two major problems. Park land had to be purchased without federal funding, since governmental authorities granted no financial appropriations. In the case of Shenandoah National Park, this problem was solved innovatively. To interest the American public in the new park, a scenic tourist road was proposed which would traverse the crest of the Blue Ridge and offer commanding views (to the east, of the piedmont, and to the west, of the Luray and Shenandoah Valleys and Massanutten Mountain). Indeed, the promise of this road (eventually constructed in the 1930s by members of the Civilian Conservation Corps, the 105-mile road was named Skyline Drive) proved to have magnetic appeal for fundraising. More than a million dollars was raised through a public donation campaign, and additional funds were contributed by the Virginia state government. This approach to fund-raising had its limitations, however: today, Shenandoah National Park is just one-third the size of original projections.

In establishing southern mountain national parks, promoters also needed to solve the issue of what to do with the people who lived on land designated for that purpose. In the case of Shenandoah National Park, the problem was solved, controversially, through the removal of over four hundred families from their ridgetop and hollow farms. Although the government paid them modest compensation fees for their often denuded and eroded properties, many people continued to harbor resentment at being subjected to the ordeal of displacement.

Despite the obstacles against its creation, Shenandoah National Park today encompasses over three hundred square miles of undeveloped forestland in the northern Virginia Blue Ridge, between Waynesboro and Front Royal; the formerly bare mountain slopes are again cloaked with trees. Because of its proximity to eastern cities and its scenic road, the park has for many years been among the most popular national parks in the United States.

The Blue Ridge Parkway

The idea of a scenic tourist road in the Blue Ridge predated the Skyline Drive by several years. In 1909, the director of the North Carolina Geological and Economic Survey, Colonel Joseph Hyde Pratt, recognizing the growing popularity of automobiles, proposed a ridgetop toll road in the North Carolina and Georgia Blue Ridge. Pratt believed that such a road would attract a large number of tourists, which he felt would help the region economically. One short section of Pratt's road was actually constructed near Pineola, North Carolina, before World War I necessitated the cancellation of the project.

Interest in constructing a scenic tourist road along the crest of the Blue

This 1937 photograph shows the Blue Ridge Parkway being constructed over a gneiss outcropping known as Alligator Back, in what is now Doughton Park (on the border of Alleghany and Wilkes counties in North Carolina). The denuded landscape in the background is the result of agricultural abuse and turn-of-the-century logging. (Courtesy of the Blue Ridge Parkway Photo Library)

Ridge was revived in the 1920s with the proposal of the Skyline Drive, which was in fact a regional example of a national trend. In the late 1920s and early 1930s, the federal government was financing the construction of scenic roads (i. e., "parkways"), generally near major cities on the eastern seaboard. In the mid-1930s, a team of politicians proposed another federal road for the Blue Ridge. The overt purpose of this road, to be called the Blue Ridge Parkway, was to connect Shenandoah National Park with Great Smoky Mountains National Park, so that a tourist might travel from one park to the other without seeing a billboard or losing the spell of the wilderness. A secondary goal of this road was to provide economic assistance to the people of the Blue Ridge, who were among the Americans most affected by the economic collapse of the 1930s. For many in the region, the Great Depression was not the cause of economic struggling—it simply exaggerated a preexistent condition of isolation and living in the margins. By the 1930s many Blue Ridge counties had seen little economic development; Floyd County, Virginia, for example, possessed no paved road before the construction of the parkway. Attempting to alleviate this situation were two federal programs, the Civilian Conservation Corps (CCC) and the Works Progress Administration (WPA) (both components of President Franklin D. Roosevelt's New Deal), which paid many residents of the region to help construct the Blue Ridge Parkway.

Completing this federal project was no easy task—the parkway took fifty-two years to finish (1935–87). A route had to be agreed upon (exhaustive and often bitter negotiations occurred between officials from Tennessee and North Carolina before the government set the route through the latter state), rights-of-way had to be obtained, funding had to be procured (from such federal sources as the Public Works Administration), and, finally, the road had to be built—over extremely difficult terrain. Beginning near Waynesboro, Virginia, at the southern terminus of Shenandoah National Park's Skyline Drive, the Blue Ridge Parkway snakes southwestward along the crest of the Blue Ridge into North Carolina. After coursing approximately 355 miles, the parkway veers westward from the Blue Ridge and, for more than 100 miles, traverses a series of adjoining mountain ranges (the Black Mountains, the Great Craggies, the Pisgah Ledge, the Great Balsams, the Plott Balsams), before it ends, approximately 469 miles from its start, at the eastern entrance to Great Smoky Mountains National Park, near Cherokee, North Carolina. World famous as a masterpiece of engineering and design, with banked curves, "natural" landscaping, intricate stone masonry in tunnels and bridge overpasses, and the avant-garde technology of the Linn Cove Viaduct, a suspension bridge on Grandfather Mountain, the Blue Ridge Parkway is maintained by the National Park Service as a noncommercial, two-lane, paved road which, since the Depression, has inspired driving for the sheer pleasure of it.

The Joyce Kilmer Memorial Forest

Most people who drive the Skyline Drive or the Blue Ridge Parkway for the first time are amazed to see so much forest growing so near the eastern megalopolis. Indeed, the parkway provides excellent access to many wild places, including, in Virginia, St. Mary's Wilderness Area, Peaks of Otter Recreation Area, and Rock Castle Gorge, and, in North Carolina, Linville Gorge Wilderness Area, Shining Rock Wilderness Area, and Middle Prong Wilderness Area, as well as the Great Smoky Mountains National Park. Among the other wild places located nearby is the Joyce Kilmer Memorial Forest, located a short drive from the southern terminus of the Blue Ridge Parkway in an isolated area of the Nantahala Mountains in Graham County, North Carolina. Arguably the most impressive of all the wilderness areas in the eastern United States and virtually the only one which is in actuality wilderness, the Kilmer Forest boasts a fascinating history, a discussion of which may serve to clarify the extent of environmental change in the Blue Ridge region since the arrival of white people. When Europeans first settled the Blue Ridge in the eighteenth century, the coves in which they built their cabins looked something like the Kilmer Forest of today.

In 1913, a simple twelve-line poem appeared in *Poetry* magazine, an important American literary journal. The poem's first couplet is as famous as any lines written in English: "I think that I shall never see / A poem lovely as a tree." Although many people today can give the title of the poem—it is, of course, "Trees"—fewer can remember the name of the poet who wrote it; after all, none of his other works are read today. Nowadays, Joyce Kilmer's name is brought up mainly in game shows (people seem amused that such a sentimental poem was written by a man named Joyce). Nonetheless, "Trees" is among the most widely known American poems. Fans of serious literature may scoff at such an assertion, but few other twentieth century American poems have been as frequently anthologized, as widely memorized, as often translated. "Trees" has been read by millions; countless others have encountered the poem as the lyrics of a popular song. Although critics have generally considered it to be a sapling in a forest of literary sequoias, "Trees" has achieved for its author an honor no other American poet can claim: an ecologically important forest is named after Kilmer.

The Joyce Kilmer Memorial Forest is the largest and most spectacular stand of virgin deciduous trees in the United States. Located just south of the Great Smoky Mountains National Park in Nantahala National Forest, near Robbinsville, North Carolina, the 3,840-acre Kilmer Forest occupies both sides of a fast-flowing mountain stream called Little Santeetlah Creek, which drains a watershed (formerly known by locals as Poplar Cove) bounded on three sides by three different mountain ranges: the Unicoi Range to the west, the Snowbird Range to the south, and the Cheoah Range to the north. Little Santeetlah Creek flows eastward into Big Santeetlah Creek, and then, after the latter stream empties into the Cheoah River, northward into the Little Tennessee River (where its waters run westward, eventually becoming part of the Tennessee River, then the Ohio River, and, ultimately, the Mississippi River). On its way out of Poplar Cove, Little Santeetlah Creek supports a magnificent, never-harvested forest featuring an amazing diversity of tree species—as many as in all of Europe. Over one hundred species of trees grow in Kilmer Forest, including yellow-poplar, eastern hemlock, red maple, Fraser magnolia, American beech, yellow birch, northern red oak, and Carolina silverbell. Individual representatives of most of these species reach near-record size in Poplar Cove's fertile, well-watered bottomland soil; for example, several yellow-poplars are so massive that it takes five or six people to reach their arms all the way around the trunks.

Many other southern mountain coves, before being logged circa 1900, contained trees as stately as those now legally protected in the Joyce Kilmer Memorial Forest. Because it was never logged, the Little Santeetlah Creek watershed is today a living museum, offering visitors the opportunity to study and appreciate an aboriginal Appalachian cove forest and its undisturbed ecosystem.

Before logging companies came to the Southern Appalachians, sheltered mountain coves like Poplar Cove permitted numerous tree species to set their roots deep and flourish. In many of these coves, for example, centuries-old yellow-poplars towered more than 125 feet high, the girth of their trunks measuring 20 feet or more in circumference. Such enormous trees dwarfed the Cherokee, who hunted game and gathered nuts beneath them long before the arrival of whites. European settlers, though, cleared the cove forests more than they hunted in them, for the trees stood in the way of their longed-for farmsteads. The destruction of the mountain forests, quietly begun by eighteenth century settlers, was dramatically increased in the late nineteenth and early twentieth centuries by logging companies. In just a few decades, using far more sophisticated technology than the early mountaineers owned, these companies harvested the vast majority of the Appalachian cove forests.

Only by a fluke of circumstance did the Joyce Kilmer Memorial Forest escape the fate of these other forests. Unlike most other mountain coves, the Little Santeetlah Creek watershed was relatively untouched by European settlers because of its remoteness; in fact, only one small homestead was ever established there. The rugged southwestern corner of North Carolina, originally the domain of the Cherokee, was settled by Europeans later and less heavily than most other sections of the Southern Appalachians. White people did not reside in the vicinity of present-day Robbinsville until 1840 (after the forced removal of the Cherokee by the U.S. government during the late 1830s), nearly a century after Europeans, journeying down the Great Valley of the Appalachians from Pennsylvania, settled other parts of the North Carolina mountains, and more than sixty years after Daniel Boone built the Wilderness Road from the Blue Ridge to Kentucky to encourage settlement west of the Appalachians.

By the first decade of the twentieth century, however, logging companies had purchased large tracts of forest in and immediately south of the Great Smoky Mountains (because of its geographical isolation, this was virtually the last southern mountain region to be logged). Continuing the process begun earlier elsewhere in the Southern Appalachians, the first companies to log near Robbinsville established railroads, which made remote cove forests more accessible. The Little Santeetlah Creek watershed was one of the targeted areas: around the turn of the century, the Belton Lumber Company bought and made plans to log all of Poplar Cove, but, as soon as its splash dams were set in place, the company went bankrupt. In 1915, the Babcock Lumber Company began to log immediately to the north of Poplar Cove, on the banks of Slickrock Creek and its immediate tributaries; Babcock had removed about two-thirds of the trees in its Slickrock Creek tract by 1922, when the construction of the Calderwood Dam on the Little Tennessee River destroyed the company's railroad access from the north. The logging of the Little Santeetlah Creek watershed, which Babcock never reached, was further delayed by the damming of the Cheoah River into Santeetlah Lake, which restricted railroad access from the east. Then, in the 1930s, with the Gennett Lumber Company ready to log the enormous trees in Poplar Cove, the U.S. Forest Service intervened.

By the 1930s, Joyce Kilmer had become an American hero—not only to those who loved his poem "Trees," but also to those who remembered his patriotism during World War I. In 1917, after the tragic sinking of the *Lusitania* by the Germans, an enraged Kilmer quit his job at the *New York Times* and signed up for the National Guard. Noted as a journalist as well as a poet, the New Jersey native was offered a position as a statistician for the U.S. Army, which would have kept him a safe distance from the battle-front, but Kilmer turned it down, opting instead to work as an intelligence officer. In that position, he was stationed, on July 30, 1918, by the front lines in France, his mission to locate enemy machine gun nests. There he died, victim of a sniper's bullet. His comrades buried him in France, among war-mangled trees quite unlike the ones he had in mind when he wrote his famous poem.

Answering the pleas of the Veterans of Foreign Wars, who wanted a memorial site in which to commemorate Kilmer, the U.S. Forest Service purchased the Little Santeetlah Creek tract from the Gennett Lumber Company in 1935. At the 1936 dedication ceremony for the establishment of the Joyce Kilmer Memorial Forest, a letter written by President Franklin D. Roosevelt was read, acknowledging Kilmer's dual role as beloved poet and war hero: "It is particularly fitting that a poet who will always be remembered for the tribute he embodied in 'Trees' should find this living monument. Thus his beloved memory is forever honored and one of nature's masterpieces is set aside to be preserved for the enjoyment of generations yet unborn."

Today, visitors to "this living monument" may not know much about its namesake, but they will certainly be impressed by the grandeur of its trees. Oleta Nelms, official hostess of the Kilmer Forest, states that "people feel awestruck when they enter this forest. I have never seen conduct here that wouldn't be permissible in church." A retired schoolteacher who lives in Robbinsville, Nelms was hired by the U. S. Forest Service to greet some of Kilmer Forest's fifty thousand annual visitors and to explain to them the significance of the place they are entering. She particularly loves to talk about the only non-Cherokee who have ever lived in the Little Santeetlah Creek watershed: her grandparents, John and Albertine Denton, who formerly lived in a small cabin just off the Stratton Bald Trail. Nelms explains that the Dentons were self-sufficient farmers who also raised their own horses, livestock, and poultry. Although she never knew them, Nelms has heard that John Denton was a master craftsman, and that the cabin he built was so solid—being held together with two-inch black locust pins—that it was able to withstand all the punishment the Dentons' nine children could give it. The cabin is gone now, having rotted away; only the chimney remains, with a yellow-poplar sapling growing through it.

When visitors first enter the Joyce Kilmer Memorial Forest on the wood-chip-blanketed foot trail, they encounter a wooden sign warning them to watch out for the trees: "This trail provides hikers a unique opportunity to observe an aging virgin forest; however, it does pass near dead or dying trees that may fall or drop limbs. Natural processes, such as trees dying, are allowed to operate freely within Wilderness."

As visitors soon discover, Kilmer Forest is no secondhand stand of trees like most of the woodlands east of the Rockies. Although many forests in the eastern United States are now federally designated as wilderness areas, very few can be considered authentic wilderness, which would mean that they possessed substantial stands of virgin timber. The logging companies' exploitation of the great eastern deciduous forests was so extensive that today virtually nothing remains of the aboriginal American wilderness.

Yet Kilmer Forest *is* wilderness, unadorned and unadulterated by humans. A stroll down the Joyce Kilmer Memorial Trail (a two-mile figure-eight loop through the heart of Kilmer Forest) will suggest to the visitor what the American wilderness was really like. From the small parking lot at the end of U. S. Forest Service Road #416, the shortest distance to the legendary big trees is the Joyce Kilmer Memorial Trail, walked in a counter-clockwise direction. The first trees that visitors see along this walk, however, are quite unimpressive—a stunted grove of yellow birch, eastern hemlock, and American beech. Growing in soil disturbed by the construction of rest rooms and a parking lot, the roots of these young trees have been exposed to the impact of heavy hiking boots, tree diseases, and insect pests. Fortunately, only a hundred yards further into Kilmer Forest, the visitor encounters far fewer traces of human interference: except for the trail itself (built by the Civilian Conservation Corps in the 1930s) and a few benches, bridges, stairs, and handrails (all constructed out of wood to blend in with the environment), the Little Santeetlah Creek watershed, having never known the environmental degradation of logging, has hardly changed since the time of Columbus. Cascading Little Santeetlah Creek still gouges out the streambed rocks as it did millenniums ago. Now, as then, huge trees, rising up through lush rhododendron thickets, continue to attain impressive girths and heights, the creek's prolific moisture encouraging them to grow to gigantic size.

And when some agent of death—old age, insects, disease, fire, or lightning—hastens their decline, these trees will still play a vital role in the forest ecosystem, providing food and shelter for numerous species of animals, especially for woodpeckers, whose holes are everywhere in Kilmer Forest. Even after these trees cease to stand, their rotting trunks, while returning to the soil that originally spawned them, will support whole colonies of smaller plants: mushrooms, moss, lichens, ferns, even small seedlings of future giants. Because they allow a new generation of forest inhabitants to gain a foothold, such trunks are aptly called by foresters "nursery logs." Examples of this regeneration are common in Kilmer Forest: perhaps the most dramatic nursery log visible along the Joyce Kilmer Memorial Trail is the decaying yellow-poplar stump (at ground level more than seven feet in diameter), out of which is growing a healthy eastern hemlock sapling. Unless it is stopped by some natural occurrence like lightning, or by some human-caused problem like the accidentally introduced insect pest known as the hemlock wholly adelgid, this sapling will someday tower over Little Santeetlah Creek like its host tree. But it will become one of the big trees only if people continue to safeguard the Joyce Kilmer Memorial Forest. For this to happen, people must continue to appreciate—in the spirit of Kilmer Forest's namesake—the beauty of *all* trees, saplings as well as giants.

The Effects of Tourism

The innovative conservation projects established in the Blue Ridge in the first half of the twentieth century (including various national forests, Shenandoah National Park, and the Blue Ridge Parkway) not only encouraged environmental recovery from exploitative logging practices, but also led to a rise in tourism, which both celebrated and threatened traditional Blue Ridge culture. After World War II, the previous years having made Americans eager for recreation, the Blue Ridge became one of the most heavily visited destinations for the new American tourism. Shenandoah National Park and the Blue Ridge Parkway were soon among the most popular units in the National Park Service system; meanwhile, already existent tourist towns in the region, like Blowing Rock, North Carolina, were swelling each summer from the influx of visitors, while major new tourist attractions were springing up, including the Grandfather Mountain attraction near Linville, North Carolina, and the Peaks of Otter Lodge and Recreation Area near Bedford, Virginia.

To attract more visitors, the agents of tourism (including the National Park Service and the managers of commercial enterprises) recognized the appeal of a traditional, rural culture to a nation grown weary of urban and suburban realities, and began to showcase the cultural life of the Blue Ridge. As a result, tourists could not only witness a mountain landscape which, through conservation efforts, was healing from the scourges of environmental abuse, but could also observe highly produced, generalized representations of the Blue Ridge people and their traditional culture. Many representations were romanticized (in "living history" dramatizations, National Park Service-sponsored talks, and regional music festivals, for instance), while others were markedly negative (especially in the tackier merchandise sold in tourist shops). By the 1950s, these representations, regardless of how they depicted the Blue Ridge people and culture, were appealing to the imaginations of countless American adults (who were seeking diversion from urban and suburban stresses by studying traditional Blue Ridge music and handicrafts) and children (who were donning coonskin caps in homage to Blue Ridge frontiersman Daniel Boone and his Tennessee counterpart, "Davy" Crockett).

The representations which attracted attention in the Blue Ridge were based on preexistent, generalized stereotyped images of Appalachian people and cultures; known collectively as the "hillbilly" stereotype, these images had been created over the previous century by the media (in popular novels, commercial recordings, movies, and television) and by the elite literary culture. The evolution of the hillbilly stereotype is a complex and fascinating story which has been explored in depth by several scholars (including, among others, Henry D. Shapiro, David E. Whisnant, and David C. Hsiung). One facet of this story which has heretofore been neglected is the significant role of one Appalachian region, the Blue Ridge, in the formation of the hillbilly stereotype. Also in need of elucidation is the fact that this stereotype took on unique characteristics when employed to represent the Blue Ridge people and their traditional culture. Indeed, media and literary depictions of the Blue Ridge have tended to reflect mainstream America's strongly ambivalent view of that region, and representations of Blue Ridge people and culture have tended to be more markedly polarized than representations of other Appalachian regions.

The "Hillbilly" Stereotype

In an essay published in 1896, American psychologist William James recounted an experience from an earlier trip to the Blue Ridge:

> Some years ago . . . in the mountains of North Carolina, I passed by a large number of "coves" . . . which had been cleared and planted. The impression on my mind was one of unmitigated squalor. The settler had . . . cut down the more manageable trees and left their charred stumps standing. The larger trees he had girdled and killed. . . . He had then built a log cabin, plastering its chinks with clay, and had set up a tall zigzag rail fence around the scene of his havoc, to keep the pigs and cattle out. . . . He had planted the intervals between the stumps with Indian corn . . . ; and there he dwelt with his wife and babe—an axe, a gun, a few utensils, and some pigs and chickens . . . being the sum total of his possessions.
>
> The forest had been destroyed; and what had "improved" it out of existence was hideous . . . without a single element of nature's beauty, ugly indeed seemed the life of the squatter . . . beginning back where our first ancestors started and . . . hardly better off for . . . the achievements of . . . intervening generations.
>
> Then I said to the mountaineer who was driving me, "What sort of people . . . make these new clearings?" "All of us," he replied. "Why we ain't happy here unless we are getting one of these coves under cultivation." I instantly felt that I had been losing the whole inward significance of the situation. Because to me the clearing spoke of naught but denudation, I thought that to those whose sturdy arms and obedient axes had made them they could tell no other story. But when they looked on the hideous stumps, what they thought of was personal victory. The chips, the girdled trees, and the vile split rails spoke of honest sweat, persistent toil, and final reward.

James was far from being the only outsider to visit the Southern Appalachians during the final decades of the nineteenth century and the first of the twentieth century, that period of painful transition from traditional to modern value systems within Appalachia. During the Civil War, thousands of nonnatives passed through the southern mountains as soldiers, and, at war's end, many of these men, upon returning home, spread rumors about the people—and the natural resources—encountered there. Before long, these mountains were being besieged by a wide range of outsiders: land speculators, railroad workers, loggers, "local color" writers, folk music and folk tale collectors, and missionaries.

Many of these visitors shared James's initial negative judgment of the southern mountain people; yet, as evidenced in the media and literary depictions from the period, few other outsiders shared James's perceptive reassessment. The popular media and cultural elites (from academicians to politicians) depicted the Southern Appalachian people as culturally archaic, helplessly foundering in rural isolation, seemingly in need of the blessings of modern industrial progress.

Some scholars have conjectured that this negative image was a concoction by late-nineteenth-century outsiders in service to the champions of industrialization. According to this line of thinking, industrialists of that era coveted Appalachia's natural resources, yet recognized that obtaining those resources in some cases (as with coal mining) necessitated the removal of people from their mountain farms (and often the creation of a pool of disenfranchised laborers), a scenario which could be more easily justified, legally and ethically, if the media had substantially marginalized the people of Appalachia and their tradition-based cultures in the eyes of other Americans.

By the early twentieth century, the stereotyped negative image of the southern mountain people—by now generally tagged with the label "hillbilly"—had become entrenched in the popular imagination. Scholar John Solomon Otto wrote:

> The hillbilly was one of the most potent stereotypes ever created by the American mass media. Unlike the Italian, Jewish, and black stereotypes, the hillbilly [stereotype] was not derived from ethnicity. Rather, [it] was based on economic status. Hillbillies were the descendants of the British-American frontiersmen who had claimed America from the wilderness. Yet, something had gone wrong. The descendants of the sturdy American frontiersman were now poor whites, living in the Southern mountains. Presumably, [as far as the American media was concerned,] the fault lay with the hillbillies [themselves], who [supposedly] lacked the strong work ethic of industrial-era Americans. Hillbillies were poor, [contended the media,] because they were lazy and not because they were the victims of extractive industries which had invaded Appalachia and Ozarkia.

In the twentieth century, this hillbilly stereotype—which assigned Southern Appalachian men such negative characteristics as stupidity, alcoholism, and laziness, and women such negative attributes as naivete, fecundity, and wildness—received seemingly irreversible reinforcement in comic strips like *Li'l Abner* and *Snuffy Smith*, in movies like *Ma and Pa Kettle* and the two movie versions of *Li'l Abner*, and in television programs like *The Dukes of Hazzard* and *The Beverly Hillbillies*.

At the same time, however, the popular media was granting the hillbilly stereotype a more positive dimension, which was generally rooted in romanticized half-truths. Early in the twentieth century, with millions of recent immigrants (many of them from eastern Europe) challenging the old Anglo-American social order and cultural assumptions, members of the Anglo-American cultural elite began to assert that the mountain people, though economically poor, were culturally rich, representing a "pure" strain of Anglo-Saxon culture which, some believed, was superior to American mass culture. Meanwhile, middle-class Americans in sprawling cities began to embrace media productions characterizing Appalachian people as America's own "noble savages," a group which, uncorrupted by the material and moral compromises of modern industrial civilization, embodied the positive values believed to have been present in pioneer America. Anglo-centrism eventually ceased being a motivating factor for the romanticization of southern mountain people, but the mountaineer-as-"noble-savage" media myth has retained a powerful grip on the American imagination throughout the twentieth century.

The ludicrous hillbilly stereotype, in both its negative and positive dresses, prevented many Americans from seeing the Appalachian people for what they were (anything but homogenous and purely Anglo-American, since southern mountain regional cultures were formed from Cherokee, Celtic, German, and African-American as well as from English cultural influences) and for what they weren't (all rural, poor, and illiterate).

An Analysis of Depictions of Traditional Blue Ridge Culture

Curiously, though the earliest settled section of the southern mountains, the Blue Ridge has received considerably less literary and media attention than have other Southern Appalachian regions. When outsiders have focussed their attentions on the Blue Ridge, they have tended (with a few notable exceptions) to see the region's people and culture through a romantic, even sentimental lens; negative stereotyping has generally been reserved for other Appalachian regions. Indeed, for much of the twentieth century, the Blue Ridge has been viewed by mainstream America as a place of romantic otherness, a bastion of rural sanctuary just on the edge of a bewildering, alienating civilization.

BOOKS

The subject of numerous nostalgic autobiographies and romanticized pop folklore books (most of which received only local or regional distribution), and of scholarly cultural studies with limited popular appeal, the Blue Ridge until recently received little in the way of serious literary treatment. Thus, few realistic and carefully considered images of Blue Ridge life have been generated to counter the stereotyped ones produced by the mass media. Before the 1960s, only one major novelist had written extensively about the Blue Ridge: Thomas Wolfe. Wolfe's early death, though, prevented his completion of a novel in which he intended to trace thoroughly his Blue Ridge roots (*The Hills Beyond* was published in fragmentary form in 1941). Neglect of the Blue Ridge among writers of serious literature continued for two more generations. In recent years, imaginative writers of considerable talent (including Fred Chappell, John Ehle, Sharyn McCrumb, Robert Morgan, and Lee Smith) have turned to Blue Ridge life and history for themes and inspiration.

Although historically underrepresented in serious literature, the Blue Ridge has long fascinated nonacademic nonfiction writers. Books which brought national attention to the region include two Depression-era books—Mandel Sherman and Thomas R. Henry's *Hollow Folk* and Muriel Earley Sheppard's *Cabins in the Laurel*—which were colorful, detailed descriptions of individual rural communities (the former was set in Virginia, the latter in North Carolina). These two books pleased Depression-weary readers in part because they romanticized mountain life, exaggerating the degree to which the people of the Blue Ridge still observed traditional folkways (by the Great Depression many people living in Blue Ridge towns and cities had been thoroughly "modernized"). Other popular nonfiction treatments of the people and traditional culture of the Blue Ridge have been published in the long-running *Foxfire* magazine and in the many *Foxfire* books, which were compiled by the staff and students of the Rabun Gap High School in northeast Georgia. Haphazardly organized and frequently lacking interpretive analysis, the ten principal *Foxfire* books nonetheless offer a mother lode of information on Blue Ridge folklife traditions (especially material culture). Each of the ten books features oral histories of Blue Ridge citizens, most of whom were elderly and all of whom obviously relished describing the details of their rural way of life to the student editors. Countless Americans of the last two generations owe their awareness of the Blue Ridge to the *Foxfire* publications.

MOVIES

Lamentably, perhaps more Americans could trace their first impression of the people and traditional culture of the Blue Ridge to another, less sympathetic source—the blockbuster motion picture *Deliverance* (1972), based on the James Dickey novel of the same name. That controversial movie, in part about the often-troubling differences in perspective between urban and rural people, features some of the most egregious examples of negative hillbilly stereotyping in the history of commercial motion pictures. Previous mass-market movies about the Blue Ridge were mostly romanticized treatments of historic figures and events (several concerned the exploits of Daniel Boone). A few movies, such as *Moonshine Mountain* (1964), had projected negative impressions of the region, but *Deliverance* was the first such film set in the Blue Ridge to attract widespread attention. Yet, while it was arguably the most influential negative depiction of the Southern Appalachian people ever projected via the mass media, *Deliverance* did not forever darken the image of the Blue Ridge people and culture in mainstream America. In fact, with the exception of *The Winter People* (1989), most subsequent movies set in the Blue Ridge have romanticized the region. *The Homecoming—A Christmas Story* (1971), *Where the Lilies Bloom* (1974) (both made by Earl Hamner, Jr., creator of the hit television show set in the Blue Ridge, *The Waltons*), and *Foxfire* (1987) are all uplifting dramas about close-knit families strongly bonded to their mountain homes. *Nell* (1994) offers a nonjudgmental portrayal of an Appalachian deviant, while *Sommersby* (1993) and *The Journey of August King* (1996) set historical dramas of national rather than regional interest against a generalized Blue Ridge background.

TELEVISION

The Blue Ridge has for many years held a secure place in television mythology, being the setting of two of the most popular and widely syndicated Appalachian-based programs: *The Andy Griffith Show* and *The Waltons*. Depicting the Blue Ridge people in generally positive terms, these shows celebrated close family and community ties, traditional morality, and the past. *The Andy Griffith Show* may have presented its more rural-dwelling hillfolk as comically backward, but the show consistently acknowledged the basic human worth of all members of its idealized Blue Ridge community (i. e., Mayberry). With an occasionally cloying sentimentality, *The Waltons* chronicled the Depression-era struggles of a family in which all generations were valued and in which effective communication was of paramount importance. If at their best these two shows possessed an endearing sense of intimacy, it was because their creators had Blue Ridge roots—Griffith hailed from Mount Airy, North Carolina, and the producer of *The Waltons*, Earl Hamner, Jr., from Schuyler, Virginia; both shows offered reconstructions of personal experiences from Blue Ridge childhoods.

RECORDINGS

The commercial recording industry, since its beginnings in the 1920s, has shown unflagging interest in the Blue Ridge and its people, a direct consequence of the fact that many of the first musicians to record Anglo-

American music in the South were Blue Ridge residents. At the famous 1927 Bristol Sessions for the Victor Talking Machine Company, which country music legend Johnny Cash has called "the single most important event in the history of country music," musicians from the Blue Ridge outnumbered those from any other Appalachian or southern region. This was partly attributable to the fact that the Bristol Sessions occurred just to the west of the Blue Ridge, and was also partly because the Blue Ridge was less affected by industrialization, its cultural traditions less compromised, than other Appalachian or southern regions. Given the influence of its musicians at the dawn of the recording industry, it is not surprising that the Blue Ridge became the subject of many recorded songs.

Generally, commercial songwriters have depicted the Blue Ridge positively. Many popular songs have extolled it as a bastion of security in a troubled world, where family is still valued and human dignity is still achievable. These idealizations are readily apparent in the most famous song about the Blue Ridge, "Blue Ridge Mountain Blues," which has been recorded by a wide range of musicians (folk revivalists like Norman Blake, country and bluegrass performers like Doc Watson, rock stars like John Fogerty, and blues musicians like the trio Martin, Bogan, and Armstrong). Written in the 1920s by Kansan Carson Robison, a former vaudeville entertainer whose persona was decidedly cowboy, the song's protagonist—a lonely, alienated man who left the mountains to find work in the lowlands—longs to return to his Blue Ridge home and family. One of many songs to echo that sentimental view of the Blue Ridge was John Denver's 1971 hit "Take Me Home, Country Roads."

A few popular songs about the Blue Ridge and its people have been more realistic or tragic than sentimental, while avoiding negative stereotyping; one of the best was an early country hit by Dolly Parton, "My Blue Ridge Mountain Boy," in which a young woman who left her Virginia mountain home for the big city (New Orleans) laments her fallen condition (to survive economically, she turned to prostitution) and her irreversible separation from her Blue Ridge boyfriend. Revealingly, only a handful of popular songs have cast the Blue Ridge in unfavorable light. One song to do exactly that was country singer George Jones's mid-1970s rerecording of his 1959 hit "White Lightning." The original hit version of the song—in which the singer remembers his beloved father, a drunken yet happy moonshiner who successfully operated a still—had been set in Jones's home state of Texas. The singer later changed the lyrics and set the song in the hills of North Carolina. Although possibly heightening audience response to the song, the new lyrics reinforced the general public's association of the hillbilly stereotype with the Southern Appalachians (and, in this case, the Blue Ridge).

Interestingly, the term "hillbilly," so often used in reference to stereotyped images of the southern mountain people, became common in mainstream American vernacular because of a group of Blue Ridge musicians. While they did not invent the term (it dates back to the turn of the century), these musicians in 1925 offered record producer Ralph Peer the moniker "hillbilly" to describe their identity as mountain people. Accordingly, the group came to be known to record buyers as Al Hopkins and the Hill Billies. Before long, national and regional record companies were employing the word "hillbilly" when referring to all commercial Anglo-American music from the rural South. When publicly associated with the misunderstood and often maligned people of rural Appalachia, the term "hillbilly" absorbed preexistent media images concerning the southern mountain people. Because hillbilly music was now inseparably linked to the hillbilly stereotype, Appalachian musicians who wanted commercial success were often obliged to adopt the highly stylized popular hillbilly persona, which meant replacing the musical and social values associated with traditional mountain music (e. g., tragic realism and intense individualism) with new attitudes: sentimentality and self-stereotyping (i. e., a performer's self-conscious manipulation of stereotypes to enhance his or her public persona). To capitalize on the new interest in southern hillbilly music, opportunistic nonnative musicians began to adopt the hillbilly persona, donning overalls, straw hats, granny dresses, and ersatz accents. Other nonnatives, while not seeking to become full-fledged hillbillies, wrote and performed songs which were evocative of the southern mountains, but which (because of most writers' unfamiliarity with Appalachia) inevitably projected stereotyped images.

Regardless of their intent or their background, all these entertainers introduced powerful, lasting stereotypes which shaped the American public's perception of the people and cultures of the southern mountains.

Verbal Folklore

For the purpose of analysis, folklorists often separate the various modes of folk expression in a given culture into three categories: verbal, customary, and material. Of these three, it is the Blue Ridge region's verbal folklore that has most fascinated mainstream America. Indeed, American popular and elite cultures have borrowed heavily from the traditional verbal folklore of the Blue Ridge people, a situation which has proven far more beneficial to the borrowers than to the providers. This usurpation of traditional Blue Ridge culture, especially of verbal folklore, by outsiders has led to considerable discussion about the ethical considerations of such "commodification." An overview of this ongoing discussion is presented later in the chapter.

Speech

For well over a century, the people of Southern Appalachia have been stigmatized by outsiders as being culturally archaic, even primitive. Much of this condescension can be traced to stereotyped portrayals of these people by the media. Such negative attitudes have also resulted from encounters in the lowland South and in northern cities between local populations and displaced Appalachian people; speech was the cultural trait which most often prevented effective communication, and therefore understanding, between the two groups. Mountain speech differed from lowland southern dialects of American English because of a greater influence within Appalachia of Scots-Irish settlement and a lesser influence of African-American settlement, and because of the region's geographical isolation and its remoteness from political and social centers of power. Thus, Southern Appalachian speech developed distinctive attributes (in terms of grammar, pronunciation, and vocabulary), which led linguists to categorize it as Appalachian English.

Whatever their Old World background, early settlers in the Blue Ridge, forced to adapt to the dominant culture in the British colonies, had to speak English; yet, the high concentration of Scots-Irish settlers in the region, and the considerable presence of non-English groups like Germans, African Americans, and Cherokees, affected the way the language was spoken. Accents, expressions, and vocabulary in the Blue Ridge stemmed as much from Scottish-English, Irish-English, and Gaelic sources as from purely English ones. In those sections of the region where German settlement was heaviest (such as in the foothill counties just west of Winston-Salem, North Carolina, where many Moravians settled), translated German expressions filtered into local speech. Where groups of former slaves relocated after the Civil War, as in foothill towns like Morganton, North Carolina, the creativity which characterized African-American dialects of English invigorated local Blue Ridge speech as well. And though Native Americans were physically removed from the region, their legacy endures in many Blue Ridge place names.

SHORTER FORMS OF VERBAL FOLKLORE

The most common shorter form of traditional verbal folklore in the Blue Ridge, proverbs have historically been utilized in everyday situations. Memorable verbal expressions conveyed through simple, familiar metaphors, these sayings clarified the moral implications of situations and instructed people in proper courses of conduct. Thus, with a proverb, a person could, directly and unambiguously, communicate to others a moral perspective or nugget of wisdom. Most of the proverbs which have circulated in the Blue Ridge since the eighteenth century can be traced to English sources, reflecting the overwhelming influence of that culture in the evolution of American English. Some proverbs, though, were brought to the Blue Ridge by other groups from the British Isles (specifically, by Scots-Irish and Highland Scots settlers), or were introduced into the region by various groups of Germans and African Americans. The proverbs of these non-English cultures sustained considerable alteration in the New World. One Blue Ridge proverb traceable to lowland Scotland, for example, can serve to illustrate the process of cultural decay. Employing a metaphor borrowed from that once-commonplace domestic activity, spinning, to make an observation about the nature of love, this Blue Ridge proverb asserted that "True love is the weft of life." Interestingly, the proverb was dramatically reduced from its original form as expressed in a Scottish dia-

Baptist churches have long been common landmarks in the Blue Ridge, as have handmade signs with verbal pronouncements regarding the location of the nearest church and the reasons people should go there. (Photo by Hugh Morton)

lect of English: "True love is the weft of life, but it whiles comes through a sorrowfu' shuttle [*sic*]." The corruption of this proverb was not a result of its imagery falling into unfamiliarity (spinning was no less important in the Blue Ridge than in lowland Scotland); rather, the proverb was a casualty of a psychological predicament: the need of an immigrant people to assimilate into a society culturally and politically dominated by people of English descent who controlled the new nation's linguistic development. Some proverbs, of course, likely originated within the Blue Ridge. Although there are relatively few with explicit regional references (e.g., place names), many Blue Ridge proverbs allude to the region's more distinctive natural and geographical characteristics and common cultural folkways.

Other shorter forms of traditional verbal folklore were riddles and rhymes. Fairly rare, riddles were used under specialized circumstances, usually when one person wished to test other people's intelligence and wit. Many Blue Ridge riddles were expressed in the form of a single sentence, and usually as a question, such as "What goes all over the world and has but one eye?" (answer: a needle). Other riddles were couched in the form of short rhymes, and generally not as a question, for example: "As I was going through the wheat, / I found something good to eat, / 'Twas neither blood nor flesh nor bone, / I picked it up and carried it home" (answer: an egg). The person to whom the riddle was directed, after some thought, would venture to guess the correct answer.

While some traditional rhymes were integral to particular intellect-challenging riddles, most regional rhymes were verbal components of folk games, primarily supporting physical action. One example is the rhyme which accompanied the Blue Ridge ring game called "frog in the meadow": "Frog in the meadow, / Can't get him out; / Take a little stick / And stir him about." In playing this ring game, participants would stand in a circle, eyes closed and singing or chanting the aforementioned rhyme, while the person who was "it" (i.e., the "frog") would run from the center of the circle and hide; after the rhyme was recited a predetermined number of times, the participants would open their eyes and commence to look for the "frog." Other rhymes would accompany dramatic games (i.e., games which tell a story through a combination of rhymes and acting), courtship games, counting games, rope-skipping games, tug-of-war games, and teasing games.

STORYTELLING

Acclaimed storyteller Donald Davis, who hails from Haywood County, North Carolina, once described the role of storytelling in his family's everyday life: "I grew up in the Appalachian mountains way back in western North Carolina. My father's and my mother's families both had come to western North Carolina from Wales and from Scotland more than two hundred years before I was born, and had lived there on the same land they received under land grants for that whole period of time. As I was growing up I was never aware of hearing stories. The mode of communication was always through story. There was never an occasion for saying, 'Let's sit down, now we're gonna tell stories.' But, all through the day, whatever was happening might prompt a story."

This penchant for creating stories out of ordinary experiences has, of course, been shared by many other storytellers, past and present, throughout the region and worldwide. In the Blue Ridge, though, the combination of geographical isolation and tight family and community ties fostered a culture of storytelling which, over many generations, produced an extensive regional repertoire of traditional stories on a wide range of subjects, including myths and legends, stories of the supernatural, animal tales, humorous yarns, and verbal sketches of all manner of people, hoodlums as well as heroes, both real and imaginary.

In any given traditional culture, a myth is a sacred story which explains the origin of deities or the creation of natural entities. Generally, both storytellers and listeners believe a myth to be true, symbolically if not literally. Virtually all the myths which were held sacred by Blue Ridge settlers were transported to the region from the Old World—specifically, they were the Judeo-Christian myths promulgated in the Bible. Indeed, the only myths which actually evolved in the Blue Ridge were those of the region's original inhabitants, the Native Americans. Generations of Cherokee, for instance, spun myths to explain the origins of the universe, the creation of the mountains, the nature and purpose of plants and animals, the emergence of humans. Many of the traditional myths of the Cherokee were collected and translated into English by nineteenth century ethnologist James Mooney, whose book *Myths of the Cherokee*, published in 1900, remains a definitive sourcebook.

If psychological allegiance to the Old World belief system of Christianity prevented development of regional myths, European settlers in the Blue Ridge did tell regional legends. Generally not sacred like myths, legends concern the things of this world—people, places, and events—and are not cosmic creation stories involving deities or totemic animals. The traditional legends of the Blue Ridge celebrated the deeds of actual historical figures like Daniel Boone and of imaginary folk characters like John Henry. Legends also elucidated the origins of Blue Ridge place names and attempted to explain unusual natural phenomena occurring in the region, including the mysterious lights near Brown Mountain or the strange winds at Blowing Rock, North Carolina. Additionally, Blue Ridge legends commemorated historic events of local, regional, and national interest, including the Wreck of the Old '97, the Hillsville, Virginia, courthouse massacre, and the Battle of Kings Mountain.

Stories of the supernatural which circulated in the Blue Ridge reflected Old World folk beliefs. The region's residents have told these stories in an effort to comprehend the meaning of human existence and to come to terms with death. Blue Ridge storytellers have not been simply entertaining listeners; indeed, many tellers have believed in ghosts and other supernatural forces. Some Blue Ridge stories have depicted ghosts as being violent and vengeful, but many have described them as being relatively benign, as returning to the land of the living to conduct some type of personal business (such as to retrieve a missing body part or to check up on an old homeplace).

Fittingly, because they were fixtures in the Blue Ridge landscape, animals were the subjects of many regional stories. These stories often depicted animals naturalistically, describing the actual characteristics of various species from the region in some detail; this, of course, reflected the Blue Ridge people's familiarity with their fellow mountain dwellers. Other stories from the region depicted animals anthropomorphically. A fox might be portrayed as epitomizing one idealized human quality, cleverness, and a dog as exemplifying the quality of faithfulness. Serving to comment on human morality, stories of the latter type were, in essence, fables.

A wide range of folktales would drive home humorous messages, and thus can be considered as jokes. Sometimes delivered as brief verbal quips and other times as long-winded "tall" tales (e.g., "shaggy dog" stories), jokes provided Blue Ridge people with a vehicle for laughing at their own foibles and for discreetly critiquing the behavior of other people, thus serving important psychological and sociological functions. The following folktale from the Blue Ridge, loosely adapted from the repertoire of the late Stanley Hicks of Watauga County, North Carolina, can serve to illustrate how a joke fulfills these two functions:

> Back in the old days everything in these mountains was woods, and there were a lot of bears at that time—quite a few bears. A little log church house stood beside a big patch of woods; a wagon road went around those woods and a path went through those woods. This preacher and one of the deacons had supper at the deacon's house, which was on the other side of that patch of woods from the church house. When they had finished supper it was getting late: they had to rush to the church house for an evening service. But when they reached the woods they were scared. The deacon said, "I'm a-going around on this road," but the preacher said, "I'm a-going straight through on this path." All week he had been preaching that, as long as you did the Lord's will, He would protect you and save you and take care of you. The deacon said, "Don't go through there, please; there are bears in there." But the preacher said, "Oh, I'm not afraid of no bear. I've done the Lord's will, so the Lord will take care of me." The deacon screamed, "Don't go through there—a bear will tear you all to pieces." But the preacher did as he pleased: he went on down the path through the woods, and the deacon went around the woods on the road. When the deacon got to the church house, the whole congregation was waiting. The preacher hadn't shown up yet, and people were getting kind of worried. Everybody waited and waited and waited. After awhile, the preacher staggered in, just a ball of strings and rags, torn all to pieces. But he went right up to the pulpit, right through the church and up to the pulpit. Then the preacher began to speak: "Folks, I've been a-preaching to you all this time that the Lord will protect you and save you and take care of you, as long as you do His will. Now let me tell you one more thing: He ain't worth a damn in a bear fight."

Its humor notwithstanding, this folktale, set in frontier days, underscored a serious concern of early Blue Ridge settlers: the importance within this rural society of all citizens respecting the laws of nature as well as the laws of God. The preacher in this story thinks he is invincible to the laws of nature, but the powerful black bear reminds him otherwise. The ultimate motivation of this folktale was not to condemn Christianity, but to point out to listeners the hubris of Christians who believe themselves immune to the earthly realities of rural mountain life.

Today, the most famous Blue Ridge stories about people are the "Jack tales," a cycle of folktales of European origin which chronicle the exploits of a boy-man protagonist. Most Americans are familiar with the cycle's best-known story, "Jack and the Beanstalk." The Jack tales feature a combination of Old and New World elements—folkloric characters from the Old World, such as giants, devils, and kings, transported to New World settings. In many of these tales the protagonist is depicted as a trickster figure, in that, though a humble country boy, Jack outsmarts all who would oppress him—whether giants, kings, or wealthy persons—through his uncanny ability to diagnose his predicaments correctly.

The Jack tales were never common within the region—historically, they were told in only a few Blue Ridge counties. Widespread familiarity with the story cycle dates back to the 1943 publication of folklorist Richard Chase's book, *The Jack Tales*. Featuring literary reworkings of eighteen traditional Jack tales which Chase collected from a handful of Blue Ridge storytellers, *The Jack Tales* remains popular today. The majority of Chase's source stories came from members of three related families—the Harmons, the Hickses, and the Wards—living in the vicinity of Beech Mountain in Watauga County, North Carolina. During the Revolutionary War era, British immigrant David Hix, a Tory (a colonist who remained loyal to the British monarchy), fled into the Blue Ridge to distance himself from militant American patriots then coming to power in lowland North Carolina. After helping to construct a fort on the Watauga River, Hix settled near the present-day community of Valle Crucis, North Carolina, where he entertained his family and his frontier neighbors by telling a set of tales (i.e., the precursors to the Jack tales) which he remembered from his youth in the British Isles. Hix's son Samuel Hicks (the spelling of the family surname was changed during this period) retold those stories to the next generation of family members, including his daughter Sabra's son Council Harmon. Apparently, Samuel Hicks made young Council the central protagonist of his version of the tales. The nickname which Hicks assigned to Council's character, "Jack," stuck, and was used in subsequent tellings of the cycle. Council Harmon (circa 1807–96) delighted in his family's stories, telling them with considerable pride to relatives and friends and to his nineteen children (by two wives) and his many grandchildren. Keeping these tales alive after Council's death, his grandchildren and great-grandchildren shared a number of folktales with various folklorists and editors. In 1923, Council's granddaughter, Jane Gentry (her mother was Council's daughter Eamaline Harmon), narrated fifteen Jack tales to Isobel Gordon Carter, who printed the texts in the March 1927 edition of the *Journal of American Folklore*, which gave this local folktale cycle publicity in academic circles. In the late 1930s and early 1940s, other outsiders, including Richard Chase, learned about this local folktale tradition. Some of Council's grandchildren serving as informants for Chase were Monroe and Miles Ward, sons of Council's daughter Sarah, and Ben and Roby Hicks, sons of Council's daughter Rebecca. In 1947, Jane Gentry's daughter Maud Long recorded several Jack tales for the Library of Congress. Later descendants of the original "Jack" have likewise been influential in the proliferation and popularization of the Jack tales. Roby Hicks's son Stanley Hicks, for instance, told Jack tales at folk festivals right up to his death in 1989, while Ben Hicks's grandson Ray Hicks, perhaps the nation's most celebrated living traditional storyteller, tells Jack tales at festivals and records them for commercial and nonprofit audio and video productions (he is the only storyteller invited every year to the prestigious National Storytelling Festival in Jonesborough, Tennessee). The National Endowment for the Arts has awarded National Heritage Fellowships to both men: to Stanley for music making and instrument building as well as for storytelling, and to Ray primarily for storytelling. Of the next generation of kinfolk, Ben Hicks's great-grandson Frank Proffitt, Jr., and Ray Hicks's nephew Orville Hicks also publicly tell Jack tales. Indeed, Ray Hicks conjectures that Orville Hicks will be telling these tales "long atter I'm gone."

THE CULTURAL COMMODIFICATION OF VERBAL FOLKLORE

From a present-day vantage point, Richard Chase's book is ethically problematic, in that Chase treated the Jack tale cycle as a slice of Americana rather than as an uncommon local storytelling tradition from the Blue Ridge. Chase might have presented the Jack tales as a written transcription of authentic regional speech (one Appalachian-English dialect from the Blue Ridge), which would have reminded readers that the tales originated in a specific cultural and historical context as verbal folklore; instead, he retold the tales in his own literary approximation of that Blue Ridge dialect. Perhaps he translated the tales into a standardized, polished prose to ensure a larger audience for his book; yet, by producing an edited, written text for traditional stories which had formerly circulated orally, Chase obtained copyright ownership of the stories, essentially becoming their "author." In his book's dedication, he justified his actions by asserting that he had the blessing of two of his primary informants, Granny Shores and R. M. Ward, to publish an accessible book edition of the Jack tales in order to reach "older American citizens" and "young Americans." Chase's patriotic overtones are understandable in a folklore collection published during World War II. Nonetheless, Chase's *Jack Tales* (as well as his *Grandfather Tales*, 1948, which featured stylized renderings from another traditional Blue Ridge folktale cycle) epitomize the commodification of traditional Blue Ridge culture—that is, the transformation of the region's traditional folkways by both nonnatives and natives (Chase happened to be of the former background) into commodities for personal or collective profit.

Commodification was again evident during the postwar folk revival, when urban and suburban audiences across the United States responded enthusiastically to pop music renditions of rural folk music. Revival fans were particularly excited by the regional music of the Southern Appalachians, and nonnative musicians, such as the members of the Weavers and the New Lost City Ramblers, performed and recorded popular versions of Appalachian songs. Since the Blue Ridge had been visited by numerous folk music collectors during the first half of the twentieth century, it is not surprising that these revivalist musicians covered traditional Blue Ridge folk songs and ballads—the materials were widely available on records and in songbooks. For example, the Kingston Trio recorded "Tom Dooley," which topped the American popular hit chart in 1959. The song's transformation from the traditional Blue Ridge ballad "Tom Dula" (based on an actual event, a murder which occurred in 1866, in Wilkes County, North Carolina, the consequence of a love triangle) to a commercial pop song illustrates the process underlying the commodification of traditional Blue Ridge verbal folklore. A collector (whether folklorist or performer) would record in the field some type of verbal folklore, then would rearrange it and copyright it in his or her own name, thereby obtaining authorship (and any subsequent royalties) for the new version. In the late 1930s, while scouting for verbal folklore in the Blue Ridge, folklorist and revivalist folksinger Frank Warner asked Frank Proffitt of Watauga County, North Carolina, if he knew any songs about hangings. Proffitt immediately thought of "Tom Dula," a ballad which he had learned from his father, Wiley, who learned it from his own mother, Adeline Pardue Proffitt, who alleged to have first heard the ballad being sung by an imprisoned Tom Dula the night before his hanging. After Warner returned to Watauga County to record Frank Proffitt's rendition of the ballad, he subsequently revised it and retitled it "Tom Dooley." In 1947, folklorist Alan Lomax included Warner's interpretation of that traditional Blue Ridge ballad in a published collection of American folk songs. This Warner/Lomax version of the ballad was the song recorded by the Kingston Trio. Denied songwriting credit for the ballad he had introduced to the world, Proffitt and his family received negligible royalties when the song became a major national hit.

The Jack tales and "Tom Dooley" are only the most glaring examples of the commodification of the region's verbal folklore. In fact, all three modes of traditional expression in the Blue Ridge were subject to commodification. For instance, in the 1950s and early 1960s, several manufacturers, taking advantage of the popular media's romanticized portrayals of Daniel Boone and "Davy" Crockett, sold huge quantities of one material object traditionally worn in the Blue Ridge frontier—coonskin caps. At least one regional customary tradition has been commodified: regional and national dance teams have co-opted traditional clogging to design the complex group dance known as "precision clogging," a highly competitive and commercially lucrative (when performed for tourists) form of popular dance. Nevertheless, of the modes of traditional expression in the Blue Ridge, verbal folklore was the most often commodified—and the most potentially profitable.

Folk Music

A vital social unifier which helped Blue Ridge settlers overcome the debilitating effects of cultural barriers, rural isolation, and economic hardships, folk music evolved within the region from the musical traditions of several cultural heritages. For more than two centuries Blue Ridge people have sung a wide range of traditional songs: British ballads (i.e., narrative songs which originated in the British Isles), native American ballads (i.e., narrative songs which, though modelled on British ballads, were composed in the New World and concern New World topics; examples include "Tom Dula" and "Omie Wise"), blues ballads (i.e., narrative songs originally created by African Americans in the South; among those sung widely in the Blue Ridge are "John Hardy" and "John Henry"), folk songs (i.e., all nonnarrative, nonreligious songs), and hymns and sacred songs. Additionally, people in the Blue Ridge have loved instrumental music, and impromptu ensembles made up of some combination of instruments—fiddles, banjos, dulcimers, guitars, and possibly some crude percussion instruments like spoons or bones—have played fast-paced instrumentals to provide the rhythmic support for many a Friday and Saturday night square dance or "play-party."

The region's traditional music, however, functioned as more than entertainment. A central activity of Blue Ridge church services, regardless of denomination, was the group singing of hymns and sacred songs (often without instrumental support), which would help to draw the community together and encourage individuals to feel closer to God. Ballads and songs, whether sung a capella or with instrumental accompaniment, were a means of communicating important cultural information (i.e., morals and values) from older to younger generations, while the singing of ballads and songs was one way for people to decrease tedium as they were working.

Traditional Blue Ridge music is steadily being replaced within the region by the more commercial musical genres (bluegrass, country music, modern gospel, rock 'n' roll) which it influenced. Nonetheless, traditional music can still be heard in the Blue Ridge today, particularly at annual folk festivals like the Old Fiddler's Convention in Galax, Virginia, where the music is performed by natives and nonnatives alike. Although interest has waned somewhat since the folk revival, traditional Blue Ridge music is still popular outside the region. Some of the best-known contemporary interpreters of traditional music, such as Mike Seeger, John McCutcheon, and David Holt, have devoted a sizeable portion of their repertoires to traditional Blue Ridge vocal and/or instrumental music. Meanwhile, the recordings of master traditional musicians who are or were native to the region, including Bascom Lamar Lunsford (a singer, song collector, and music promoter from South Turkey Creek, North Carolina), Tommy Jarrell (a fiddler and banjoist from Round Peak, North Carolina), and Etta Baker (a blues guitarist from Morganton, North Carolina), are being heard by new audiences. Reissued and unreleased material on compact discs, video documentaries, folk festivals, and the word-of-mouth of traditional music aficionados are together ensuring that traditional Blue Ridge music will endure into the twenty-first century, both within the region and worldwide.

CECIL SHARP AND TRADITIONAL BLUE RIDGE BALLADRY

> As I went over London's bridge
> One morning bright and early,
> I saw a maid forbide the way
> Lamenting for poor Charlie.
>
> It's Charlie's never robbed the king's high court,
> Nor he's never murdered any,
> But he stole sixteen of his milk-white steeds
> And sold them in old Virginia.

On September 14, 1916, in Hot Springs (Madison County, North Carolina), Jane Gentry sang the above traditional ballad in the parlor room of

Members of a Blue Ridge family sing the gospel. (Photo by Hugh Morton)

Sunnybank Inn, her boardinghouse. Sitting near Gentry were English folklorist Cecil Sharp and his assistant, Maud Karpeles, both of whom were quite excited—they were hearing a New World variant of "Geordie," a ballad they knew from their native country. It is highly doubtful that Gentry knew when or if the events she was singing about had actually happened—the ballad had long before been transported across the ocean by anonymous British settlers—but she was nonetheless moved by the pathos of the ballad's narrative and by the beauty of its melody. That day, Gentry intoned for her appreciative visitors several other traditional ballads. Listening attentively and grasping notebooks, Sharp noted the melody of each ballad while Karpeles transcribed the lyrics.

If not for Sharp's and Karpeles's visit to Sunnybank Inn, Gentry's version of "Geordie" might have been forgotten, along with her versions of other traditional English ballads, including "The Cherry-Tree Carol," "Young Hunting," and "Lamkin." In honor of the historic event which occurred there, Elmer Hall, proprietor of Gentry's former Sunnybank Inn (now called the Inn at Hot Springs), maintains Gentry's parlor as a music room. A state historical marker positioned not far from the house informs passersby of the important roles Sharp and Gentry played in the preservation of traditional Appalachian ballads (though it omits Karpeles's name).

Gentry was their most prolific informant, but Sharp and Karpeles, during their travels in the Southern Appalachians, collected folk ballads and songs from nearly three hundred other traditional singers. During brief stays in Blue Ridge communities like Burnsville and Hot Springs in North Carolina and Buena Vista and Meadows of Dan in Virginia (as well as in eastern Kentucky), Sharp and Karpeles located and transcribed remnants of traditional English music—especially ballads, the finest of which Sharp believed compared favorably with the greatest poetry. They only spent portions of three summers in the region, but Sharp's name will always be associated with its traditional ballads.

Many of the ballads that Cecil Sharp collected in the Blue Ridge are still sung today, by interpreters of traditional mountain music like Jim Trantham. Born in Swannanoa, North Carolina, and raised in nearby Haywood County, Trantham happened upon Sharp's book *English Folk Songs from the Southern Appalachians* in the Haywood County Library in the 1950s. Ever since then, Trantham has considered Sharp's work a major reason for his own deepened appreciation of his Appalachian heritage. When a college student, Trantham had felt that his mountain background was a stigma to be overcome, but Sharp's book led him to sense that, as he puts it, "The Appalachian culture I grew up in, despite its warts and freckles, was actually superior to what I saw in the melting pot." He began to listen to radio broadcasts of traditional Appalachian music, especially Saturday night broadcasts from Renfro Valley, Kentucky. As his enthusiasm for traditional music deepened, he started to sing some of the ballads his aunt and uncle had sung when he was a child. Trantham also taught himself how to make and play Appalachian instruments—banjos and dulcimers—to accompany his singing. Formal music training enabled him to read Sharp's musical notations and gave him a critical ear for discerning the distinction between commercial country music and traditional music. Trantham observes that "Nashville music is not our music."

Since first reading Sharp's book, Trantham has dedicated much of his spare time to collecting and performing traditional Appalachian music, especially ballads. By performing ballads like "Barbara Allen," "Little Maggie," and "Pretty Polly" at folk festivals, libraries, and campgrounds, Trantham hopes to keep alive for mountain people their real musical heritage.

Principally interested in preserving and performing the traditional ballads of the Southern Appalachian region, Trantham also hopes to foster appreciation for the work of Cecil Sharp. According to Trantham, Sharp was his era's most trustworthy collector of traditional Appalachian folk music. Unlike many of his contemporaries, "Sharp made no attempt to exploit the mountain people," says Trantham, "because he was not motivated by career or commercial gain. He was always gracious to the mountain people for sharing their ballads with him. He was only there to write their ballads down."

Sharp's collection of traditional ballads, however, might never have happened. Only by sheer chance did Sharp learn that many of the traditional ballads he had encountered in his native England—which survived there only in fragmented form, sung by relatively few elderly people in rural areas—were actually thriving in the Southern Appalachians.

At the dawn of the twentieth century, Sharp, then in his forties, was working in England as a composer and professor of music, when he developed a passion for traditional British music and dance. Recognizing that these traditions might soon disappear with the decline of folk communities in England (a country which by then had felt the impact of industrialization for over a hundred years), Sharp committed his time exclusively to the study and preservation of England's folklore. Meanwhile, he eked out a living by teaching English folk dances to university students and by publishing some of the traditional ballads he had collected, to the acclaim of folklore enthusiasts on both sides of the Atlantic. A decade later, Sharp was forced to abandon his fieldwork in England when World War I wrested away most of his students, and he could no longer afford to collect in his native country. Furthermore, there was little left to collect. "In England," Sharp lamented, ". . . no one under the age of seventy . . . possesses the folk-song tradition." In need of employment, Sharp in 1915 accepted an offer to direct the choreography for a New York production of Shakespeare's *A Midsummer Night's Dream*. He returned to the United States a year later, this time hired to lecture on English folk dances. Towards the end of this visit, during the month of June, 1915, after giving a lecture in Lincoln, Massachusetts, Sharp met Olive Dame Campbell, an amateur folksong collector from New England. This chance meeting was to change the course of his life.

From Campbell, Sharp first learned about a place called Appalachia and its people, many of whom were of British ancestry. Having spent a decade traversing the Southern Appalachians with her missionary husband, John C. Campbell, Olive Dame Campbell knew that, because of the region's isolation, many remnants of British culture remained relatively intact. She told Sharp that "there is a great amount of material untouched here, 'ballets,' as they call them, of all sorts new and old."

Familiar with his reputation as England's foremost folklorist, Campbell invited Sharp to join her in seeking and recording these ballads, before they disappeared in the wake of industrialization. As Campbell saw it, her project would benefit from Sharp's musical expertise as much as from her knowledge of the region and its people.

Sharp quickly volunteered to assist Campbell. Soon, however, Campbell decided that she could no longer work in the field, and Sharp agreed to accept full responsibility for collecting the ballads. Because the project "would in a sense complete the work upon which I have been engaged so long in England," Sharp eagerly returned to the United States in the spring of 1916. After completing several lecturing obligations, Sharp and his assistant, Maud Karpeles, headed for Asheville, which was to be their base for field trips into western North Carolina.

Toward the end of July, 1916, John C. Campbell escorted Sharp and Karpeles to "the Laurel Country," near the North Carolina-Tennessee border, an area which the Campbells believed harbored several local ballad traditions. Heading first towards Hot Springs, Sharp and Karpeles found Madison County's few roads to be in extreme disrepair from the flood of 1916. "Good roads were scarce or non-existent," Karpeles recalled many years later. "[O]ccasionally the creek-bed itself would serve as a roadway for a few miles. . . . Whenever possible we walked, although this was a tiring business when it meant a tramp of fifteen or sixteen miles in great heat over a track so rough that it was necessary to pick every footstep. . . . If luggage had to be carried we hired a boy and a mule, and hung our two suitcases and my typewriter across the mule's back."

In an era before paved roads were commonplace in the Blue Ridge region, travel through the mountains was extremely challenging; and, as Karpeles admitted in retrospect, "[T]here was certainly nothing of the adventurous, resourceful pioneer about either of us." In a letter home Sharp described their fear of crossing streams on footlogs: "There was one [footlog] we had to cross on the way to Carmen [in Madison County, North Carolina], quite high up over a rushing stream, only about 14 inches wide, but 16 or 17 yards long and very springy—no hand rail of course! The first time I went across I didn't like it at all, but didn't say anything to Maud for fear of making her nervous too. Coming home I felt it worse than ever, and when she followed me she stuck in the middle and frightened me awfully. However she summoned up her courage and got over all right. Then I told her what a funk I had been in[,] and we decided we couldn't risk it again. . . . So we finally decided . . . we would wade at the ford. . . . You would have laughed if you had seen me cautiously picking my way across with a tall sort of Alpine stock in one hand and my umbrella in the other."

Sharp and Karpeles experienced other hardships in traveling through the region. Because of their urban middle-class perspective, which influenced their judgments of what they encountered, they could not accept or adjust to all aspects of the mountain way of life. Neither Sharp nor Karpeles, for example, cared for the mountain people's diet. To Sharp in particular, who was a vegetarian, their food was "monotonous and unpleasant, mainly owing to its greasiness. . . . Cooking meant frying, and all things, even apples, were served swimming in fat." To survive, Sharp carried his own food supply, which included chocolates and raisins. Karpeles complained more of the mountain people's different "standard of cleanliness" and their tolerance for large swarms of flies. As she later remembered it, "[M]any was the time we thanked Providence for having placed eggs inside shells."

Despite the hardships of collecting in the region, Sharp and Karpeles were committed to finishing the project. For one thing, they liked the people they met, whom Sharp lauded not only for their independence and self-sufficiency, but also for their hospitality and good manners. In many respects, Sharp's and Karpeles's views of the mountain people bore little resemblance to the stereotyped image of Appalachian people then held by many nonnatives. Although some northern contacts had forewarned the two folklorists of alleged violence in the mountains, Sharp refused to carry a gun. After finally meeting native mountain dwellers, Sharp wrote that they were "a leisurely, cheery people in their quiet way, in whom the social instinct is very highly developed. They dispense hospitality with an open-handed generosity and are extremely interested in and friendly toward strangers, communicative and unsuspicious. 'But surely you will tarry with us for the night?' was said to us on more than one occasion when, after paying an afternoon's visit, we rose to say good-bye."

The two English folklorists' initial apprehensions about travelling in the mountains were soon forgotten when they encountered a profusion of ballad singers in Madison County. After only three days there, Sharp wrote, "There is no doubt that I am going to add some wonderful stuff to my collection. I have never before got such a wonderful lot in such a short time." In his excitement Sharp exclaimed, "It is the greatest discovery I have made since the original one in England sixteen years ago." He later added, "I could get what I wanted from pretty nearly every one I met, young and old. In fact, I found myself for the first time in my life in a community in which singing was as common and almost as universal a practice as speaking."

Sharp grew to appreciate the Blue Ridge region as well as its people. "It is a paradise," he wrote; "I don't think I have ever seen such lovely trees, ferns, and wild flowers. . . . If I had not my own special axe to grind I should be collecting ferns or butterflies or something."

Although thousands of miles away from his family and his London home, Sharp felt welcome in the log cabins and frame houses he visited. His contacts liked him because he was not condescending. He eagerly talked at length with ballad singers about whatever topic concerned them—crops, politics, or the latest news about the world war then being waged across the Atlantic. One woman, intrigued by what Sharp had to say, commented, "I could go on listening for hours to Mr. Sharp talking. He is so educating."

The Appalachian people were rarely suspicious of Sharp and Karpeles. Only during their visit to Virginia in the summer of 1918 did mountain communities question their presence, accusing the two English interlopers of being German spies. Sharp and Karpeles good-naturedly laughed at the absurdity of such accusations, and the allegations were promptly forgotten.

In all, Sharp and Karpeles recorded more than five hundred ballads, an impressive accomplishment considering their lack of tape-recording equipment. At the time, such equipment was costly, bulky, and unreliable, and it also required power sources frequently unavailable in the mountains. Sharp and Karpeles were forced by necessity to record the ballads by hand, with Sharp transcribing the tunes of the ballads and Karpeles recording the lyrics. Since singers often ran through a ballad only once, Sharp and Karpeles had to be both quick and careful in their transcriptions.

Upon meeting his first ballad singers in Madison County, Sharp compared them with the rural balladeers he had known in England. "The [Blue Ridge] singers," he wrote to his family, who had remained in London, "are just English peasants in appearance, speech, and manner. . . . Indeed it is most refreshing to be once again amongst one's own people." He added in another letter: "Although the people are so English they have their American quality [in] . . . that they are freer than the English peasant. They own their own land . . . so . . . there is none of the servility . . . of the English peasant. With that praise I should say that they are just exactly what the English peasant was one hundred or more years ago."

Here Sharp betrays a prejudice that affected the outcome of his project. His analysis of the plight of rural English peasants—that they had lost their land during the rise of industrialization in England—was correct; however, his claim that the people he met in the Blue Ridge were such peasants transplanted was only partly correct. Sharp's work was well intentioned, but this assessment overly simplified the Blue Ridge people, denying them their diverse cultural heritage. In his quest to find traces of English culture in the New World, Sharp ignored the other cultural influences in the region: Scots-Irish, Highland Scots, German, African-American, and Cherokee.

Because of "his preference for materials of provable English origin" (as folklorist David Whisnant put it), Sharp overlooked many important forms of musical expression which did not descend directly from English sources, such as religious songs (hymns and spirituals), instrumental tunes, and commercial songs of the pre–World War I era. By not extending his enthusiasm to other aspects of the region's culture, Sharp limited the utility of his book. His outstanding collection of Appalachian ballads is too narrowly focused to be considered a definitive study of traditional Blue Ridge music.

Despite its flaws, *English Folk Songs from the Southern Appalachians* is ar-

Natives of Avery County, North Carolina, Lulu Belle and Scotty Wiseman went to Chicago during the 1930s and became country music stars on the radio program *National Barn Dance*. Scotty wrote a number of popular songs, including "Remember Me (When the Candle Lights are Gleaming)," "Have I Told You Lately That I Love You?" and the words to "Mountain Dew." (Photo by Hugh Morton)

guably the greatest collection of preindustrial Southern Appalachian verbal folklore. According to David Whisnant, Sharp was "the best-trained, most humane and open-minded collector working in the area at the time." Folklorist Bertrand Bronson even pronounced Sharp's book to be the best folklore collection from any region in the United States. Many years after her expedition with Sharp into the Blue Ridge, Maud Karpeles commented, "With the eye of the artist Cecil Sharp saw beneath the surface, and where some might have seen only poverty, dirt and ignorance, he saw humanity, beauty and art."

Country Music and Bluegrass

After the introduction of portable recording equipment in the 1920s, nonnatives heard Blue Ridge music for the first time. Record companies sent producers to scout throughout the South, with the aim of locating and recording talented musicians, both whites and African Americans. Perhaps the most important of all these scouting missions, in terms of influence on subsequent musical developments, occurred in the summer of 1927. Ralph Peer, a producer employed by the Victor Talking Machine Company, ventured to the city of Bristol (on the Virginia-Tennessee border just west of the Blue Ridge) to record mountain musicians for the expanding "hillbilly" record industry (which then was less than four years old). Upon arriving in Bristol, Peer explained to the local media the purpose of his visit: "In no section of the South have the pre-war melodies and old mountaineer songs been better preserved than in the mountains of east Tennessee and southwest Virginia, experts declare, and it was primarily for this reason that the Victor Company chose Bristol as its operating base." During his two weeks in Bristol that summer, Peer recorded nineteen different musical acts (solo artists as well as musical groups), most of whom were lured to his makeshift studio by the promise of cash payments. Not all of the musicians who showed up in Bristol, though, were from the mountains. Among the seventy-six performances committed to wax master discs during Peer's Bristol sessions were the first recordings by Jimmie Rodgers, a Mississippi native who that summer was working in Asheville, North Carolina. Closer to home were the Carter Family, a southwestern Virginia trio composed of group leader and songwriter A. P. (Alvin Pleasant) Carter; his wife, Sara Dougherty Carter, who sang lead; and, on vocals, guitar, and autoharp, the teenaged Maybelle Addington Carter, who was married to A. P.'s brother Ezra.

Peer's recordings catapulted both Rodgers and the Carter Family into country music history. Released commercially in the fall of 1927, the best of the Bristol recordings introduced to national audiences some masterful regional musicians—many of them from the Blue Ridge—whose work was traditional and at the same time highly personal. Subsequent generations of musicians, including numerous people living far from the Southern Appalachians, imitated the Bristol musicians and their regional styles. Removed from its original regional, rural contexts, the traditional music of the Bristol musicians evolved into mainstream country music.

Bluegrass music, an offshoot of country music, has long been popular in the Blue Ridge region, though it did not originate there. Owing its origins to the string band music which proliferated throughout the rural South during the early years of the twentieth century, bluegrass's first significant stylist was songwriter/singer/mandolinist Bill Monroe. Exposed to the music of both African Americans and whites while growing up in rural western Kentucky, Monroe became a professional musician while still a teenager, joining forces with his brothers at the start of the Depression. In the late 1930s, Monroe went solo, fronting his own group, the Blue Grass Boys. By the early 1940s, he was making records and performing around the South in concert and on radio, most prominently on the Grand Ole Opry. Monroe's music—which combined frenetically paced instrumental renditions of standard string band tunes, harmonized versions of sentimental songs and popular hymns, and his own instrumental and song compositions—was immediately popular. It wasn't until after World War II, though, that this new style of music was named "bluegrass" (in honor of Monroe's Kentucky roots). By the late 1940s, southern musicians were forming their own bluegrass groups, which usually, after Monroe's model, were composed of mandolin, banjo, guitar, fiddle, and bass. These groups often borrowed from Monroe's repertoire and copied his improvisatory manner of playing. Among the many Blue Ridge musicians devoting their energies to this new style were Monroe's former sideman Earl Scruggs (from Shelby, North Carolina), Carter and Ralph Stanley (from Stratton, in southwestern Virginia), Don Reno (from Spartanburg, South Carolina), Red Smiley (from Asheville, North Carolina), and Mac Wiseman (from Virginia's Shenandoah Valley). Bluegrass was from the start a commercial music, its diffusion highly dependent upon commercial recordings, radio, and formal concerts, yet the aforementioned musicians incorporated into their interpretations of the genre certain thematic and stylistic elements from their traditional musical culture. For instance, the Stanley Brothers, who next to Monroe were the most influential musicians in bluegrass, included traditional Blue Ridge folk songs and instrumentals in their repertoire, while Carter Stanley's original songs achieved distinctiveness by drawing upon such traditional Blue Ridge themes as unrequited love, respect towards elders, and reverence for and displacement from the land.

Among the first generation to play bluegrass were a handful of Blue Ridge musicians, such as Jim and Jesse McReynolds (from southwestern Virginia), Ola Belle Reed (from Ashe County, North Carolina), and Ernest V. Stoneman (from Carroll County, Virginia), who were influenced less by Monroe's music than by other kinds of traditional and commercial music, a scenario which ensured wider stylistic possibilities for future bluegrass musicians. The McReynolds brothers, for instance, were strongly influenced by the smooth two-part harmonies of the various "brother" duet groups active in the South during the McReynolds' initial years of music making, while Reed's and Stoneman's family groups incorporated elements of traditional Blue Ridge music into their bluegrass.

The Blue Ridge figured quite differently in the music of such second-generation bluegrass musicians as Bill Clifton, the Country Gentlemen, the Seldom Scene, and the Bluegrass Cardinals. Mostly from urban backgrounds, the musicians in these groups all played pivotal roles in popularizing bluegrass among urban and suburban audiences during the folk revival (particularly in the 1960s and the early 1970s). In their repertoires and stage personas, these bluegrass musicians often employed the Blue Ridge as a thematic touchstone, to appeal to people suffering the rootless discomfort of modern cities and suburbs.

The Blue Ridge is usually credited as being the site of the first outdoor bluegrass festival (in Luray, Virginia, in 1961, organized by Bill Clifton), a concept which has since become a primary vehicle for marketing bluegrass throughout the United States. Today, musicians from the Blue Ridge—including leading groups like the Virginia-based Lonesome River Band and Lost and Found and individual musicians like Doc Watson (from Deep Gap, North Carolina)—are producing some of the best third-generation bluegrass. In short, while the region did not directly spawn bluegrass, the Blue Ridge has undeniably influenced the music's directions.

Etta Baker

Etta Baker (born March 31, 1913) has spent most of her life in Morganton, North Carolina, where the fertile and flat piedmont meets the foothills of the Blue Ridge, and her music embodies both the African-American musical traditions of the Carolina piedmont and the Anglo-American musical traditions of the southern mountains. Before the 1991 release of Baker's recording *One-Dime Blues*, fans of southern music were likely to hear her extraordinary guitar playing only at one of her concerts, on the rare 1975 album *Music from the Hills of Caldwell County*, or on the album *Instrumental Music of the Southern Appalachians*. Baker's five tracks on the latter recording, made in 1956, enchanted many folk music enthusiasts during the folk revival of the 1950s and 1960s. As folklorists Wayne Martin and Lesley Williams recently explained: "Etta's performances [on the anthology] caught the attention of listeners, especially some of the young, urban musicians who were part of the folk revival. Within this circle, her rendition of 'One-Dime Blues' was considered such a consummate performance that those who could emulate it were said to be 'One-Diming it.'"

Baker was unable to play an active role in the folk revival. As a married woman raising a large family while holding a full-time job, she was forced to politely deflect much of the attention she received during those years.

Doc Watson, from Deep Gap in Watauga County, North Carolina, overcame the handicap of being blind to become one of the nation's more popular and influential musicians, performing and recording a wide variety of music—traditional folk, country, bluegrass, blues, and rock 'n' roll. (Photo by Hugh Morton)

However, by the mid-1970s, the circumstances of Baker's life had changed dramatically—her children had grown up and set off on their own, her husband, Lee, had died, and she had retired from her job at a local textile mill. Finally in a position to perform away from her Morganton home, Baker began to accept invitations to play her guitar both inside her home state of North Carolina and elsewhere.

For the last twenty years, Baker has been a featured performer at numerous schools, festivals, and special events, where audiences have been privileged to witness her intricate fingerstyle guitar playing and her diverse repertoire. Although she does not sing much, she plays a variety of instrumental tunes, from piedmont blues to fiddle tunes, ragtime pieces to stringband breakdowns. Baker spent her formative years at the base of the North Carolina Blue Ridge and in the tobacco fields near Richmond, Virginia, and her repertoire seamlessly combines the musical traditions of rural southerners, blacks and whites alike.

It is important to note that Baker's music is neither strictly traditional nor strictly of her own devising—it is both. Although solidly based in the rural musical traditions that she learned from her father, from other family members, and from friends in the communities where she has lived, her music is also unique. In her performances, Baker recasts each traditional tune so that it takes on a degree of complexity unattainable for less skillful musicians, and she also composes original tunes.

Baker's fellow musicians have long appreciated her unique guitar playing. Over the years, she has performed with such musicians as Ray Charles, Taj Mahal, Sparky Rucker, Doc Watson, David Holt, Guitar Slim (James Stephens), John Jackson, John Cephas, Phil Wiggins, and Howard Armstrong (of the African-American string band Martin, Bogan, and Armstrong).

With the release of *One-Dime Blues* and the accolades recently bestowed upon her by prominent folklore organizations, Baker is currently receiving more attention than ever before. In 1991, she was one of sixteen traditional artists to be awarded the prestigious National Heritage Fellowship from the National Endowment for the Arts. In recent years she has also been given the Brown-Hudson Folklore Award from the North Carolina Folklore Society, the John Henry Award from the John Henry Foundation, and the Outstanding Achievement Award from the city of Morganton. Her festival and workshop appearances include the 1980 National Folk Festival, the 1982 World's Fair, the Banjo Institute, and the Merle Watson Memorial Festival. More recently she has performed in Europe.

As Etta Baker's guitar playing reaches new and larger audiences, many people will be curious to know more about this master musician. To learn more, I interviewed Baker in July 1992, in the house she has called home for half a century.

I've played the guitar for a good long while, since I was two months of being three years old; that's about seventy-seven years. My daddy taught me how to play—I learned by watching him. He'd take a lot of time to show me where to set my fingers and everything. By the time I was three I knew the three basic chords. He taught me until I was old enough to hold a guitar myself. Those were the only lessons I've ever had.

My daddy played country-style guitar. He liked to play all the old tunes, and he knew a bunch of them, like "Railroad Bill," "Never Let Your Deal Go Down," "Bully of the Town," and "Turkey in the Straw." He also played "John Henry," with a slide. My daddy never did sing that much, I guess that's why I don't like to sing much.

My daddy played the guitar, but he also played the banjo, because his daddy played the banjo. His daddy, my granddaddy Alexander Reid, did not play the guitar, and I never heard mention of him playing any other instruments. I just heard my daddy say that my granddaddy was a good banjo player and that he'd play tunes like "Sourwood Mountain" and "Johnson Boys." I hardly knew him, and I never was around him very much. When I was born, he lived near where my parents lived, in a tiny little town called Collettsville in Caldwell County. But when I was the age of two, my parents left town and moved away from there. Some friends of my daddy went to live in Chase City, Virginia, and they got my daddy in the notion to go, too. That's where I was raised. We made one trip back from Virginia to see my granddaddy. Shortly after that, he passed.

We stayed in Virginia about seven or eight years, maybe longer. But my daddy didn't like picking tobacco out in the field, so we returned to Caldwell County. We lived in a tiny little house in the country, near Collettsville. My daddy had a couple of acres that he tended, so we always had a garden. He also had some pretty woodland. This made my daddy really happy, because he loved to hunt. I really liked learning the different herbs and flowers around the house—I really liked that a lot.

It might have been hard times then, but I never did know of it being hard. I guess being a child I wouldn't have known hard times like my daddy and mama did. It seemed like happy times to me. Whenever everybody had time to get together, we'd be making music together and fixing big dinners. My parents had about as many white friends as black friends—everybody was just one big family there in Collettsville. It was a real happy little place.

My daddy, Boone Reid, was Indian and Irish. He might have been named after Daniel Boone, I don't know. My mama, Sally Reid, was Indian, full blooded Indian; a lot of her people lived over in Johnson City [Tennessee].

She could really play harmonica. She didn't play very much blues, but she could play all the fiddle tunes and she loved to lead dances. I never could play the harmonica like her.

My parents had seven children, and we all made music. I had three brothers: Robert, Jay, and James—they've all passed. And two of my sisters, Minnie and Mattie, have also passed. I don't have but one sister left—that's Cora [Phillips]. We still play together when we get the chance.

All of my daddy's brother's children played instruments: guitars, banjos, and fiddles. And my daddy's sister had a daughter who played guitar and banjo real well. We would get together and play all the old tunes. Sometimes somebody would come up with a new tune, and then somebody else would learn it and keep it going; and it would go from there.

Soon after we returned to Caldwell County from Virginia, I met Lee Baker. Lee played piano. Since we didn't live too far apart, we began to play music together. We would play at square dances and other entertainments around Caldwell County. We would play a lot of [old-time] country music and some blues—we tried to mix it up, because not everybody likes the same thing. Sometimes we were paid, other times we would just play for the fun of it. But when we played for parties at Brown Mountain Beach, the white people who owned the cabins on the river there paid us real good.

Later, Lee and I married and started a family. Lee found a job at a furniture factory here in Morganton, at Tablerock and Drexel. I found a job here at Skyland Textiles, where I worked for twenty-five years. It was hard work—all those machines running all the time. They made children's clothes; my job was to do domestic work, to keep everything in order and clean up.

It was really hard to raise a family while both of us were working so hard. But our children were good kids, and they did everything they could to help out. When they were old enough, they would have my supper ready when I got home from work.

It was hard, yes, but we had our fun, and we always found time for music. All my children learned to make music. Lee gave piano lessons to some of our daughters. Our baby girl Joanne learned to play the piano before she was three. Our daughters Darlene and Irene also got pretty good at the piano.

I never did care very much about the piano, so I taught some of our sons how to play the guitar. Edgar can play my style of music on electric guitar, and John can play my style on acoustic guitar. Our second son, David Baker, also played the guitar pretty good. We lost him in Vietnam.

Our son Francis doesn't play either the piano or the guitar, he plays the drums. Our daughter Dorothy doesn't play any instrument, but she is the only one of all of us who can sing. I tell her she carries her music with her at all times.

I just never did like singing. Sometimes I try to sing, but I really don't like it. My sister Cora, she loves to sing. She's eighty-six years old now. We've played together all our lives—she sings, I play.

While I was raising my family, I couldn't go very far from the house to play music. Now and again, when my sons and their band would take breaks during their concerts, I would play to hold the crowd. But mostly I worked weekdays at Skyland and stayed with the family the rest of the time.

Sometimes our family would all go on a trip somewhere. We often took trips up the Blue Ridge. Morganton is just about as far into the mountains as I want to live, but I love to visit up there, it's beautiful. Lee and I took the children for a little ride into the mountains one day in the 1950s; I met [folksinger] Paul Clayton that day. He was playing his guitar at the Cone Manor House, near Blowing Rock. Lee walked up to Paul and told him that I could play too. Paul wanted to hear me play, so he lent me his guitar. He must have liked what he heard, because he came to Morganton shortly after that and recorded me playing some tunes on my guitar. Those tunes came out on that album [*Instrumental Music of the Southern Appalachians*], alongside some of my daddy's and my brother-in-law's banjo playing.

I lost Lee in the 1960s. I gave his piano away to the Carolina Center for Children. I was on my own, the children were all grown up and gone. I had more time to play my music.

After I retired from Skyland [in 1973], I started to play more away from home. Since then, I have played a lot of different places. I played at the World's Fair in Knoxville [in 1982], where I wrote my "Knoxville Rag." I dreamed the chords of that tune. At the World's Fair, there was good music going on everywhere; and when I hear music like that, I don't sleep real good, I just can't get the music out of my mind. I want to do something with it. So I got up at quarter to three that morning, went out on the porch of the hotel there, and put my new tune together. It was kind of like putting a crossword puzzle together: whenever a little piece fit, I just put it in there. When I went back over the next morning and told the audience that I had a brand new tune for them, they told me that if I would play it, they would name it. And because we were in Knoxville, they named it "Knoxville Rag."

When I play the guitar, I don't brush the strings or strum them, I just play with my fingertips, what they call fingerstyle. I don't use fingerpicks, though, because I'd hit too many strings if I did. But when I play "John Henry," I use a steel slide.

To be better heard when I play, I usually use an amp. I play a Les Paul guitar when I play at home and when I record, though I don't tour with it—I take a Takamine guitar on tour. I've been offered in the thousands for that Les Paul, but money's not that good. I just want to hang onto it. I don't ever take it on trips, I'm afraid the airlines will mess it up.

I played the fiddle quite a bit a long time ago, but I just laid it down. When you quit on an instrument, it just gets away from you. Now I have another fiddle, so I'm taking it back up.

A couple of years ago, a friend sent me a banjo. I never really played the banjo as a kid, but I remember watching my daddy play it. I memorized his tunes, so all I have to do now is to figure out how he played them. I would like to get some good help from somebody who really plays the banjo; meanwhile, I'm going to keep trying to learn on my own.

When I won that award [National Heritage Fellowship], Wayne Martin gave a party for me here in Morganton. A lot of my people were there, my sister-in-law and her family were there. But I don't care what I play or where I play it, no black people will come out, they just won't come out. One black man told me, "I don't like your style of music." I said, "I'm just playing to suit the one who's paying me." I told that man I didn't expect any black people to come out—that's all up to them. It really doesn't make my business bad if they don't show up.

I have a bunch of grandkids and great-grandkids, a bunch of them—I wouldn't dare try to keep up with how many I have. *They* like the music I play. One of my grandsons is learning to play the old tunes on his guitar. And my two-year-old great-granddaughter is just crazy about my music. One time when I was playing at the courthouse here in Morganton, she came out and cut her a good shine right out on the floor in front of me!

These days, when I'm not out playing music, I'm gardening. It keeps me going, keeps me busy. My garden hasn't done too well this summer—all the days I've been gone; but I'm real happy with the ripe tomatoes I did grow. And I've already harvested some big onions.

I was really happy with the award they gave me last year [the National Heritage Fellowship], it was really nice. Playing my daddy's music for others is something I have always wanted to do, and I'm glad people like it. I have been trying to make the best of what my daddy gave me. He would have wanted me to stay with the music. It makes me really happy to know that I have.

Walker Calhoun, Cherokee Song and Dance Man

When Walker Calhoun was a child growing up in Big Cove, a Cherokee community within the Qualla Boundary (the Cherokee Indian Reservation) in western North Carolina, his uncle, Will West Long, taught him a number of traditional Cherokee songs and dances. Now nearing eighty, Calhoun has not forgotten what his uncle taught him.

It is something of a miracle that these highly ceremonial songs and dances survived into the twentieth century, because in the eighteenth and nineteenth centuries the encroachment of American civilization into Cherokee territory severely endangered traditional Cherokee culture (this was especially true after the U. S. government displaced many Cherokee to Oklahoma during the infamous Trail of Tears in the late 1830s). Recognizing this threat, several individuals (some Cherokee, some non-Cherokee) at the end of the nineteenth century worked to preserve essential aspects of Cherokee culture. The best known of these people was an ethnologist employed by the U. S. government, James Mooney, who in the 1880s conducted fieldwork among the Cherokee. No less important in the preservation of traditional Cherokee culture (though less often acknowledged) was Calhoun's uncle, Will West Long (1870–1947). According to folklorist Michael Kline, "Long became a pivotal 'informant' to investigative scholars, collaborating with them in documenting Cherokee life. He is credited with recreating for various ethnologists the ceremonial life of the nineteenth century and earlier." Similarly, Long shared his knowledge of traditional Cherokee culture with his Big Cove neighbors and relatives, sparking in many of them a renewed interest in their Cherokee traditions, such as their ceremonial songs and dances.

As a child in the 1920s, Calhoun began to take part in performances of these traditional Cherokee songs and dances, and by the age of ten he had memorized much of his uncle's repertoire. Although Long taught these songs and dances to others of his nephew's generation, Calhoun was virtually the only one to defy the trend toward cultural assimilation by carrying the songs and dances into the 1990s. Calhoun's extraordinary enthusiasm for the tradition he learned from his uncle has ensured the tradition's survival.

Calhoun has received considerable recognition for his efforts, including the Cherokee Nations' Sequoyah Award (in 1988), the State of North Carolina's Folk Heritage Award (in 1990), and the prestigious National Heritage Fellowship from the National Endowment for the Arts (in 1992). Calhoun's cassette *Where the Ravens Roost*, which features his recordings of some songs he learned from Long, was selected by the Library of Congress for its "Best Folk Recordings List" of 1991.

In June 1992, while working as a National Park Service ranger for the Blue Ridge Parkway (on the section of the parkway nearest Cherokee, North Carolina), I was assigned the task of organizing a folk festival with a very modest budget. Having read about Walker Calhoun in an article by Michael Kline in *The Old-Time Herald* magazine, I wanted to invite Calhoun to perform at the festival. Obtaining his phone number from the Qualla Arts and Crafts Cooperative in Cherokee, North Carolina, I tried to call him for several days, but there was no answer. When his wife, Evelyn, finally picked up the phone, I learned that Calhoun was performing at a folk festival in another state. I realized then that Calhoun was much in demand, and I began to fear that he and his dancers (the Raven Rock Dancers, a group composed of family members) would not be able to perform at my festival for the small fee I could pay them. So I decided to concentrate on inviting lesser-known performers. Within a week, however, I discovered that one of my ranger colleagues, Tony Welch, was related to Calhoun. After I informed Tony that the parkway's festival was to be a celebration of local mountain folk culture, he stated that Calhoun would probably be delighted to participate, since, as Tony put it that day, "the Cherokee were the original mountain people." Tony even agreed to contact Calhoun for me.

On the day of the festival, August 2, 1992, Calhoun and his dancers were there (not on the stage, but right in front of it on a grassy lawn) performing those ancient Cherokee songs and dances. I watched and listened in fascination, along with the other festival attendants—approximately two thousand people in all. Toward the end of their set, all the dancers disappeared behind the stage, and Calhoun reappeared with a banjo, which for about fifteen minutes he picked with great flair.

Shortly after the festival, on August 13, curious to learn more about those songs and dances and the man who kept them alive, I interviewed Walker Calhoun at his home in Big Cove. The oral history printed below is edited from our three-hour conversation.

I was born May 13, 1918. My father's name was Morgan Calhoun, my mother's was Sally Ann Calhoun. I was the youngest child, the baby, in a family of twelve children. One of my six brothers and one of my six sisters died young, and the rest lived at least until middle age. Now it's just me and my sister— she's about eighty, I'm seventy-four.

I have lived in Big Cove all my life. Growing up here, we always raised all our own crops . . . except coffee, sugar, and salt, which we would buy. And we would sometimes buy flour, but flour was a luxury. Mostly we ate corn, beans, potatoes, and other vegetables. We also ate a lot of pork. In those days, everybody would just turn their hogs loose in the woods and let 'em go, and they would go wild. And then, anytime someone wanted pork, he would just kill one—it didn't matter if it was his hog or somebody else's, because everybody owned some.

When I was a child, few people around here owned horses. A horse then was just like a car is now—real expensive. Instead of horses, most of us farmed with steers. A steer cost about twenty dollars. Now, that might not sound expensive, but at the time twenty dollars was a lot of money, because we didn't have any.

The [Great Smoky Mountains] National Park is half a mile from here. Before there was a park, many of my relatives (including my three oldest brothers) worked in these parts as loggers, so I used to think that logging was okay.

But now I think, if the loggers wipe out all the forest, there will be no place for the animals. I really like animals. I often sit in my backyard and watch the rabbits and squirrels and deer. I used to hunt, but now I realize I don't have to—you can buy meat. I don't hunt just for sport, that's no good. There's no point in killing animals anymore.

I used to go with my mother and my brothers and sisters to a lot of dances held at Will West Long's home. He lived about a quarter of a mile from here. His picture is on the wall there [Calhoun points to a portrait mounted on the wall]. Will West, who was my father's half brother, left the reservation to go to college, and he was gone a long time. He studied agriculture, but he really wasn't interested in getting a job as a college man; he wanted to return to his family and farm.

Will West learned about dancing and singing from his father, John Long. If you go to the craft shop [Qualla Arts and Crafts Cooperative in Cherokee, North Carolina], you can see a medicine man mask made by John Long. Anyway, every Saturday evening, starting a month and a half before the start of the Indian fair [an annual event held in Cherokee, North Carolina, from 1914 to the present], we would prepare for the fair's dancing competition by practicing around a big fire we would build in the yard. My family and my friends would all be there—some of them would walk all day from the other side of Cherokee just to take part. Once everybody had arrived in the late afternoon, we would get right to the dancing—we weren't there to eat or talk, we were there to dance. We kids would dance too, right beside our parents. While it was still daylight, we would do the animal dances; then when it got dark we would do some other dances, like the Friendship Dance. We would dance until ten or eleven o'clock at night, then quit.

On the day of the fair, we would leave early in the morning for Cherokee. We would walk down to Raven Fork, where we would meet the one person in the community who owned a Model T. There were very few cars in those days, and only wagon roads to travel on. We had to ford streams several times. It took a long time to get to the fair.

I was pretty young then, I don't really remember the fair. I do remember I got to ride the merry-go-round one time. At the fair were people from the different Cherokee communities—Big Cove, Wolf Town, Paint Town, Soco, Bird Town, Big Witch, Snowbird—and each community had its own dances and dance teams. Each year at the fair, these different communities would compete with each other in dance contests, and most of the time Big Cove would win. The winner of a dance contest would win some money, two dollars or something like that. I didn't participate in these competitions, because Will West didn't use kids in competitions, he used grown-ups. But I watched.

When he died in 1947, Will West was pretty old—in his eighties. After he died, people lost interest in the songs and in the dances. No one stepped forward to keep the tradition going, and so it began to die out fast. I was very interested in the tradition, but I couldn't do anything about it right then—I was too busy.

During World War II, the army drafted me to go to Europe. I was in Germany almost a year, as a combat engineer (mostly I checked the supply lines). While there, I remember seeing a lot of abandoned German tanks—I guess the men had been killed or captured. The army was training me to go to the Pacific after Germany. Then Truman dropped the atomic bomb on Japan, and the war was over. The army changed my orders from going to the Pacific to going back to the States. They sent me to California.

When I finally got back to these parts I was too busy working to get back to performing the songs and dances I learned from Will West. My wife, Evelyn, and I had to keep ten children fed, and we were too busy to even think of other things. For a while, I was employed by the North Carolina Department of Highways. I'd often be gone seven weeks at a time, working for a number of private contractors hired by the state. After awhile, I wanted to be closer to my family, so for about twenty years I worked for a plant in Cherokee. When I turned sixty-two, I retired—that was about a dozen years ago.

Even though I was retired, I didn't get back to my uncle's songs and dances for the longest time. Then, about six or seven years ago, I began to think about everything I had learned from Will West. I knew that no one was performing those songs and dances anymore, and I realized that many Cherokee born after 1947 had never known them. So I decided I should teach the songs and dances to all the kids (I have ten children, twenty-five grandchildren, and eight great-grandchildren). I know I can't stop kids from getting interested in rock and country music, but I've discovered that a lot of the kids come around to learn about the tradition—they realize it is something they should know.

Today, when I perform the old dances, I use the little ones because they're the ones I can teach. We call ourselves the Raven Rock Dancers. When I try to use grown-ups, they get drunk on me. I can't depend on grown-ups. It's a shame, but that's the way it is. There are some other people my age who grew up with the tradition and who know some of what I know, but they don't care anymore. They are church-goers, and I guess the preacher tells them that it's not right to sing the old songs, to dance the old dances. So they think of the old dances as sinful, but really they aren't, they're sacred. The Bear Dance was very important to the ancestors because the bear was a big source of food. They ate bear meat and used the hides for clothing, so they had to thank the bear for giving itself to them. Dancing and singing was their way of doing it.

I didn't learn all of the Cherokee dances. I used to play stickball (the game was real rough then—blood flew . . . nothing like the way they play now), and so I have watched the Ballplayer's Dance being performed, but I didn't learn the songs. And I didn't learn the Groundhog Dance, the Snake Dance, or the Frog Dance. I don't know half of what Will West knew.

I do remember the Friendship Dance and the eight or nine songs that go with it. I also know the Quail Hunter's Dance and the one song that goes with it, the Bear Hunter's Dance and the four songs that go with it, and the Beaver Hunter's Dance and the four songs that go with it. (The last song of the Beaver Hunter's Dance—that's when they go beaver hunting—is the hardest to sing. The couples branch off from the main dance and go around and around. I have to sing throughout their dancing. It's exhausting.)

And I remember the Medicine Song, a song that doesn't accompany a dance. The ancestors sang that song on clear mornings when the sun hit a particular treetop. The song was supposed to protect them from all death and evil. They would see the sun and drink water, then wash their chests and faces, and that would guard them for the day.

A lot of white people have become interested in the tradition now. And some Cherokee. Last night, for example, a crowd came up here, some Oklahoma Cherokee. They wanted to talk with me about how things used to be, and to buy copies of my tape. They didn't know many of the traditional Cherokee songs and dances, and they wanted to learn them.

In the late 1980s, [folklorist] Michael Kline became interested in what I do. He said he would help me make a tape of the songs I know, to preserve them. I said "Okay," so we went to the Cherokee museum to record it. Michael turned off all the electric lights, because they made too much noise, and I sang by candlelight. It took a couple of hours to record everything. Afterwards, Michael asked me about the songs and dances, and he wrote the information down in the notes to the tape. For example, I told him that many of the lyrics I sing when I perform Cherokee dances can't be translated—they're just sounds that help to carry the tunes.

After the tape came out, Michael asked me if he could enter me in some contests. I didn't really know what they were all about, but he said I had a chance of winning, so I said "Yes," then forgot about them. Some time later, someone called to tell me my tape had won an award in Washington [it was selected for the Library of Congress's 1991 "Best Folk Recordings List"]; very soon after that, someone else informed me that I had won another award [the 1992 National Heritage Fellowship from the National Endowment for the Arts].

People want to know about this tradition nowadays, but when I was a child, everybody wanted us to forget our Cherokee traditions. Looking back on it now, I think the schools and the schoolteachers were trying to turn us against our old ways. You see, when I was a child, most of us spoke only Cherokee (Will West's wife was just about the only one around here who spoke much English). The teachers were white people, and they would teach us in English (and, before class would start, they would lead prayers in English). I never understood what they were talking about. They would punish us if we spoke in Cherokee. I didn't learn much at school because I would run off most of the time. When I was nine years old, I stopped going to school for good so I could work around my parents' house. In those days, it was important to get the farm work done, because the person who raised his crops properly was a rich man.

I learned to speak English, of course—I had to. We had to survive. Many Cherokee people my age, though, have just about given up on the old ways. But my family hasn't. My great-granddaughter, for example, can't remember all the original English words to "Amazing Grace," but she can sing it all the way through in Cherokee. And I've got a grandson, about twenty years old, who can sing most of the songs I know. He practices out there in the field. He's learning the songs of the Beaver Hunter's Dance—he has already led a performance of it. He's also learning the Quail Dance. But he has been slacking off since he started school. I tell him, "That's how the Cherokee language got forgotten." Maybe he'll be the one to keep alive the tradition I taught him. He had better! [Calhoun laughs.]

I'm usually hired to perform Cherokee songs and dances, but sometimes I bring my banjo with me and play old string-band tunes like "Redwing," "Under the Double Eagle," and "Down Yonder." I've played the banjo since I was half his age, I guess [pointing towards his young great-grandson, who is playing on the floor]. Two of my brothers owned banjos, and they kept them hanging on the wall. They didn't want me to touch their banjos or take them down, but one day while my brothers were at work, I took a chair and stood there and strummed the strings. After that, I would often sneak down one of the banjos and play it, and I would put it back before my brothers got home. I learned how to play the banjo by watching my brothers pick out simple tunes like "Little Brown Jug," and, later, by listening to old hillbilly and bluegrass records. But mostly I taught myself how to play [the banjo]. Nowadays, when I perform the songs I learned from those 78s, like "Coming 'Round the Mountain," "Going Down the Road Feeling Bad," and "Wabash Cannonball," I don't sing because I can't ever remember the words. I just pick out the tunes on the banjo. My family doesn't always like to hear me play my banjo—I have to go outside to practice. [He laughs.] But some people out there do like my banjo playing, because this year the people at the Banjo Institute in Tennessee wanted me to perform there.

As a young man, Will West sang some Cherokee songs for a scholar [ethnologist Franz Obrechts], who recorded them on wax cylinders (that's all there was to record with back then). A tape recording of those wax cylinders is kept at the museum in Cherokee [Museum of the Cherokee Indian]. A couple of years ago, Michael Kline took me there to hear Will West's recordings for the first time. It was a moving experience—I'm real glad I got to hear them. Yet there was so much static on those recordings, you can hardly hear Will West. So, I'm very glad that I've helped to bring Will West's songs and dances back to life.

Customary Folklife

The term customary folklife refers to traditional behaviors which generally possess both nonverbal and verbal (and sometimes material) components. The Native American presence in the region produced some fascinating customary traditions, all of which are now absent from the Blue Ridge (though some of the customary traditions of the Cherokee still survive in the Qualla Boundary, the tribe's landholdings in the nearby Great Smoky Mountains). For three centuries, the Blue Ridge has harbored different yet equally interesting European-American customary traditions; some of these died out in the wake of modernization, some linger tenuously in the region's more remote areas, and some are still widely practiced today. This chapter discusses the most characteristic of these customary traditions, including religious rituals and ceremonies, folk beliefs, social customs (for rites of passage including birth, courtship, marriage, and death), holiday celebrations, festivals, dances, and games.

Footwashing and Full-Immersion Baptism

Many of the region's customary traditions reflect the central importance of religious experience in the lives of the Blue Ridge people. One traditional religious ritual in the region, footwashing, was associated with an important rite of passage: the sacramental communion of the individual Christian with God. By participating in footwashing the sinful individual might be initiated into the community of believers. Historically practiced in the Blue Ridge by various Baptist sects and Holiness groups during communion services and at the end of church meetings, footwashing took literally Christ's biblical edict, as conveyed in John 13: 14–15: "If I then,

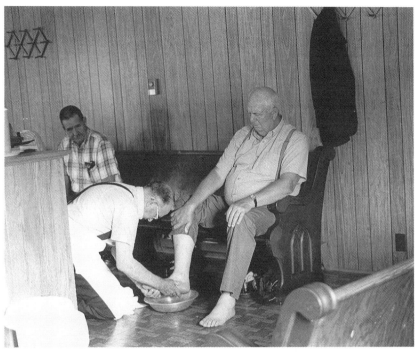

The ritual of footwashing being administered at Stoney Creek Primitive Baptist Church, near Elizabethton, Carter County, Tennessee. (Photo by Howard Dorgan)

your Lord and Master, have washed your feet; ye also ought to wash one another's feet. For I have given you an example, that ye should do as I have done unto you." A religious rite widespread in the South during the late eighteenth and the early nineteenth centuries (a period often called the Great Awakening for its climate of religious fervor), footwashing was employed during revival meetings by preachers, for the efficient conversion of large numbers of people. By the middle of the nineteenth century, though, with the rise of organized religious councils in the South (most notably, the Southern Baptist Convention), footwashing fell out of favor in the lowland South—many Baptists there began to view the ceremony as primitive, a remnant of a less civilized era. Many Blue Ridge congregations, however, continued to practice footwashing well into the twentieth century, and some still make it a regular part of their services.

The survival of footwashing in the region is the result of specific historical circumstances. Early Blue Ridge settlers—specifically, anti-institutional German Anabaptists (Mennonites and Dunkards) and independent-minded Scots-Irish—set the region's mold for noncompliance toward establishment Christianity. In the nineteenth century, many regional Baptist congregations refused to affiliate themselves with organized religious councils, which these congregations saw as irrelevant for their communities' needs. Spared from having to conform to centralized by-laws, they were free to design their own worship services. Some Blue Ridge congregations chose to retain footwashing in their services, as well as another old-time Christian communion ceremony, full-immersion baptism.

Conducted in Blue Ridge streams and rivers since the eighteenth century and still observed today among the region's more fundamentalist Baptist sects (including the Freewill, Missionary, and Old Regular Baptists), full-immersion baptism ceremonies have served as metaphorical re-creations of Christ's baptism in the River Jordan. A person requesting baptism would submit him- or herself for a total dunking in the cold water of a mountain tributary; in so doing, that person's soul would be metaphorically washed clean of his or her sins, purified by water which had been declared holy by the preacher presiding over the event. Full-immersion baptism ceremonies would most often take place in the summer, on special Sundays after the

A Separate Baptist baptism in the cool waters of the North Fork of the New River, near Warrensville, North Carolina. (Photo by Howard Dorgan)

morning worship service. On such an occasion a congregation would gather by a stream or river, at a spot deep enough to allow for full immersion and accessible enough so that all age groups could participate. Since the ceremony was always a central event in the lives of believers, already-baptized congregation members would gather by the stream, where they would offer encouragement to the new initiates, recount happy memories of their own spiritual redemption (which may well have occurred at the same site), and sing and pray. The preacher, after inspecting the stream or river to make sure it was adequate for dunking, would meet the congregation by the bank and offer some appropriate words for the occasion—a prayer or a brief sermon, sometimes a hymn. Then the preacher and one or more male helpers would lead the first initiate slowly into the stream or river to the baptism site. Women initiates, to prevent the awkward billowing up of their clothing in the water, would often have tied or sewn weights into their dresses. The preacher or one of his helpers would cover the mouth and nose of the initiate with a handkerchief, since the person to be baptized would be bent quickly backwards into the water. Then the preacher would offer a special baptism prayer, while the helpers braced the initiate, who was now closing his or her eyes. Finally, the immersion would occur. Underwater for only a few seconds, the initiate would be lifted back up, and the handkerchief over his or her face would be removed to allow breathing. Cold, wet, yet emotionally excited, the now-baptized person would return to shore, often displaying outward signs of exuberance—shouting, crying, flailing arms, and uncontrollable moving of the body. When he or she reached the shore, women would offer towels, whereupon the person would dry off while being greeted by family and friends. The preacher would then begin the baptism of the next initiate waiting on the bank. When all initiates had been baptized, the preacher would close the ceremony with one last prayer, and everyone would disperse.

Other Religious Rituals

Religious fervor in Appalachia gave rise in the early twentieth century to a now notorious religious ritual: snake handling. Probably originating near Ooltewah, Tennessee, in 1908, allegedly after George Went Hensley had a vision in which God directed him to take literally a biblical verse advising true believers to "take up serpents" and to observe other "signs" as a way to prove their faith in God (Mark 16: 17–20), the practice of handling snakes (i.e., poisonous snakes, particularly rattlesnakes) as a way to publicly express one's faith eventually became, for some fundamentalist Pentecostal-Holiness congregations, an important ritualistic activity associated with special worship services. Never very common in the western ranges of the Southern and Central Appalachians, snake handling has been even rarer in the Blue Ridge. Frequently outlawed by state and local authorities, the ritual would generally be conducted covertly, and thus it is difficult to trace the exact range of its dissemination; nonetheless, snake handling has been practiced by a handful of Pentecostal-Holiness congregations in north Georgia and western North Carolina (Haywood County, for instance, has been the site of relatively recent snake-handling activity).

At one of these special worship services, collective emotion would be raised high among the congregation by a combination of religious music, preaching, testimonials (often spontaneously delivered), and "speaking in tongues" (another of St. Mark's "signs," this phenomenon, also known as glossolalia, involved the uttering of unintelligible speech-like sounds— thought to be the voice of God channelled through a person experiencing the ecstasy of spiritual communion). Then someone among the congregation would reach into storage boxes and remove by hand one or more vipers. To a background of hymn singing, instrumental music, and ecstatic outcries from congregation members, willing participants would hand, and sometimes toss, the snakes amongst themselves while publicly professing their faith in God. At these same special worship services, some congregation members would also drink poison (usually strychnine), another of St. Mark's "signs." Participants in both of these rituals believed that, if their faith was strong enough, God would protect them from the effects of the poisoning. Another ritual associated with certain Pentecostal-Holiness groups was the touching of fire (in the form of hot coals and embers or a fire-blowing torch); as with the aforementioned rituals, faith in God, it was believed, would protect practitioners from being hurt.

Folk Beliefs

Given the slowness with which many modern American values entered the region, the Blue Ridge remained fertile ground for traditional folk beliefs well into the twentieth century. Many people would cling to these beliefs because of the culture's adherence to fundamentalist Christianity, which encouraged acceptance on faith (i.e., empirical proof is not required). Of course, no group, however formally educated or intellectually "enlightened," is free of folk beliefs, and not every belief incorporates incorrect logic—indeed, some involve correct (and often insightful) analyses regarding the cause and effect relationship of two actions or two phenomena.

Blue Ridge beliefs reflected folk ideas about many aspects of everyday life within the region: food ("Don't eat cherries or any kind of fruit with milk or cream. It's dangerous"); health and sickness ("Never think of warts or look at yours, and they will disappear"); and medicine ("Slice and dry Indian turnip and mix with honey. This cures T.B."). Beliefs also concerned social relationships ("If you see a redbird that is not flying, you will meet your future husband [or wife]"); domestic realities ("If your left foot itches, you are going to get a new pair of shoes"); and economic affairs ("If you hear the first whippoorwill to your front, you will go forward all the year and all will have plenty that year"). Additionally, there were many traditional beliefs regarding the interrelationship between the natural world and human life, including observations about the weather ("It is bad luck for a girl to get married when it is snowing"); animals ("It is an ill omen for a squirrel to cross the road before you going toward the left"); and celestial bodies ("Count seven stars for seven successive nights, and the first person of the opposite sex who shakes hands with you afterwards will be your future mate"). These beliefs, and the thousands of others which once circulated in the Blue Ridge, were probably not endemic to the region; most were transported to the New World by European settlers, while others were probably introduced to the mountains by travellers from the lowlands (including African-American migrant laborers). Despite the abundance of folk beliefs in the region, it is likely that many Blue Ridge residents were highly suspicious of some, if not most—including those strongly religious people who refused to believe what was not mandated by the Bible. Other individuals no doubt renounced all such beliefs on principle.

PLANTING BY THE SIGNS

Every European who settled in the Blue Ridge brought to the region knowledge of numerous customary traditions from his or her country of origin. While many of these traditions did not take root in the New World soil, some did. One of the more intriguing Blue Ridge customary traditions of Old World origin was known as "planting by the signs," which likely evolved in ancient times out of the universal desire to understand the fluctuating environmental conditions in which humans are forced to live. Like many other rural populations worldwide, the people of the Blue Ridge embraced folk beliefs in an effort to influence their predicaments; thus, some farmers in the region have turned to astrology for tips on how to gain an edge on nature. In addition to acting upon hearsay, observation, and intuition, Blue Ridge farmers would sometimes heed the predictions of commercial astrological charts, which were generally obtained through the mail. Offering farming advice based on the accumulated folk wisdom of western astrology (which for centuries has interpreted a mystical relationship between the earth and the stars involving the earth's position relative to constellations in the zodiac belt), these charts advised that each of the twelve zodiac signs controls a few days each month. Since, figuratively speaking, each sign was thought to have its own identity, each day controlled by a particular sign was believed to possess some of that sign's characteristics. For instance, days ruled by the "water" signs—Cancer, Scorpio, and Pisces—were thought to be ideal for planting crops, since the soil would then be especially fertile, while days ruled by the "fire" signs— Aries, Leo, and Sagittarius—were deemed bad for planting crops but good for plowing a garden or field.

A related astrological belief involved considering the phases of the moon when planning farming and other activities. For example, many people believed that they should avoid planting crops when the moon was new. Some believed that they should plant crops only when the moon was waxing, except for root crops, which were to be planted during the waning of the moon; the latter time was also good for harvesting crops. Farming was not the only activity for which many in the Blue Ridge sought celestial counsel. For believers, the zodiac signs and the moon provided insight regarding the best times for activities ranging from butchering hogs, hunting, chopping logs, and painting barns to having one's teeth pulled.

Planting by the signs specifically and astrology in general were easily justified—after all, many people could claim to have personally witnessed their effectiveness. The famous biblical passage from Ecclesiastes (3: 1–2) lent additional credence: "To everything there is a season, and a time to every purpose under the heaven: A time to be born, and a time to die; a time to plant, and a time to pluck up that which is planted." Planting by the signs is steadily disappearing in the Blue Ridge—less because of the weight of scientific evidence against it than because of the availability of up-to-the-minute weather forecasting. Farmers in the region today consult radio and television weather reports more often than they do astrological charts.

FAITH HEALING

Several customary traditions in the Blue Ridge region were born out of a fusion of fundamentalist Christianity and secular mysticism. Many people there have believed that, with proper faith, they could summon the power of the Lord, who would cure sicknesses and injuries. In a rural and isolated region which until recent years possessed few hospitals, such faith healing was often a substitute for formal medical attention. Faith healers had the power to cure thrush (a fungus affecting the digestive tract, particularly of children), to reduce the impact of burns, and to stop bleeding. To cure thrush, a faith healer, feeling empowered by the Lord, would cradle the child with one arm and then would cup his or her free hand over the child's mouth and nose and try to suck the thrush out of the child's mouth, whereupon the healer would safely dispense with the bad air containing the thrush germ. Stopping the pain of a burn involved drawing out the fire which was believed to have entered the victim's skin at the time of the burn; this magical rite was accompanied by the faith healer's silent recitation of a special Bible verse. By uttering a different biblical passage, a faith healer could stop bleeding. Faith healing was most often learned directly from an experienced healer who understood the magical aspects of healing and who knew that the right to practice was exclusively granted by divine authority. Such a healer, who was generally an elder, would share with an initiate (usually a person of the opposite sex) such aspects of faith healing as proper attitude, appropriate biblical passages, and procedures. Initiates would be advised never to divulge this secret knowledge publicly or face losing their healing powers. Certain people were believed to have been born with the power to heal by faith, including those whose fathers had died before their own birth and those who were born a seventh son or daughter. As with planting by the signs, faith healing endured because many people claimed to have witnessed its beneficial effects. Because of the ongoing influence of fundamentalist Christian beliefs within the Blue Ridge, and because of a deep-seated suspicion of formal medical science among many individuals (particularly the elderly), faith healing is still practiced today in some parts of the region.

Birth

Many of the beliefs and customs which evolved in the Blue Ridge region concerned the great mysteries of birth and death (for practices related to death, see below). For example, many midwives, who witnessed both of these realities at close hand, believed that the sight of a yellow-colored bee on the morning of a birth assured the safety of mother and baby; however, they also thought that the sight of a black-colored bee shortly before a delivery portended bad luck. Such beliefs probably arose out of midwives' unconscious recognition that they might at some time fail to save a mother or baby during a delivery. Deaths, of course, did occur, and a midwife might have felt a psychological need for transferring responsibility for such an outcome to the forces of fate, sparing herself the psychic guilt which otherwise would hinder her effectiveness in future deliveries. A midwife might want a means for assigning ultimate responsibility for a death to some other source, such as to black bees, which were not uncommon in the region. Such a projection would enable a midwife to remain emotionally balanced. More empowering were the regional beliefs which encouraged midwives to believe they could magically control the forces of life and death. One such belief directed the midwife to place an axe under a pregnant woman's bed and a knife under her pillow—acts which would alleviate the patient's pain, the midwife believed. This practice may have owed its origin to European folk beliefs which maintained that iron was a guard against witchcraft, and that adults might keep supernatural creatures from stealing human babies by placing iron tools and weapons in nurseries. It is also possible that this belief stems from an actual, though unrecorded, incident in which a midwife, doing everything within her power to help a suffering patient, set the axe and knife in the aforementioned locations. When the woman's condition suddenly improved, likely a coincidence, the midwife, making a direct correlation between her action and the subsequent change in the patient, spread the word about her discovery to other people; another midwife, facing a similar predicament, might have followed that midwife's advice immediately before her own patient's condition improved. By such a scenario an individual belief resulting from a specific situation might become widely held.

Perhaps not surprisingly in a region requiring self-reliance among its inhabitants, elaborate customary traditions evolved in the Blue Ridge for virtually all aspects of everyday life, including birth. Before a hospital or clinic was built to serve a particular community, a pregnant woman within that community was either transported to the nearest facility or had to give birth at home. In more remote areas the slowness of communication and the difficulty of travel often rendered impossible the timely arrival of formally trained doctors or nurses. Fortunately, there was, in virtually every locality, a midwife (sometimes called a "granny") who could dependably deliver a baby. In the old days, most Blue Ridge midwives had little or no formal training, though more recently some would receive training from licensed doctors at government-sponsored programs in nearby towns and cities. Twentieth-century midwives did not necessarily distrust modern medicine, and many would recommend that a pregnant woman obtain a check-up from a doctor in advance of the expected delivery date, so that potential problems could be diagnosed; if deemed to be at risk, the woman was advised to forgo a midwife and instead travel to a hospital before going into labor. However, a lack of facilities in many areas and the reality of sudden labor necessitated that midwives handle difficult as well as uncomplicated deliveries.

When a woman went into labor, the nearest midwife was summoned; she would journey, night or day, on foot, by horse, or by car, to be by the expectant mother's side. A midwife would carry a bag containing aprons, towels, cloth for diapers, and scissors, but generally no commercial medicine or pain relievers. She would usually bring a laundry basket, which would serve as a makeshift crib for the baby. Local women would assist the midwife with her work. After the baby was born, the midwife would cut the umbilical cord and tie up the navel, then wrap the baby in cloth. Sometimes a newborn would need immediate attention; if he or she was born with croup, for instance, the midwife would improve the breathing by shaking the baby and blowing into his or her mouth. If the baby was born with hives, the midwife might administer some herbal tea (usually catnip tea). Once the safety of the baby and mother had been assured, the midwife would pick up the placenta and umbilical cord and promptly bury them outside. Although often lacking formal training, midwives were in general conscientious and skillful, providing Blue Ridge communities a crucial service for little or no financial recompense. Having attained the most respected position for females in premodern Blue Ridge society (some felt empowered enough to smoke corncob pipes when not working), midwives were frequently honored with the title "Aunt"; many female babies were named after the "grannies" who eased their passage into the world.

Courtship and Marriage

Interestingly, courtship and marriage in the Blue Ridge involved far fewer customary behaviors than birth, death, and spiritual salvation; in fact, the process of establishing marital unions within the region might be characterized as decidedly unromantic. Courtship would begin sometime after boys and girls reached their teenage years. Since the local church served as both the religious and social center of a Blue Ridge community, a young person would often meet his or her love interest there. Thus, the first stage of courtship, which people in the Blue Ridge called "talking," would frequently occur following a Sunday service, at which time a young man would walk a young woman home from church—after obtaining permission from her parents, of course. The second stage of courtship, often referred to as "sparking," involved the young man escorting the young woman to church on subsequent Sundays, as well as bringing her gifts at her parents' house and visiting her there, under supervision. (In some sections of the Blue Ridge, the courting couple might sit on the front porch without parental supervision if they would jointly play the "courting dulcimer," an Appalachian instrument constructed with two fretboards, each facing in the opposite direction; so long as the nearby parents could hear both sets of strings being strummed, they could leave the couple unobserved, knowing that the teenagers were preoccupied.) During this stage of courtship, a woman, in preparation for seeing her boyfriend, would don her best clothes and apply makeup (perhaps rouge). Nevertheless, strict, if informal, behavioral codes in Blue Ridge social life rendered it inappropriate for a single woman to make more overt advances toward her suitor, and in general she was expected to act coyly.

The third stage of courtship—premarital sexual activity—was the most problematic. Despite religious strictures which officially prohibited Christians from yielding to the temptations of the flesh, sexual activity outside marriage was rather common, and most people were surprisingly forgiving of the consequences of such behavior. Conceiving a baby out of wedlock would generally lead to a hastily arranged wedding. If social pressure or legal action failed to force the responsible man into compliance, the young woman would remain single, and her parents would raise the illegitimate child with their own children. If a wedding was held, it was seldom an elaborate ceremony, and would often occur away from the bride's and groom's communities—perhaps hastily administered by an unfamiliar preacher or justice of the peace in another county. Once the homefolk had adjusted to the new social relationship, a celebration might be offered in honor of the newly married couple, featuring music and some kind of dancing, as well as food and liquor.

Later, if a marriage proved unworkable, a couple might separate, though in the old days this action did not necessarily lead to legal divorce. Many people could not afford a lawyer, and, furthermore, the county courthouse was often quite inconvenient to the divorcing couple. Some people, ignoring the formality of filing for an official divorce, would remarry, undaunted by the fact that they were, according to civil laws, committing bigamy. People in the Blue Ridge were flexible regarding human relationships, because, in an environment of geographical and social isolation, all adults were in principle equally important to the survival of the community; thus, forgiveness and acceptance were essential social values.

Death

Death being inevitable, several customary traditions in the Blue Ridge addressed this phenomenon and the related quest for life after death. Historically, since hospitals and funeral homes were not a factor in most parts of the region until the twentieth century, Blue Ridge inhabitants died at home, where their bodies would be prepared for burial; the wake would also take place at home, while the funeral and burial would be held at a nearby churchyard. In short, death was not softened or sanitized. When a person died, family members would inform neighbors about their loved one's passing by tolling the bell at the local church—usually one ring for every year of the deceased person's life. Knowing who had died by the number of times the bell tolled, neighbors would go straight to the house of the deceased to comfort the grieving family; work would often be postponed until after the burial. The family of the deceased would immediately arrange for a craftsman within the community to construct a wooden coffin. Then, perhaps with the help of a family friend or the local preacher and his wife, members of the family would prepare the body for burial, a process which involved closing the eyes (often placing coins there to keep them closed), straightening out the corpse and dressing him or her in fine clothes, wiping the face and hands with soda water or alcohol (to prevent the skin from changing color), and storing the body in a cool place. In the days before the telephone, the family would promptly write letters to relatives and friends not residing nearby to inform them about the death (traditionally, a black border would be drawn around the edge of the envelope to call the recipient's attention to the letter's serious and timely message).

Shortly afterward, usually the evening following the death, a wake would be offered so that the living might show their respect for the dead. The wake not only enabled those in attendance to verify that a person was indeed deceased, but also served to protect the corpse from animal predators which, if they fed on the body, might endanger the dead person's soul. During the wake, the corpse would be placed in the parlor room (either on a table or in the coffin if it was finished). Relatives and members of the community—old and young alike—would gather near the body to eat, talk, and sing hymns; some people might cut locks of hair off the deceased for keepsakes. The wake would eventually grow quite festive, with people participating in such activities as music making, storytelling, card playing, game playing, and courting. A coffin completed during the wake would be brought directly into the house so that those attending might participate in the placing of the corpse into it (coffins were made of oak, chestnut, pine, or poplar, and were lined with cloth and padded with cotton). The wake festivities would end sometime after midnight, at which point most neighbors would go home; at least one relative or close friend, however, would stay to comfort the grieving family, who would be "sitting" with the deceased. Such wakes are rare in the Blue Ridge today. Nowadays, many people die in hospitals or nursing homes, and, even when a person passes away at home, ordinances and modern practice require his or her body to be promptly taken to a funeral home for embalming. Loved ones and neighbors may come to the funeral home for a short public viewing, but a family seldom "sits" all night with their deceased kin as in the old days.

Generally, the funeral service and the burial would be held the morning after the wake (if close relatives were unable to arrive in time, the burial would take place promptly, and the funeral service would be postponed until the next community homecoming, Decoration Day gathering, or family reunion). The coffin bearing the deceased would be loaded onto an animal-drawn wagon, and the animal or animals (horse, mule, or ox) would be led toward the church house. A tolling of the bell would announce the arrival of the coffin to the church, whereupon relatives and members of the community, dressed in black, would quickly gather for the funeral service. The coffin, usually opened, would be placed in front of the pulpit, and the preacher would speak in honor of the deceased, read aloud from the Bible, and, finally, lead a round of prayer. After a final viewing of the deceased by all members of the community, the coffin would be transported to the cemetery for burial. Once the coffin was placed beside the grave (already dug by relatives or friends), a short, highly emotional committal service on behalf of the deceased would be conducted. This service gave the family and close friends a last chance to view the body. After the preacher offered a final prayer and a few last words, the lid would be attached, and the coffin would be carefully lowered into the hole. The loose dirt would be shovelled into the grave and packed down, at which point relatives and friends would go home and get back to the business of living. Before long, a gravemarker would be placed at the head of the grave to commemorate the deceased. This service was usually done for little or no payment by someone in the community, as a gift to the family. Made of either wood or stone and often carved by hand, the gravemarker would bear the deceased person's name, vital dates, and sometimes a heartfelt epitaph, either words taken from scripture or a stock expression, such as "Gone Home," to soften for the living the pain of their loss. Since many people in the region received only intermittent formal education before the twentieth century, gravemarkers often contained phonetic rather than standardized spellings of English words.

Annual Celebrations

DECORATION DAY

Although the people of the Blue Ridge have observed most of the same holidays as other Americans, these celebrations within the region have often been markedly different in character from the national versions. Many people in the Blue Ridge, for example, still refer to Memorial Day as Decoration Day, the original name of the late-nineteenth-century holiday which gave a grieving nation a chance to remember Civil War casualties. Decoration Day was not always observed in late May: well into the twentieth century, people would gather in cemeteries on any convenient Sunday between spring and fall (sometimes after the crops had been harvested) to remember their deceased relatives and close friends. Once a date had been decided upon, people would visit the family cemetery (usually near the local church house) a few days before the holiday and clear debris off the gravesites of kith and kin, cut the grass, repair gravemarkers and fences, and remove old flowers. On the morning of Decoration Day, members of a family and/or community would gather at the cemetery and place on the graves of loved ones bouquets of newly picked wildflowers—or, in recent years, artificial flowers. Then would ensue a lengthy, sometimes daylong, emotional service officiated by one or two preachers. Around noontime, preaching would be interrupted for a traditional group picnic, a "dinner on the ground," in which a generous array of foods would be spread out on blankets on the grass (folding card tables are commonly used today to help keep food out of the reach of ants and beetles). In the afternoon, after the preaching was over, participants would conclude the conversations they had begun during the dinner on the ground, then would disperse.

Historically, Decoration Day was a good occasion for family reunions. The out-migration of many people from the region in the twentieth century, combined with the increase in organized perpetual-care cemeteries, has led to the decline of daylong Decoration Day ceremonies. Today, many cemeteries are overgrown with weeds and otherwise neglected.

EASTER

People in the Blue Ridge have generally celebrated Easter as other Americans have, with special church services and egg hunts. After helping children gather and paint eggs with natural dyes, adults would hide the eggs in the churchyard grass, often inside the cemetery. This location held strong symbolic value, with the presence of eggs among graves underscoring the significance of Easter: the emergence of life after death.

FALL HOLIDAYS

The best-known fall holidays—Halloween and Thanksgiving—were observed in the Blue Ridge much as they were nationally, in large part because both holidays were formally introduced into the region from the outside (the former through the pressures of commercial interests, the latter by the edict of the federal government). More unique to the region were the various annual celebratory events occasioned by the harvest season. In the Blue Ridge, the fall routine of converting sorghum cane into molasses spawned a social event known as a candy pulling, intended primarily for young people. The adults overseeing the process at the sorghum mill would

Members of Stoney Creek Primitive Baptist Church (near Elizabethton, Carter County, Tennessee) enjoying a dinner on the ground. In the Blue Ridge, this traditional communal feast is an integral part of Decoration Day and homecoming Sunday celebrations. (Photo by Howard Dorgan)

boil down a small quantity of molasses into hard candy, which they would give to youths. Boys and girls would take the opportunity of eating (i.e., "pulling") the molasses candy to socialize and court. Another event practiced during the harvest, cornshucking, ensured that this chore got done, and, through the activity's cooperative nature, reconfirmed community ties. Hosting one- or two-day-long cornshuckings each fall, a farmer would pick his corn a day or two before, and pile the unshucked ears in an accessible spot. Since he was obligated to feed his helpers, the farmer also would butcher and begin to cook a hog. On the day of the cornshucking, while the farmer's wife and several neighbor women were preparing a full meal (to be eaten after all the work was done), the farmer and male neighbors would make short work of the pile. In one custom associated with cornshuckings, the farmer would place a jug of moonshine at the bottom of a pile of unshucked corn ears; in another, the farmer would permit a helper, whenever he shucked a red ear of corn, to kiss his wife or girlfriend (or, depending upon the rules established in advance, the closest woman). The first custom, of course, served as an incentive for helpers to work more efficiently, while the latter provided an element of excitement to an otherwise tedious task. After the corn was all shucked, the ears would be carried to the corncrib for storage, and the shucks and stalks would be saved for composting and other uses, including the making of toys (such as corn-shuck dolls and cornstalk constructions). When the work was done, people would eat and socialize, which included talking, drinking, music making, and dancing. Participants would then disperse, often to gather together again a few days later for a cornshucking at another neighbor's farm.

CHRISTMAS

The most popular holiday in the Blue Ridge was Christmas, which was celebrated with little or none of the crass commercialism found in main-stream America. Historically, poor access to commercial decorations, gifts, and food forced many people in the region to improvise when preparing for the holiday. For Christmas trees, Blue Ridge residents would generally harvest whatever species grew best in their locality. In higher elevations, people would cut Fraser fir or red spruce (in several western North Carolina counties today, these two trees are grown as commercial Christmas trees), while people in lower elevations would use less picturesque red cedar, American holly, or eastern hemlock. The trees were decorated with a com-bination of natural and artificial products—sycamore balls, strings of pop-corn, shredded cotton, and ribbons of crepe paper and cellophane. Over the years, seasonal house decorations have included bouquets of dried grass and wildflowers, clusters of Galax leaves and Christmas fern fronds, bowls of apples and oranges, and red- and green-colored ropes strung around the house. In the old days, gifts were simple—perhaps a handmade toy or a store-bought pocketknife for youths, and, for adults, an article of clothing, a tool, or a book; owing to the scarcity of stores in those days, it was com-mon for people to give gifts which had already been used.

On Christmas Eve and well into Christmas morning, many young people would roam through their rural Blue Ridge communities "serenading" their neighbors; this traditional activity involved much more than the singing of Christmas carols, though that was a part of it. When serenading, youths would approach houses in the dark and scare the occupants with loud noises (screaming, clanging cowbells, exploding firecrackers, or blast-ing guns); the occupants would subsequently open their doors and let the youths inside for singing and for the giving of various treats. Although Christmas was an occasion for good will, these serenaders would sometimes play pranks on their neighbors, an example being the rearranging or hiding of possessions such as tools. At other times, young people would play a game associated with serenading: if they could sneak up to a house and shout "Christmas gift!" without being noticed, the occupants would be obligated to give them a gift; however, if the occupants spied the serenaders before the shout could be made, then the young people would have to give them a gift.

Festivals

The Blue Ridge is the site of numerous annual festivals which acknowledge the region's diverse folklife traditions, celebrate its many landmark historical events, and/or honor its most prominent citizens of yesteryear. Among the best known of these are several with national reputations, including the National Storytelling Festival, the Old Fiddler's Convention, the Singing on the Mountain, and the Grandfather Mountain Highland

Mr. Joe L. Hartley, with hat and Bible in hand, was the founder and chairman of the annual event at Grandfather Mountain known as Singing on the Mountain. According to locals, Hartley believed that this handmade sign was the main reason people knew about the festival. In truth, entertainer Arthur Smith plugged the event on television for years, in every major market between Texas and Baltimore. (Photo by Hugh Morton)

Games and Gathering of Scottish Clans. The National Storytelling Festival, held on the first weekend of October in Jonesborough, Tennessee, has, since its inception in 1972, showcased acclaimed local, regional, national, and international storytellers. The Old Fiddler's Convention (often called the Galax Fiddler's Convention since its base is Galax, Virginia) was founded in 1935 as a local event offering friendly competition for folk musicians and old-time string bands. Each contestant in various musical categories performs a short selection, while a group of anonymous judges listens, evaluates the performance, and awards prizes to those deemed most accomplished. By the 1960s, the Old Fiddler's Convention had been adopted by fans of the folk music revival, whose enthusiasm helped to transform the event into one of the nation's largest regularly occurring folk music contests. Today offering formal competitions in folk, old-time string band, and bluegrass music, as well as in traditional dance (clogging and flatfoot dancing), the Fiddler's Convention, held each August, also serves as the site of numerous informal jam sessions which continue on into the night, long after the day's official competitions have ended. An opportunity for the free exchange of ideas about musical style and repertoire, these jam sessions also encourage understanding between the two socioeconomic groups which regularly attend the festival: older Blue Ridge natives and the younger urban- and suburban-born, college-educated audience. Despite their cultural differences, these groups find common ground at Galax through a mutual appreciation for the traditional music of the Blue Ridge.

The Singing on the Mountain and the Grandfather Mountain Highland Games and Gathering of Scottish Clans are both staged at the base of Grandfather Mountain, the highest peak in the Blue Ridge (Mt. Mitchell and Mt. Rogers have higher elevations, but are technically part of adjacent mountain ranges). Held in June since its inception in 1924, the Singing on the Mountain combines gospel singing by musicians with local, regional, and national reputations with preaching by a wide range of evangelists and Christian entertainers (from local ministers to television personalities). With no admission fee—even celebrities have volunteered their time in order to join their fans in worship and fellowship—the Singing on the Mountain is "dedicated to the Glory of God." The Grandfather Mountain Highland Games and Gathering of Scottish Clans, the largest event of its kind in the New World, celebrates the region's (and the nation's) Scottish cultural heritage. Since 1956, the July festival has featured competitions in traditional Scottish athletics (such as stone- and hammer-throwing), traditional Scottish music (including individual piping and drumming, as well as band contests), highland dancing (traditional sword and fling dances), and animal training (specifically of the famous Scottish breed, the Border collie). The festival also offers several noncompetitive traditional activities,

Reverend Billy Graham preached at the 1963 Singing on the Mountain, attracting
the largest crowd ever assembled in the mountains of North Carolina. (Photo by
Hugh Morton)

such as Scottish country dancing (traditional Scottish social dancing), Cei-
lidhs (akin to a variety show of Scottish music and dance, a Ceilidh accen-
tuates audience participation), and the annual meetings of many Scottish
clan associations.

Other celebratory events in the Blue Ridge, while not as nationally renowned as those mentioned above, nonetheless attract sizeable crowds.
Events which acknowledge historical occurrences of regional and national
significance include the Days of Revolution in Roanoke, Virginia (April),
the Wilderness Trail Festival in Christiansburg, Virginia (September), and
the Moravian Love Feast in Mount Airy, North Carolina (December). Also,
each May in New Market, Virginia, a costumed reenactment commemo-
rates the 1864 Battle of New Market, in which Confederate troops forced a
larger Union command to retreat northward up the Shenandoah Valley.
Other Blue Ridge events honor individual regional figures who had an
impact on American political or cultural history. These include the Historic Birthday Parties, held in January in Lexington, Virginia, honoring

The Hammer Throw is one of several Scottish athletic competitions offered each July at the Grandfather Mountain Highland Games and Gathering of Scottish Clans, the largest event of its kind in the New World. (Photo by Hugh Morton)

Thomas "Stonewall" Jackson; Jefferson's Birthday Commemoration, held in Charlottesville, Virginia, in April; the Patsy Cline Festival, held in Winchester, Virginia, over Labor Day weekend; and the Thomas Wolfe Festival, held in Asheville, North Carolina, at the end of September.

Among the many celebratory events in the Blue Ridge which are community efforts to remember the region's folklife traditions are the Folk Arts and Crafts Festival in Weyers Cave, Virginia (May), the Blue Ridge Folklife Festival in Ferrum, Virginia (October), Fall Pioneer Living Days in Weaverville, North Carolina (September), Foxfire Folk Skills and Tradin' Days in Dawsonville, Georgia (August), and Blue Ridge Divide Arts and Crafts Festival in Mountain City, Georgia (October). The region's dependence on agriculture, past and present, is acknowledged in events such as the Shenandoah Apple Blossom Festival in Winchester, Virginia (May), the Virginia Mountain Peach Festival in Roanoke, Virginia (August), the Page Valley Agricultural Fair in Luray, Virginia (August), the Cabbage Festival at Meadows of Dan, Virginia (August), the Washington County Fair and Burley Tobacco Festival in Abingdon, Virginia (September), and the North Carolina Apple Festival in Hendersonville, North Carolina (Labor Day weekend).

Other events promote traditional and contemporary Blue Ridge music, storytelling, and dancing, including several in North Carolina: Merlefest (otherwise known as the Merle Watson Memorial Festival) in Wilkesboro (April), the Sandburg Folk Music Festival in Flat Rock (May), the Albert Hash Memorial Festival in Jefferson (June), the Mountain Dance and Folk Festival in Asheville (August), the Bascom Lamar Lunsford Festival in Mars Hill (October), and the Black Mountain Folk Festival in Black Mountain (October). Although certain other regional events are more mercantile than celebratory, they nonetheless fulfill a traditional function of bringing people together for community interaction; one such example is the Gun Show and Flea Market in Hillsville, Virginia (sponsored by the local chapter of the Veterans of Foreign Wars), one of the largest flea markets in the United States, with approximately twenty-five hundred exhibitors and many more customers gathering over the Labor Day weekend to buy, sell, bargain, and socialize.

Dancing

Although the homogenizing forces of the modern world threaten the survival of most traditional Blue Ridge customary activities, the region's traditional dances have been co-opted by nonnatives and thus will likely endure, albeit in altered form. Historically, dancing was officially viewed within Blue Ridge communities as a forbidden activity which celebrated the body and encouraged the physical intermingling of the sexes. Many people, though, ignored moral denunciations, since dancing not only challenged physical coordination but also provided inhabitants of the rural Blue Ridge with opportunities for camaraderie and courting. Thus, people in the region would dance whenever possible—at celebratory events (such as at various harvest-time activities) and at Friday and Saturday night get-togethers (including the dances known euphemistically as "play-parties").

A play-party was a socially condoned dance for youths and young adults. This "dancing," usually supervised by older adults, involved participants acting out (through the use of gestures) the lyrics of traditional play-party songs. These lyrics were simple, generally evoking the everyday routines and realities of rural life, and thus were easily acted out. The lyrics of the play-party song "Hog Drovers," for example, featured familiar agricultural imagery. In performing "Hog Drovers," a group of young men and women would sing to each other in a call-and-response manner, while mimicking the physical motions used in herding and farming. The girls would start by chanting rhythmically, "Hog drovers, hog drovers, do you come here / A'courting our daughters so neat and so fair?", all the while motioning with their hands for the boys to step forward. The boys would respond by imitating first a finicky horse, then a man loading a wagon and turning away, while singing: "Our horses ain't hungry, they won't eat your hay, / Our wagons are loaded and rolling away." "Hog Drovers" not only concerned courtship, of course: its gesture-filled "dancing" served the vital psychological function of affirming the participants' rural experience (likely the reason for the continued survival of play-parties, despite their resemblance to dances).

While play-parties were popular among younger people, most adults in the Blue Ridge favored various traditional social dances, which borrowed elements from such European dances as English reels, French quadrilles, and Scottish country dances. Many traditional social dances in the Blue Ridge required groups of couples to form one or more squares, with each square needing four couples. However, if the number of couples wanting to dance rendered impossible full participation in a square dance, dancers might opt for either a circle or a line (actually two parallel lines of people facing each other) dance. All types of traditional Blue Ridge social dances employed a caller, who would stand apart from the dancers and guide them through a sequence of maneuvers. Most dances were designed to alter the formation of groups of dancers in a recurrent pattern (e.g., from a square shape to a star shape and back again to a square), until the caller either ended the dance or ordered the groups of dancers into a new pattern of formations.

Blue Ridge social dances were usually tagged with colorful, descriptive names, such as Dive and Shoot the Owl, King's Highway, London Bridge, Ocean Wave, and Wagon Wheel (though a "revivalist" dance from the region might bear the name of the place where it originated or the person who created it), with each dance featuring a generally accepted sequence of maneuvers. Nonetheless, a caller would often improvise during the course of a dance, compelling dancers to pay attention to his or her every word. The best callers had individualized performance styles, delivering directions through some combination of talking, chanting, and singing. In the old days, social dancing would usually be accompanied by live music (whether a lone fiddler or a full string band); in more recent times, people have frequently danced to recorded music on tape players or phonograph/ compact disc players (music transmitted via the radio has proven much less useful for organized dancing, since it is not programmable).

Blue Ridge social dances have received both national and international attention. In 1939, promoter Bascom Lamar Lunsford arranged for a Haywood County, North Carolina, dance team (the Soco Gap Square-Dance Team led by Sam L. Queen) to present a program of traditional regional social dances at the Roosevelt White House for the visiting king and queen of England; and, in the 1940s, the leaders of the national folk dance revival began to incorporate regional dances into the popular square dance repertoire.

Clogging is the most visible group dance in the Blue Ridge today. Less a social than a team dance, clogging incorporated elements of another traditional regional dance, buckdancing. Combining elements from Cherokee tribal dancing, Irish jigs, and African-American flatfoot dancing, buckdancing was a solo dance designed to encourage individualism and improvisation; it demanded the rhythmic alternation of the feet and the fluid movement of the legs, with arms playing a less significant role. While echoing buckdancing's emphasis on the lower torso, clogging, being a team dance, accentuated cooperation and careful choreography. Although originally danced in traditional circumstances (in living rooms, on front porches, and at community gatherings), clogging, because of its competitive and showy nature, proved popular at the early stagings of Bascom Lamar Lunsford's Mountain Dance and Folk Festival (held annually in Asheville since 1928). Recognizing that clogging pleased audiences, other promoters soon hired teams to perform at other formal events within the region. The new marketability of clogging had the effect of heightening the dance's competitive aspect, which led teams to design ever more sophisticated, showy routines. To enhance the impact of their performances, clogging teams began to wear taps on their shoes, to don color-coordinated costumes, and to employ amplified music. Initially, this straying from tradition upset purists; nonetheless, precision clogging, as this new approach to clogging came to be called, has continued to draw large, paying audiences, both within and without the Blue Ridge.

Traditional Games

Involving verbal, material, and customary components, traditional games in the Blue Ridge were taught through demonstration and discussion. In general, the verbal and material aspects of these games augmented the customary aspect, which remained the central purpose of the game. Through game playing, participants could enjoyably pass the time, while (depending on the game) exercising their physiques, improving their motor control, challenging their mental powers, and/or learning social skills.

INDOOR GAMES

Some traditional regional games were meant to be played indoors, by individuals or groups forced inside a house or other building because of inclement weather or darkness, and by people observing some special occasion (such as a holiday, birthday party, or wake). Appropriately, indoor games could be played in limited space, and most possessed simple rules which permitted people in a range of ages to play together. Some indoor games were intended for two people, rendering them useful for such circumstances as a caregiver needing to preoccupy an ill youth or an elderly person. One traditional two-person game, with rules reminiscent of checkers and featuring corn kernels placed on a homemade board, was called fox and geese. A mill customer might challenge a miller to a round of fox and geese while he waited for his corn to be ground. Most indoor games, though, necessitated larger groups of players. Some of these games were more tactile than verbal and thus were ideal for the very young; these included blindfold, in which a blindfolded person had to locate and identify other people in a room without the benefit of sight, and relay, in which two or more teams competed to be the first to walk across a room carrying pieces of fruit or balls between their knees. While these were specifically designed to develop participants' motor control, other multiple-player indoor games were a challenge to the imagination; games such as bum, bum, bum, Old Granny Wiggins is dead, and Old Granny hum bum all required participants to tell and interpret stories using pantomime. Still other games, like the farmer in the dell and club fist, tested players' memories by requiring that they recite traditional verses while performing ritualized motions with their bodies.

OUTDOOR GAMES

The majority of traditional games in the Blue Ridge were played out of doors. The most common, the free-form play of children, was not really a game at all, in that it usually possessed no rules or formal structure. Nonetheless, this play—which involved climbing trees, running through woods and fields, swinging from ropes and vines, and other noncompetitive interactions with the natural world—had a customary aspect, in that youths with different levels of physical development would play in groups, with clumsier children improving their agility by watching and imitating more graceful children. Most traditional outdoor games, though, were overtly competitive, with participants observing an agreed-upon set of rules (players either already knew these rules, rendering formal instruction unnecessary, or agreed to the rules immediately before play). The object of most games was to win, either for oneself or for one's group. In many games the first individual or team to take a turn was determined by finding out who was "it." Techniques for deciding this matter included choosing straws (the person who picked the short straw was "it"); flipping flat stones (one person would spit on a side of the stone and flip it into the air, with the other person guessing whether it would land on the wet or on the dry side); and saying traditional rhymes (which would consist of nonsense words spoken by one player, like "eeny meeny myny moe," or of a short verse containing lines spoken in alternation by all players, with the player or team speaking the last line or word either "it" or "out" of the game).

The most common traditional outdoor games in the Blue Ridge were various chase games, which were popular because they required little equipment and because they sanctioned mingling between the sexes. In the chase game known as buck, the person who was "it" would chase and try to tag the other participants, who were scattered in the woods; if tagged, a person would have to help "it" capture the others. In the game known as fox and hounds, the person who was "it" would flee from a starting spot into the woods, then would try to return to that spot without being tagged by the other players who were chasing him or her. Another chase game, crows and cranes, was played within the boundaries of a makeshift rectangular court: two teams (one called crows, the other cranes) would face each other across a center line, with each team's own safety zone located a short distance behind it. A neutral referee standing outside the court would randomly yell the name of one of the teams, whereupon that team would attempt to retreat to its safety zone without being tagged; the referee could reverse the call at any time during play. The winner of the game was the first team to tag all the members of the other team. Two chase games long played in the Blue Ridge which were also popular nationally were kick the can (based on hide and seek, but with a faster tempo and the added element of teamwork, since the person who is "it" has to defend a can against all other participants, who conspire together to outwit "it") and soup pot (in which two teams try to enter each other's territories; this was a forerunner of capture the flag, a modern game popular at Blue Ridge summer camps).

Many traditional outdoor games, including two long-popular ones, horseshoes and marbles, required specific equipment. Horseshoes remains popular in the region today, particularly among elderly people, while marbles, formerly a favorite game of Blue Ridge youths, is steadily declining in popularity. Rope or tightly bound rags would be used for the game of jump rope (a solo or multiple-person activity, rope jumping was frequently accompanied by various traditional rhymed verses chanted repeatedly until the jumper missed a beat). Some games required sticks, one being knock the stick, in which participants used their walking sticks to bat a short stick into the air; the winner was the person who could hit the short stick the furthest, or, in another version of the game, the person who could more accurately estimate the distance the stick would be hit. In the old days, people in the Blue Ridge would make virtually all such equipment by hand, though many opted for glass marbles and commercial rope when they became available, as these were much more durable than handmade clay marbles and homemade rope. Another game, mumbly peg, involved the ordinary pocketknife. The winner of a game of mumbly peg was the first person who could, with his knife, hit a stationary target—often a small circle drawn in the ground—from all required positions. One incentive for winning the game was that the person would get to strike three times with his knife onto the head of a thin peg, with the goal of pounding that peg into the earth. The loser would have to remove that peg with his teeth, which might mean a mouthful of earth (hence the game's name). Once functioning to train young people in the skillful handling of knives, this game is seldom played today because of ordinances against weapons in schools and other public areas.

BALLGAMES

Several traditional outdoor games formerly popular in the Blue Ridge were those in which balls were primary equipment. These balls were often made by wrapping thread or yarn around a rock, or, in later years, a rubber ball, then sewing a piece of cotton flour sack around the object. In the game anty over, played with a large ball, people would divide into two teams which would hide from each other on opposite sides of a building. Yelling "anty over!" the team with the ball would throw it over the roof of the building toward the other team, who would try to catch it. If members of the other team didn't catch the ball, they would yell "anty over" and throw it back over the building. However, if one team member did catch the ball, he or she would run to the other side of the building and try to hit members of the opposite team with the ball; those struck with the ball were now members of the other team. If the members of the first team could avoid being hit by the ball, and if they could run to the opposite side of the building, they could not be captured. The two teams would take turns throwing the ball over the building to the other team, until the game was called or one team had captured all its opponents. Anty over not only strengthened players' physical quickness but also tested their reaction time to constantly changing stimuli.

In the nineteenth century, before baseball became America's national pastime, people in the Blue Ridge played several similar games involving balls, bases, and bats. In catball, fieldball, and townball, a pitcher would throw a ball toward a catcher, while a batter holding a handmade wooden bat would try to hit the ball. The rules of all three games were not standardized, and much local variation occurred. Catball, which could be played with as few as three people, challenged players individually. A pitcher would throw the ball toward a catcher squatting behind a base, while a batter standing beside the same base would attempt to hit it; if the batter did hit the ball, he would try to run and touch a second base and return to the original base without being tagged with the ball by the other players. If the batter swung without hitting the ball three times in a row (a strikeout), or if the other players could catch a ball hit by the batter before it touched the ground or within one bounce, or if the players could tag the batter before he reached the original base, then the batter was out, at which time another player would bat. If a batter could successfully hit the ball and touch both bases, he was awarded a point (a run) and was allowed to bat again. After all participants had the chance to bat, the winner was the player with the largest number of runs. Fieldball and townball were team sports which tested not only individual ability but also group cooperation. Fieldball could be played with as few as six participants (divided into two equal-sized teams), while townball was played with a slightly larger number of players. Both games used four bases, as in baseball. In both fieldball and townball, all members of one team would bat consecutively, and then the next team would bat, with each batter getting to hit one pitch. In both games, if a batter did not make contact with the ball or if the other team's fielders caught it on the fly or after one bounce, the hitter was out. In fieldball, a batter hitting the ball would run the bases, going as far as he or she could without being tagged or hit with the ball; as in baseball, a player was safe while standing on a base. The winner was the team which scored the largest number of runs. Similarly, the object of townball was to score the most runs, though runs were obtained differently. The team that was batting would position three runners on first base, and the batter would try to hit the ball so that the three runners could run the bases safely and score runs. The team on the field would try to get out every member of the batting team, while the batting team would try to score all three of its runners from first base; if the latter was achieved, the batting team could bat again.

By World War I, baseball, with its standardized rules, had gained a foothold in the Blue Ridge. Professional, semipro, and amateur baseball teams were forming in regional communities like Asheville, Spartanburg, and Elizabethton, leading young players to daydream about major league stardom. Other games with standardized rules, particularly football and basketball, rose to prominence shortly afterward. As the twentieth century wore on, the lives of young people in the Blue Ridge became increasingly routinized, as they attended school and did homework, played organized sports sponsored by schools and local civic clubs, assisted parents with the everyday yard and farm chores, and, later on, watched television. Traditional games fell further and further out of favor.

Cherokee Stickball

The earliest cultural traditions in the Blue Ridge, of course, were those of Native Americans. European settlement and the U. S. government long ago forced aboriginal groups from the region, but these former residents are commemorated in place names like Chestoa View (an overlook along the Blue Ridge Parkway, taking its name from the Cherokee word for rabbit) and Swannanoa (named after the historic Shawnee town Swannano, formerly located on the banks of what is now called the Swannanoa River). Today, some Cherokee live just west of the Blue Ridge in the Great Smoky Mountains; there, despite centuries of oppression and assimilation, traditional Cherokee folkways have survived, albeit often in a compromised state. One of the best known of these folkways is the traditional game of stickball. Although countless outsiders have witnessed this customary tradition, few have comprehended how complex the game really is—or was. The following discussion of stickball suggests the complexity of the customary life of this most influential Native American group.

"Here comes the ball, down in this direction," said Jerry Wolfe over the public address system. "Big Jeff Toineeta has the ball and . . . down he goes, somebody tackled him. Now I believe one of the other Wolftown Wolves has the ball—Bill Reed, in the red trunks, has the ball. He's looking for some help, some blocking, he's taken down by a Bear almost to his goal . . . oh, they may have worked a score through—yes, they have: it is now 6 to 3 Wolves."

While the Wolves and their rivals, the Big Cove Bears, made their way back to the middle of the field, Wolfe, the play-by-play announcer, began to describe the game he knows well and obviously loves: "There's a little bit of wrestling, a little bit of blocking, a little bit of boxing. . . ." Before Wolfe finished his thought, a tourist on the sidelines yelled, "And a little bit of killing!" Other tourists clapped and laughed loudly—as if they too had heard about stickball's reputation for violence.

Despite the interruptions, Wolfe continued: "This is an exhibition game for you visitors to see how the game of stickball was played; but if the old-timers ever returned and saw a game played like this, they'd probably laugh us off the field."

I didn't understand what Wolfe meant by his statement. It was October 1988. I was attending my first Cherokee Fall Festival—held annually in the eastern shadow of the Great Smoky Mountains—and this game certainly looked impressive to me. It was, however, my first exposure to stickball, and I knew no more about the game and its traditions than the rest of the tourists. Wolfe's comments made more sense to me a few weeks later when I stumbled upon a photograph of the 1888 Wolftown team in an old anthropology journal. Only a hundred years had passed since that photograph was taken, historically not much time in the life span of a traditional culture, but the chubby players I had watched at the 1988 Cherokee Fall Festival bore little resemblance to the quick, muscular men in this photograph. A few years later, I found a passage in John Finger's *Cherokee Americans* that further clarified Wolfe's criticism of the 1988 exhibition game. According to Finger, stickball was already in decline by the time of the First World War:

> The ballplay of the 1920s was only a pallid reflection of the earlier game. Conjurers still performed secret rites to support their favorite team or undermine an opponent, and an athlete might still "go to the water" and endure ritual scratching for purification or perhaps even observe certain dietary and sexual restraints before competing. Yet such practices were voluntary and probably more a cursory bow to tradition, a welcome break from the Cherokees' routinized life, than part of any deeply ingrained belief. And even though there was considerable enthusiasm for rough play, with occasional broken limbs, the contests were no longer the "little brother of war." Compared with college football, at least, Frank Kyselka believed the ballplay was

a model of decorum. In 1910, when fatalities among collegiate athletes had become a national scandal, he expressed the belief that football's rule makers could learn "valuable points from a study of this Indian game."

Cherokee stickball was formerly much more than an exhibition sporting event: it was a ritualized contest between townships and tribes to settle arguments that otherwise might have escalated into feuds and wars. And stickball was once anything but the "model of decorum" it had become by the 1920s. When James Mooney, an ethnologist for the U. S. government, lived among the Cherokee in the 1880s, he watched a version of stickball remarkably different from the one Finger claims was in existence only a few decades later. Of the game he saw in the 1880s, Mooney wrote: "It is a very exciting game as well as a very rough one. . . . Almost everything short of murder is allowable in the game, and both parties sometimes go into the contest with the deliberate purpose of crippling or otherwise disabling the best players on the opposing side. Serious accidents are common."

Today, despite the decreased intensity with which it is played, stickball survives as a remnant from the Cherokees' aboriginal past. It is a very old game. Hernando de Soto witnessed a ballgame during his explorations of the 1540s, but Mooney thought that the game was much older. He conjectured that the Native American "shaped the pliant hickory staff with his knife and flint and twisted the net of bear sinew ages before visions of a western world began to float through the brain of the Italian dreamer." Although it is not possible to trace the game's exact origin, it was probably played in some form millenniums ago, perhaps before the aboriginal peoples crossed the Bering Strait and dispersed over North America. We do know that numerous tribes played stickball and that the game was widespread; reliable witnesses before Mooney observed the game in different parts of the continent: Powers in California, Schoolcraft in Michigan, and Catlin in the Deep South. And, according to Wolfe, French Canadians imitated the basic rules of Indian stickball when they devised the game of lacrosse.

When Mooney began to study Cherokee stickball during the 1880s, few non-Cherokee had previously observed the game—and, of those who had, none had yet identified correctly the game's underlying significance. Of the handful of writers who had watched a stickball game, Mooney wrote: "All these writers . . . appear to have confined their attention almost entirely to the play alone, noticing the ball-play dance only briefly, if at all, and seeming to be completely unaware of the secret ceremonies and incantations—the fasting, bathing, and other mystic rites—which for days and weeks precede the play and attend every step of the game."

Because of his deep commitment to understanding Native American cultures, Mooney became the first non-Cherokee observer to note the complex ritualism of the game, which in the 1880s was surprisingly intact among the Eastern Band of the Cherokee. Originally composed of those Cherokee who in the 1830s refused to be forcibly relocated by the U. S. government to Oklahoma, the Eastern Band survived persecution by hiding in the rugged Great Smoky Mountains along the North Carolina-Tennessee border. Eventually, no longer hounded by the federal government, the Eastern Band purchased its own "reservation," known as Qualla Boundary, and continued to practice traditional Cherokee folkways, such as stickball. Thus, during the last half of the nineteenth century, while many other tribes across the nation were surrendering themselves and their traditions to the forces of modernization, the Eastern Band flourished.

Although Mooney is, more than anyone else, responsible for recording and interpreting the traditional rules and ceremonies of Cherokee stickball, an earlier nineteenth century observer, Charles Lanman, preserved in writing the game's basic rules. A travel writer, Lanman in one of his columns described a stickball contest he watched in 1848 as an invited guest of the Cherokee. Although he was not shown all the pregame and postgame ceremonies that James Mooney was later allowed to see, Lanman's presentation of the rules governing the game itself was very detailed and clear.

More vital to our knowledge of Cherokee stickball, however, was the fact that Mooney both learned the Cherokees' language and earned their trust; thus, he was able to record the myths and secret formulas associated with the game as well as its rules. Capable of understanding some of the complex symbolism and ritualism behind the game's ceremonies, Mooney provided, in his 1890 essay for *The American Anthropologist*, a full account of Cherokee stickball.

Listed below, compiled from Lanman's column and Mooney's essay, are the traditional rules and ceremonies of Cherokee stickball:

Pregame ceremonies

1. The medicine man begins conjuring upon the announcement of the game
2. For seven to twenty-eight days before the game, all players abstain from "sensual appetites," such as taboo foods, sexual activity, liquor, etc.
3. The night before the game, all players participate in the ballplayers' dance
4. After the ballplayers' dance is completed, players "go to the water" in a nearby river
5. Players return home to rest and to keep out of sight until the game begins

Game ceremonies

1. The players "go to the water" separately
2. The players prepare equipment: the two sticks made of hickory with web-

bing of bear sinew, and the ball made of deerskin and stuffed with deer hair (about 1 1/2 inches in diameter)

3. The team waits in seclusion and discusses the coming game
4. The medicine man delivers an inspirational speech promising victory
5. The players walk to the ballfield
6. The medicine man diagrams strategies
7. The players strip to their loincloths
8. The medicine man "scratches" the players
9. The medicine man gives the players a root "to which he has imparted magic properties by the recital of certain secret formulas"
10. The players mark their bodies with paint and charcoal and wear symbolic ornaments
11. The players "go to the water" but do not enter
12. The medicine man tries to jinx opposing players by such divination rituals as bead rolling
13. The players return to the ballfield
14. Stones and debris are removed from the ballfield
15. Spectators arrive late in the morning
16. The medicine man erects two poles at each end of the field, about six hundred yards apart, which serve as goals
17. The challenging team emerges at one end of the field and whoops loudly toward the other team
18. The opposing team emerges and whoops
19. The two teams march toward the center of the field, alternating whoops and taunts
20. The wives and girlfriends of the players run onto the field and offer their "favorite champions" small items they are willing to wager on the game
21. The medicine man matches each player to a same-sized player on the opposing team
22. Players lay down their sticks at the feet of their matched players and stand before them
23. The medicine man admonishes the players to obey the one strict rule—that no player should physically harm his matched player
24. The two teams stand in parallel lines facing each other and reclaim their sticks
25. A medicine man tosses the ball vertically between the tallest member of each team (who try to bat the ball with their sticks toward their opponents' goal)
26. Players on the team that wins the ball toss-up try to scoop up the ball with their "spoony" sticks—they may use their hands only to carry the ball, not to pick the ball up

27. The player who has possession of the ball attempts to carry the ball through the opposing team's goal
28. Each ball that breaks the plane of a goal scores one point
29. The players return to the center of the field after each point is scored, and a medicine man tosses up the ball again to start a new round of play
30. To help their own teammates score points, players may block, tackle, and wrestle their matched opponents
31. Each team has two drivers who are allowed to follow the ball and point out its location with a stick but who are not allowed to score
32. There is no fixed number of players: as few as six and as many as sixty players have been recorded
33. The first team to score twelve points wins the game
34. There is no time limit: once begun, a game is played through to the end
35. The game is never called because of inclement weather

Postgame ceremonies

1. The players rush to the river to remove ritually any vengeful incantations of defeated enemies
2. The players dress
3. The players feast
4. A chief awards the players from the winning team the prizes waged before the game
5. The defeated team generally challenges the victorious team to a rematch
6. The spectators disperse to prepare for the evening dance
7. Men, women, and children participate in the evening dance at the court-house, each person "fantastically dressed" and dancing to "his own music"
8. The presiding chief addresses the crowd "on the subject of their duties as intelligent beings" and then closes the ballgame activities by asking every-one to return to their homes, shops, and fields

No printed source of stickball rules exists from the first half of the twen-tieth century. This was a crucial period of change for the Eastern Band of the Cherokee; it was then that the abrupt arrival of industrialization in western North Carolina forced change immediately outside, and then in-side, Qualla Boundary. After logging companies abandoned the region, leaving much of it treeless, the Great Smoky Mountains National Park was created by an act of Congress in 1926; because of the Qualla Boundary's proximity to the new park, roads were subsequently paved through Chero-kee land. Suddenly, millions of Americans were driving hundreds of miles to "see the bears," and, while they were there, to "see the Indians." During the Great Depression and after, the Cherokee learned they could obtain white people's currency by catering to their needs (selling lodging, food, gas, and various trinkets to tourists). Economic survival, however, had its dark side: some Cherokee made money by donning the elaborate feather headdresses seen in Hollywood movies and posing for tourists' photographs in front of Sioux tepees. Called "chiefing," this was, of course, an inauthentic depiction of traditional Cherokee culture.

Another result of assimilation was the steady decline of stickball, which was played less often during the first half of the twentieth century, with less emphasis on its traditional rules and ceremonies. The Cherokee themselves are partly responsible for this. After the U. S. government banned stickball around 1900 (reasons given being the game's roughness, the spectators' rowdiness, and the excessive wagering on the outcome of the game), the Cherokee introduced a revised version. Proving to be a popular feature at the First Annual Cherokee Indian Fair of 1914, this tamer version of the game was offered as an exhibition sport at subsequent Cherokee-sponsored events, such as the Cherokee Fall Festival. Thereafter, with the economy of Qualla Boundary becoming dependent on tourism, stickball increasingly functioned as a money-making exhibition sport; yet, since stickball in its exhibition form needed to appeal to white people's standards of propriety, the game's elaborate ritualism was not performed for tourists. Consequently, younger Cherokee were soon more familiar with exhibition stickball than with the original version of the game.

Thus, the stickball game most often played after World War II was a greatly simplified version of the original. Following is a list of the rules of stickball that was printed in the July 22, 1966, edition of *The Cherokee One Feather*, the newspaper of the Qualla Boundary. It leaves out entirely the pregame and postgame ceremonies that were a vital part of the original game:

1. Twenty players, ten per team, is the normal number of participants, though the game can be played with two or three players per team
2. Two sets of posts are stuck into the ground about 150 yards apart
3. The two teams advance onto the field from opposite directions, "yelling defiance at each other"
4. The two teams meet in the center of the field and face each other
5. A medicine man (referee) tosses up the ball
6. The tallest members of each team, called centers, jump for the ball, and play begins
7. Each center attempts to strike the ball toward the opposing team's goal
8. The players try to catch the ball on the run or scoop it up off the ground
9. The team that has possession of the ball moves it toward the opposing team's goal

10. The team that does not have possession of the ball attempts to take it away by blocking or tackling, by stopping their opponents physically
11. The teammates of a ball carrier try to clear his way by tackling, wrestling, or blocking the opponents
12. If a ball carrier gets through his opposing team's goal, a point is scored for his team
13. A player may throw the ball through the opposing team's goal if obstacles are in his way
14. The first team to score twelve points is the winner

By 1978, the printed rules of the annual exhibition stickball game had been simplified even further (see below), though, to be fair, it should be said that they appeared in the pamphlet *Cherokee Fair and Festival* and were intended for tourists. Nevertheless, Jerry Wolfe, who knows the game as well as anyone, openly admitted to hundreds of tourists at the 1988 Cherokee Fall Festival that most Cherokee today do not understand or appreciate stickball as much as their ancestors did.

1. The "few rules of play" are agreed upon before the game begins
2. There are "not less than ten men" per team
3. No substitutions can be allowed; and if a player leaves the game for any reason, his opponent must leave also
4. Each team has its own drivers and medicine men, who take an "active part" in the game
5. The players are chosen from the reservation to form "well-balanced teams"
6. All participants will be rewarded financially for their efforts

The game of stickball will likely continue to decline. As the ceremonies associated with stickball disappear with the deaths of the medicine men who understood them, only the skeletal rules of the game will remain.

A few "old-timers" like Wolfe still remember the great stickball athletes of long ago. There was Standing Turkey Wolfe, "the strongest ballplayer ever," who once wrestled the whole opposing team down and won the game single-handedly. And there was the ballplayer known as Columbus, "the fastest man here on the reservation," who once challenged and beat a prize-winning racehorse, then rode all over town on horseback as his reward. Those men are gone now.

CHAPTER 5

Material Culture

In *Pattern in the Material Folk Culture of the Eastern United States*, folklorist Henry Glassie observed that, since the middle of the nineteenth century in the United States, "[T]he most usual result of the influence of popular upon folk material . . . has been the replacement of the traditional object by its popular equivalent. The popular object has been accepted by the innovative individual because it saves him time, is more quickly produced or bought, and is easier to use than the traditional object—and also because it is new." Despite the general decline in traditional material culture across the United States, traditional (i. e., handmade, nonstandardized) material objects are still valued in certain sections of the country. One such region is the Blue Ridge.

Of all the regions in the Southern Appalachians, the Blue Ridge, though the first to experience industrial activity (in the form of early nineteenth-century commercial gold mining), was ultimately the least affected by industrialization. This was in part the result of geographical circumstance. The region harbored no coal deposits, and thus was spared the environmental devastation the coal industry caused elsewhere in Appalachia. Also, the National Park Service's acquisition of Southern Appalachian land during the first half of the twentieth century (in an effort to conserve natural resources and promote tourism) affected traditional folklife in the Blue Ridge far less than it did in the Great Smoky Mountains. The national park established in the Smokies displaced many residents and caused the erosion of much traditional culture. Although Shenandoah National Park did displace some residents in a sliver of the northern Blue Ridge, the establishment of the other major National Park Service unit within the region, the Blue Ridge Parkway, routed largely along a narrow strip of sparsely settled ridge crest, proved less disruptive of traditional folklife. By offering timely economic relief (providing federal jobs and encouraging tourism), the parkway allowed a number of Blue Ridge residents to remain in the region during the Depression and through the lean years of World War II.

Many of the traditional material objects discussed in this chapter are still being made and used in the region; others, once integral to everyday life in the Blue Ridge, are today rarely found outside of museums, attics, and storage sheds. Historically, traditional Blue Ridge handicrafts possessed significant stylistic variation because of the region's geographical isolation: local designs often had limited influence on craftspeople elsewhere. Before the twentieth century, the Blue Ridge was like a long string of islands separated by prohibitive gulfs; contact between communities was often minimal, and people only a dozen miles apart as the crow flies might communicate little or not at all. With a scarcity of outside influences, the region's craftspeople developed strongly localized traditional designs.

Blue Ridge craftspeople traditionally utilized accessible materials to construct a variety of material objects to make their lives easier and more enjoyable. With wood they themselves harvested from the forest and cut by hand or in a local sawmill, people built various structures necessary for survival (houses, barns, outbuildings, mills, and fences), wagons as well as furniture (tables, chairs, stools, chests, and bedsteads) to enhance their domestic lives. Wood also allowed craftspeople to pass the time pleasantly, making intriguing carvings, toys, and musical instruments. Combining wood and metal, they designed farming tools and rifles which enabled them to put food on the table. Using animal hair, they spun yarn and wove cloth for clothes, blankets, coverlets, rugs, and quilts. Animal skins and hides provided craftspeople with materials for shoes, coats, and saddles. In a few locales, clay was shaped into pottery; more widespread was the fashioning of wood and vines into baskets.

Log Structures

No aspect of material culture is more often associated with southern mountain people than log cabins. This type of house dominated the Blue Ridge landscape during the first century and a half of European settlement in the region, and then was steadily replaced by more spacious and comfortable wooden frame houses. The log cabin evolved out of the architectural traditions of several cultures. Scandinavian and/or German settlers venturing into the Appalachian frontier probably introduced wood construction techniques to settlers from the British Isles (where constructing houses entirely out of wood was uncommon). The influence of Scandinavians in the Blue Ridge is debatable in that relatively few left their primary settlement area along the Delaware River. The German influence on the region, though, is indisputable, since thousands of Germans left their primary settlement area in southeastern Pennsylvania (where they were known collectively as the Pennsylvania Dutch, a corruption of their German name, Deutsch). Trekking southwestward into Virginia as early as the 1730s, these settlers (many of whom were members of fundamentalist protestant sects) entered the region to escape overcrowded conditions and religious discrimination in Pennsylvania. The earliest of these settlers established often prosperous farmsteads in the Shenandoah Valley; later arrivals, finding the fertile valley land claimed, headed into the Blue Ridge, where they utilized their Old World knowledge of log construction in a restrictive New World environment.

Working with the region's most abundant natural resource, wood, German (and possibly Scandinavian) settlers were the first Europeans in the Blue Ridge to construct cabins by joining logs together with V-notches (this occurred especially in Virginia) or half-dovetail notches (particularly in North Carolina and Tennessee). Logs were generally notched only on the bottom, minimizing water build-up which might cause rot. During construction, cabin builders would cut off sections of logs which extended beyond the walls of the house, so that there would be no protrusions. Favored trees for building cabins included such hardwoods as chestnut, oak, ash, walnut, poplar, and hickory. Logs would be hand-hewn flat on front and back (very few logs were unhewn). Blue Ridge settlers would often close the spaces between horizontal logs with some combination of mud, stones, clay, and lime (this practice, chinking, was probably of Scandinavian or Slavic origin) or would block them by nailing up rails or boards. In an effort to shield cabin dwellers from the weather, builders would nail roofing boards horizontally across the top of the structure, and against these would be nailed split shingles, often made of white oak. Some cabins had dirt floors, while other cabins possessed puncheon floors constructed out of hewn logs or adze-cut boards. Blue Ridge cabin builders incorporated a few design features of British origin, including external stone chimneys, gabled roofs, and add-on kitchens.

Two basic shapes of cabins were commonly found in the Blue Ridge: square and rectangular. Frequently measuring sixteen feet by sixteen feet (with many variations) and most likely based on a design of English origin, the square cabin design was probably transported to the eastern slopes of the Virginia Blue Ridge from the Virginia piedmont. The rectangular cabin design, ranging from fourteen to eighteen feet in width and twenty to twenty-six feet in length, was a modification of either a Scandinavian or an Irish design, probably carried by settlers from Pennsylvania down through the Great Valley of the Appalachians to the North Carolina Blue Ridge. Alterations of cabins often occurred as Blue Ridge families grew larger. Occupants could increase the space within their cabins by building second stories (i. e., lofts). In some cases, additional rooms were joined to the main structure. In other cases, a second building would be added beside the main one, with the two often connected by a covered breezeway known as the dogtrot. Sometimes this second structure was a kitchen, separated from the main building to keep it from becoming uncomfortably hot during the warmer months.

Scholar Terry G. Jordan asserts that the style of log construction transported to the Blue Ridge from Pennsylvania, which he describes as consisting of "a relatively small number of basic techniques and floor plans, most of which are rather simple or even crude by European standards," was a prototype for the popular midland American style later found in other regions to the south and west.

In most parts of the Blue Ridge, people had abandoned log cabins for frame houses by World War I (and in many cases much earlier). As the Blue Ridge economy improved toward the end of the nineteenth century and many commercial sawmills began operating in the region, people began to favor frame houses, which were not only more spacious and comfortable, but which also symbolized a family's increased social and economic status. Although reflecting a trend toward self-conscious aesthetic standardization, frame houses nonetheless retained some of the characteristics of traditional Blue Ridge log cabins, including the attachment of additional rooms to the main structure and the construction of external stone chimneys.

The traditional designs for other types of utilitarian structures found in the Blue Ridge—barns, outbuildings, and mills—were likely brought to the region by German settlers from Pennsylvania. Some barns were multifunctional, serving as storage sites for grain, hay, equipment, and tools, and as places in which to house livestock. Other barns were specialized, including drover barns, which in the old days were constructed along major drover routes to provide temporary shelter for large numbers of animals being transported to market. Springhouses protected water sources and preserved perishable foods, while root cellars, corncribs, apple houses, henhouses, blacksmith shops, smokehouses, pigsties, and outhouses fulfilled the particular functions suggested by their names.

Mills

Another important utilitarian structure in the region was the mill, which, by exploiting the power of a natural watercourse, fulfilled the twin

In the nineteenth century, this log cabin, the Polly Woods Ordinary, was an inn: the Woods family provided "ordinary" services for those passing through what is now the Peaks of Otter Recreation Area (along the Blue Ridge Parkway north of Roanoke). The architectural features of the Polly Woods Ordinary—hewn logs, chinking between the logs, flush corners, external stone chimney, and loft—were found in most traditional Blue Ridge log cabins. (Courtesy of the Blue Ridge Parkway Photo Library)

functions of grinding corn and cutting lumber. Some mills were built right in the path of a stream; for those that were not, water had to be diverted from a stream by means of a trough (usually lined with wooden boards) known as a flume. Regardless of its proximity to a stream, a traditional mill would feature one of two mechanisms for tapping the energy of running water: the tub wheel or the waterwheel.

The tub wheel mill was simpler to build because it did not involve gears but was powered exclusively by water pressure. To operate the tub wheel mill, water would be channelled from its source via a flume into a large wooden holding tank which stood beside the mill. Most of the time, a door at the bottom of the tank was kept closed; water overflowing the tank would continue flowing downstream and reenter the stream. However, when the miller opened that door, the water, with great pressure, would rush down a wooden chute and spill directly onto the tub wheel. Round,

One of several utilitarian structures on display at the Humpback Rocks Pioneer
Exhibit, this root cellar exemplifies the simple yet effective architectural design
traditionally employed in the Blue Ridge: the door allowed for summertime
ventilation and prevented animals from entering, while the gaps between the logs
in the second story ensured the escape of hotter air which otherwise might damage
the various crops stored in the cellar. (Courtesy of the Blue Ridge Parkway Photo
Library)

made of stone or wood, and carved with blades radiating out from the center, the tub wheel resembled a fan. Positioned horizontally and fixed on a
stationary point (often made from a pine knot), the tub wheel would turn
whenever water was spilled onto its blades. The rotating tub wheel would
subsequently rotate a tall vertical shaft, which would turn, many feet
higher, the uppermost of two millstones (circular pieces of granite which
actually ground the grain) positioned on the mill's main floor. The lower
millstone, though aligned immediately below the top millstone, was not
connected to the shaft and thus would remain stationary. When the top
millstone was rotating, the miller would pour whole grain—usually corn—
into a hopper, which, functioning like a funnel, would feed the grain between the millstones, where the kernels would be ground into meal. The

rotating movement of the top millstone would push the meal outward to the edge of the millstones, whereupon it would pour out into the meal chute. A container (often a flour sack) would catch the meal as it exited the chute. Although it might belong to one individual, a mill would serve an entire community: a farmer could bring his own grain to the nearest miller, who would grind and bag it, usually keeping a portion (often one-half) for his fee.

A waterwheel mill featured a large vertical wheel lined with wooden steps. Water which had been diverted through a flume would pour onto the steps and turn the waterwheel, which would set in motion a series of geared wheels connected to the waterwheel, ultimately rotating the uppermost of two millstones. As with the tub wheel mill, grain would be ground between this millstone and the lower, stationary millstone. There were three water-wheel designs: the overshot wheel (turned by water pouring from above the wheel), the breast wheel (turned by water hitting the wheel toward its middle), and the undershot wheel (turned by water striking near the base of the wheel).

One famous waterwheel mill in the Blue Ridge is picturesque Mabry Mill, located beside the Blue Ridge Parkway near Meadows of Dan, Virginia. Constructed just before the First World War, this mill is one of the most photographed structures in the United States. In its day, Mabry Mill served as both a gristmill and a sawmill (it possessed a water-powered jigsaw and jointer). Fluctuating water sources and a decline in business during the Depression forced the original owners to abandon the mill. Later acquired and restored by the National Park Service, Mabry Mill operates today as an exhibition gristmill for tourists.

By the early twentieth century, mill builders tended to bypass traditional mill mechanisms in favor of commercial turbines, since the latter were simpler (involving no intricate system of wooden gears), smaller, and more efficient (producing, for a given flowage of water, more energy than traditional mills).

Fences

In the earliest years of settlement in the Blue Ridge, livestock roamed freely, feeding in the fields and forests surrounding a homestead. Increased settlement, however, necessitated the building of fences to control the movement of livestock. Some fences were built out of stone, though this was a labor-intensive procedure. More commonly, people exploited the region's abundant supply of trees and built wooden picket fences and three major types of split-rail fences: the snake-rail fence, the post-and-rail fence,

Mabry Mill, one of the most photographed buildings in the United States, as it
appeared in the winter of 1944, its flume and wheel covered with ice. Operated as
a combination gristmill and sawmill by its builder, E. B. Mabry, from 1910 until
his death in the mid-1930s, Mabry Mill was renovated in the 1940s by the National
Park Service. Just to the left of the mill is the Blue Ridge Parkway. (Courtesy of the
Blue Ridge Parkway Photo Library)

and the buck fence. These rail fences are possibly variations of a Scandinavian prototype brought to the Blue Ridge from Pennsylvania. Historically,
fence makers favored chestnut wood for its resistance to rot; after the decline of that species in the early twentieth century (because of the chestnut
blight), people used other durable woods, especially black locust. The easi-
est fence to build, the snake-rail fence, was ideal for temporary situations
since it could be quickly disassembled and moved. This type of fence consisted of a zigzag arrangement of stacked rails which were angled to keep
them from falling; pairs of vertical posts kept the upper rails from slipping
off in the wind or from contact with animals or people. To prevent rot,
stones would be regularly placed beneath ground-level rails. The post-and-
rail fence took more time to build, yet it was stronger and required less
wood than the snake-rail fence. To construct a post-and-rail fence line,
pairs of vertical posts would be set a few inches apart into the ground along
the fence line; the ends of horizontal rails would then be inserted into

these posts (alternately positioned, with each rail heading in an opposite direction along the fence line). The buck fence—so named because it looked like a sawbuck—was ideal for difficult topography, because it did not require posthole digging; instead, it made use of regular crisscrossed (i.e., X-shaped) posts, sometimes anchored by rocks, into which were wedged diagonal rails, which supported the posts by bracing them. While rail fences served to control livestock, picket fences, with much smaller gaps than rail fences, were preferred for protecting garden plots from foraging animals, domestic and wild. Today, the various traditional Blue Ridge fence types can be seen along the Blue Ridge Parkway, especially at Groundhog Mountain near the Virginia-North Carolina border.

Wagons

At the start of the Civil War, roads were rare in the Blue Ridge. With few roads and fewer navigable waterways in the region, carrying any substantial load of gear posed a problem—steep foot and horse trails were often the only way to travel from one community to another. To haul loads too large and heavy for backpack or horse, the people of the Blue Ridge used a traditional vehicle: the horse-, mule-, or ox-drawn wagon. Requiring a thorough knowledge of both blacksmithing and woodworking, wagon building was a lengthy process. Generally limited to hand tools, the wagon maker would utilize a felloe saw to cut wooden felloes (the pieces which fit together to form the rim of the wheel) and a drawing knife to carve out wooden spokes. Aged oak was preferred for both felloes and spokes. If lacking the proper tools or skills, a wagon maker might commission a local blacksmith to produce the metal parts necessary for the construction of the wagon, including the circular metal strips which rimmed the wheels and the metal rods which constituted the wagon's brake system. Wagon makers would connect many of the wooden parts with a combination of homemade and store-bought metal parts (such as plates, clamps, nuts, and bolts), though certain wooden pieces would be joined without metal connectors or glue, but rather by means of an arrangement in which projections (tenons) in one piece of wood would be fitted into equal-sized holes (mortises) in another piece. Hauling heavy loads on rugged roads would daily test a wagon maker's craftsmanship. Weight would bend down the wagon's axles, thrusting the hubs outward; to ensure that the wheels were stable enough to carry the heaviest loads—whether a pile of wood or all of a family's worldly possessions—wagon makers would bow the spokes inward. These durable wagons played a vital role in the settling of the Blue Ridge and the establishing of trade there.

Furniture and Other Wooden Objects

Historically, Blue Ridge craftspeople made furniture, including tables, chairs, stools, benches, and bedsteads, for their own use. Some regional furniture makers consciously continued Old World traditions. Early in the twentieth century, for example, Jim Gosnell of Tryon, North Carolina, practiced a chair-making tradition which he had learned from a circle of visiting English furniture makers; formally untrained and illiterate, Gosnell built furniture out of wooden pieces which he cut after measuring them with a stick bearing the precise dimensions of pieces favored by his English contacts. Many Blue Ridge furniture makers, though, developed recognizably New World styles, giving rise to local traditions which in some cases have proved commercially marketable. The Woody family of Spruce Pine, North Carolina, has made excellent furniture for nearly two centuries, and the family's signature ladder-back chair is much sought after by consumers nationally.

Harvesting trees near their houses and shops, Blue Ridge furniture makers used particular species of wood for specific purposes. For chair making, many people preferred white oak for seats, sugar maple for posts, and shagbark hickory for rungs. Sourwood was often used for the bottoms of rocking chairs because of its curved grain, while black walnut was sometimes chosen for the same purpose, since its rough grain minimized sliding on wooden floors.

Before the twentieth century, lathes, planes, drawing knives, and chisels were luxuries within the region. Most craftspeople made furniture with basic equipment: axes, saws, pocketknives, braces, and bits. A distinctive feature of much traditional Blue Ridge furniture was the absence of nails, screws, and glue; instead, the various wooden parts of a piece of furniture were carefully crafted to fit together without external support. For instance, in the construction of chairs, well-seasoned rungs were inserted into holes bored in the freshly cut posts; as they seasoned, the posts would enclose the rungs, making a tight fit which could endure heavy use. Although usually soiled from the lack of finish or paint, chairs and other handmade furniture products were so well built that they often lasted for several generations.

After World War I, Blue Ridge furniture makers realized they could capitalize on the growing national interest in traditional furniture. In a region which then offered few ways of earning money, many craftspeople, of all skill levels, began to produce furniture in large quantities. Guilds and organizations such as the Shenandoah Community Workers in Bird Haven, Virginia, and the Artisan Shop in Biltmore Forest, North Carolina, assisted furniture makers in this endeavor by offering more efficient technology, formal instruction, and channels for distribution; all these factors led to a greater emphasis on streamlined production and modern style.

Also constructed from wood were utilitarian objects like baskets and hampers (commonly made of white oak splints), bowls (cherry, maple, and walnut), boxes (the aforementioned woods plus holly), tool handles (ash and hickory), and lamp bases and candlesticks (holly and sourwood). Whittling was a popular hobby in the Blue Ridge, and decorative items such as animal figurines were carved from tight-grained woods like apple, maple, cherry, and walnut, as were toys, ranging from bows and arrows, stilts, and spinning tops to limberjacks and whimmy diddles. Traditional wooden musical instruments included some that were easily constructed, like whistles (made from smooth-barked sticks of maple, sourwood, and willow), as well as those requiring considerable craftsmanship, like fiddles, banjos, and dulcimers.

Other Crafts

INSTRUMENTS

Historically, the predominant instrument in the Blue Ridge was the fiddle, which could be heard at a wide variety of occasions, such as play-parties, weddings, and music festivals. A fiddle consisted of several component parts: the top (a modified figure eight, most often carved out of spruce), a similar-sized bottom (made of maple), the "ribs" (i. e., the sides, made of premolded maple), two blocks (usually maple, placed inside the fiddle to hold the ribs in place), the neck/head (one piece of maple, with the head featuring either a standard fiddlehead or some original design), pegs (often made of boxwood and tapered to fit snugly into holes near the end of the neck), the fingerboard and tailpiece (both made of some strong, fine-grained wood, such as boxwood), and the sound post and bridge. Fiddle makers would clamp these pieces together, using glue. Constructing fiddles required considerable patience, for the process involved selecting the right woods, cutting separate pieces, planing them to the correct thickness, curing them for approximately a year, and then shaping them, all before actually assembling the instrument. Next, the fiddle maker would fashion a bow out of a piece of curved hardwood, with horsehair strung along its length. Given the fiddle's complex design, a person who could make the instrument was usually admired as much as the person who could play it expressively (in the Blue Ridge these two people were often one and the same).

The banjo, an instrument of African origin, was brought to the Southern

Appalachians in the nineteenth century by slaves, black migrant laborers, and white entertainers (e. g., minstrels). By the twentieth century, the banjo had become nearly as popular in the Blue Ridge as the fiddle. Few generalizations can be made about the traditional designs of banjos constructed in the region: they ranged from the simple and ephemeral (gourd or tin-can bodies and animal-skin heads) to the sophisticated (built with more lasting materials and sometimes extensively decorated). Occasionally, banjo makers would produce personalized instruments with idiosyncratic design features, like Kyle Creed's fretless banjo, which utilized Formica for a fingerboard. Many twentieth century pickers favored commercial banjos purchased in stores or from mail order catalogs. During the urban folk revival of the 1950s and 1960s, though, Blue Ridge craftspeople discovered that there was a market for handmade banjos and fiddles, as well as for several other wooden instruments, including the Appalachian dulcimer, the hammered dulcimer, and the guitar.

TOYS

Before modern forms of entertainment (e. g., radio, phonographs, television, and video games) entered the region, people in the Blue Ridge passed the time by playing with a wide range of toys, many of which were handmade from both natural and artificial materials. Some toys, such as noise-makers, were intended primarily for unreflective amusement, but most were overtly functional—i. e., educational (puzzles), utilitarian (toy wagons), or social (playhouses). Toys that served to help children develop their musical aptitude included motion-makers, whistles, and songbows (a green stick held in a bow-like shape by a single steel string, placed near a person's mouth; the string was plucked, and players changed the pitch of the resonating drone by altering the size and shape of their mouths). Females favored certain toys, such as dolls, while males preferred others, including toy weapons like the slingshot. Children of both sexes enjoyed playing with cornstalk constructions (animal figurines, toy airplanes, and toy fiddles made out of cornstalks). Toys were primarily, but not exclusively, the domain of children: adults assisted in the making of these objects, and some took considerable pride in their handiwork, achieving unsurpassed craftsmanship (especially among dollmakers). Some toys were integral components of games; such games, though including material objects, were taught orally and through demonstration and thus involved verbal and customary folkloric elements (see chapter 4).

SHOEMAKING

Before the late nineteenth century, when improved transportation facilitated the distribution of commercial products into the Blue Ridge, shoes and clothes were usually made by hand. With materials chosen for maximum durability, regional shoemakers would make shoes individually tailored to the exact configurations of the wearer's feet. While many would make only enough shoes to serve their family's needs, others would produce a surplus to trade or sell in their communities. To obtain leather with which to make shoes, many shoemakers would raise and slaughter their own cattle and tan their own hides; some would raise their own cattle but hire a tanner to prepare the leather (by this arrangement, shoemakers would surrender some of their leather to the tanner); still others would purchase (or barter for) leather directly from a tannery.

The preparation of leather involved several steps: first, the soaking of animal hides in lime to loosen the hair; second, the scraping off of the hair and flesh with a long dull knife; third, the washing of the hides in salt water and then in fresh water; and, finally, the tanning, which involved placing the hides in a large vat between layers of ground-up tannin-rich bark peeled from chestnut, chestnut oak, and hemlock trees (water was poured into the vat so that the hides would soak in a tannin broth). After a few months, the tanned hides would be hung out to dry in the open air. Once dry, they would be softened with grease made from animal tallow and fish oil and then split along the line where the animal's backbone had been. Thus, each cow would yield two pieces of leather. Tanning was so time consuming (it took many months to produce finished leather) and so laborious that many shoemakers preferred to leave that task to the tanner. Blue Ridge shoemakers were careful in choosing materials, knowing that specific sections of the hide were ideal for particular parts of a shoe. The high-quality leather from the hip area of a cow, for instance, was best suited for the soles. Shoemakers would use the highest quality thread available to them, such as the kind made from flax grown in the Deep South. Shoelaces would be cut from pliable cow leather or from strips of tanned groundhog hide.

The first step in constructing a pair of shoes was to make precise measurements of a person's feet, from which the shoemaker would design same-sized wooden lasts (assuming the shoemaker did not already own a last with those measurements). Shoes constructed around these lasts required seven pieces of leather: sole, insole, heel, "vamp" (the toe-and-tongue section, which was shaped like the head of a shovel), two pieces known as "quarters" (resembling home plate on a baseball field), and the leather cap (for the toe section of the shoe). In the old days, shoemakers would use hand-tools exclusively: saddle hammers (hammers with long, thin heads for driving wooden pegs into leather), pegging awls (to make holes into which the pegs were inserted), knives specifically designed for leather cutting (including a gauge knife to cut leather into strips of a particular size), nippers (for adjusting the various leather pieces over the wooden lasts), steel needles, and hog bristles (for sewing through curved holes). Experienced shoemakers could make shoes in different styles and for different purposes, from work boots (brogans) to women's dress shoes. To preserve the shoes and render them nominally waterproof, a coating of freshly melted beeswax and beef tallow would be rubbed on the leather. The life span of a pair of handmade shoes was one to five years, depending on the quality of construction and the frequency of use.

SPINNING AND WEAVING

Before the twentieth century, the people of the Blue Ridge manufactured much of their own cloth, generally from sheep they themselves raised. Like hogs, sheep were generally marked for identification and allowed to forage in nearby woods and fields during summer months; during the winter they would be retrieved and herded into a barn and fed hay and corn. Twice a year, in spring and fall, people would utilize hand shears (more recently, electric shears) to cut wool from healthy sheep. The wool would be washed in hot (but not boiling) water, dried on clean rocks, then put in storage for future use. To make cloth, a person would separate the wool fibers with two pairs of handheld wooden combs (cards), the first pair breaking up the wool into fibers and the second aligning the fibers into rolls. The spinning into thread of these rolls of wool involved wrapping one end of the roll around a bobbin (often made out of a cornshuck) which had been inserted onto the spindle of a spinning wheel. The wheel would be turned clockwise, rotating a rope around the spindle (resembling a bicycle chain moving around two cogs); the spinning motion of the spindle would turn the bobbin, which would pull the strands of wool together into a tight spiral, forming thread. When one roll of wool was consumed, another would be added, until the bobbin was fully wound with thread, whereupon the new ball of thread would be removed from the spindle. At this point, the craftsperson would transfer the thread directly to spools by means of a hand-cranked mechanism known as a spooler. Some thread, before being wound on a spool, would be dyed. In the old days, dyes were produced by boiling sections of a variety of plants; mordants were often added to ensure that colors would last. In recent times, people in the region have relied upon commercial dyes, which produce more reliable tones.

Making cloth from thread required of Blue Ridge weavers a thorough knowledge of a complex process, as well as precise motor control and great patience. The machine traditionally used to convert thread to cloth—the loom—was one of the most sophisticated examples of folk technology in the region. The first step in using the loom was to establish the warp (all

Mrs. Elijah Greene demonstrating weaving in the Rocky Knob District of the Blue Ridge Parkway, 1956. The National Park Service and various regional craft organizations and schools have long sponsored demonstrations of traditional Blue Ridge handicrafts. (Courtesy of the Blue Ridge Parkway Photo Library)

the threads running lengthwise in a piece of cloth, to be crossed later with threads running widthwise and known as the weft or woof). After a weaver decided upon the approximate length of the desired piece of cloth (and, concurrently, the thread count necessary to yield the piece), the warp would be established by means of a warper (a large rectangular wooden frame lined on four sides with regularly positioned pegs). Getting the warp in place required the careful counting and placing of threads on the warping frame. After the warp was set, it was rolled onto the loom. The threads at one end of the warper were carefully passed through the eyes of heddles (strings or wires connected vertically to the part of the loom which can be manipulated up and down). After passing through the heddles, the warp threads would be tied down. By depressing the loom's foot pedals, the weaver could control the relative positions of the warp threads, thus creating a repeatable pattern of high and low threads. With a wooden shuttle the weaver could pass a weft thread across the warp; then, after repositioning the warp threads, the weaver could pass the shuttle back across the warp, thus securing another weft thread. By repeating this procedure again and again, the weaver would produce cloth which, depending upon the thickness and texture of the thread, could yield clothes, towels, sheets, blankets, bedspreads, coverlets, and rugs. Many weavers adorned their creations with various traditional designs, some of which were remarkably intricate. Handwoven clothes were quite durable, often lasting for years despite heavy use and rough hand washing, which involved beating them with wooden paddles, then boiling them in an iron pot.

QUILTS

One material culture tradition in the Blue Ridge (generally thought to be of German origin) which has consistently been the domain of women is quilting. Although their primary purpose was to keep people warm on cool nights, patchwork quilts also fulfilled the decorative function of brightening the otherwise drab interiors of cabins and houses. In the old days, given the difficulty of obtaining commercial cloth, quilters would use available scraps of material, including salvageable pieces of cloth from old dresses, blankets, and rags. The top of the quilt, which bore the design, was usually constructed by a woman working alone. When fabric was scarce, a quilter might sew pieces of cloth together randomly, producing what was commonly termed a "crazy quilt" (one bearing no predictable design pattern). When a quilter had more material to work with, many designs were possible, some geometrical and some representational. The designs of regional quilts were sometimes traditional, like the Log Cabin, the Friendship Star, and the Drunkard's Path; others were original artistic statements by individual quilters. For visual impact, most quilt designs—whether simple or intricate—featured a contrast between dark and light colors.

Historically, after the top was finished (i. e., the design was selected and the pieces of cloth cut and sewn together), the individual quilter would gather with fellow quilters for a bee, at which time the top would be sewn to the bottom (with a layer of stuffing—leaves, scraps of cloth, or cotton—in between). In addition to ensuring the completion of a quilt, a bee granted participants a much-appreciated opportunity to gather and talk (one of the few times when Blue Ridge women were able to meet without the presence of men). During the bee, the sides of the quilt would be attached to a wooden frame resembling a table without a top, which would hold the material taut. Some quilts would be sewn in the middle, while in others the three layers would be tied together in numerous spots with short sections of yarn. The final stage of quilting involved the binding together of the edges.

POTTERY

Interestingly, pottery making, which was a traditional craft integral to the folklife of other regions in the South, was relatively rare in the Blue

Ridge, owing to the lack of extensive, high-quality clay deposits and the remoteness from potential markets. While most other traditional crafts were spare-time activities, pottery making required a significant time commitment, involving numerous steps: building the kiln and the mud mill (a wooden apparatus used to smooth the clay), constructing the potter's wheel, harvesting the clay and running it through the mud mill, making the glazes with a handmade glaze mill, gathering the firewood for heating the kiln, shaping the clay into pottery and firing it, and then hauling the finished products to market. Although survival in the region necessitated many activities, most Blue Ridge residents were, first and foremost, farmers. Some craftspeople might have justified the time-consuming work of pottery making if they could have located a significant market for their creations, but the region's geographical distance from large populations rendered that moot. For all these reasons, during pioneer times, folk potters (both individuals and families) avoided settling in the Blue Ridge, opting instead for the piedmont and coastal regions, where proper materials could be readily obtained and a network of distribution more easily established. For these same reasons, traditional Blue Ridge craftspeople, though proficient at making other material objects, over the years have been disinclined to start making pottery. Historically, only a few potteries of any size were founded in the region. One of these was located in Buncombe County, North Carolina, and another near Rabun Gap, Georgia. Consequently, well into the twentieth century, most of the pottery objects (bowls, churns, crock pots, jars, jugs, and plates) which served the daily needs of Blue Ridge residents were not locally made, but instead were produced in the lowlands and transported into the region by wagon, train, or truck. In recent years, numerous nonnative potters have chosen to work in the Blue Ridge. While exhibiting considerable skill, most of these potters produce wares primarily for commercial sale, and their aesthetic is more idiosyncratic than traditional.

Marketing Handicrafts

Although it brought long-term cultural change to the region, tourism initially revived the Blue Ridge people's interest in their traditional culture. Tourists' fascination with this culture created a market for such material objects as quilts, baskets, folk toys, dulcimers, and banjos. To satisfy this new market, Blue Ridge craftspeople were forced to change their approach to producing traditional handicrafts. Whereas once they made material objects occasionally, primarily for their own use, craftspeople now had to step up production and appeal to the aesthetic standards of outsiders. Traditionally, a material object needed to serve some utilitarian purpose and to satisfy the aesthetic standards of the maker and his/her family and community. While the aesthetic beauty of a handicraft's design was, of course, important, it did not matter as much as the object's usefulness and durability. Whether or not a particular handicraft was "art" became an issue only in the twentieth century when craftspeople began to compete for tourist business. Craft guilds, museums, and stores in the region promulgated the idea of "folk art." Artistic self-consciousness replaced utility as the primary consideration in the making of handicrafts.

As demand for traditional crafts increased after World War I, formal organizations emerged in the Blue Ridge, part of an effort to promote the products of regional craftspeople more effectively. These organizations included Allanstand Cottage Industries, founded in Asheville, North Carolina, in 1917; the Southern Highland Handicraft Guild, founded in Asheville in 1929 (into which Allanstand later merged); the Shenandoah Community Workers, founded in Bird Haven, Virginia, in 1927; and Penland Weavers and Potters, founded in Penland, North Carolina, in 1923. Penland's mission statement might serve to illustrate the philosophy of most of these organizations, suggesting their mix of missionary zeal and economic self-determination: "[T]o revive and perpetuate the native arts and crafts of a mountain community, and . . . to provide for the people of this mountain community an opportunity of supplementing the products of their small farms with a little cash income."

When orders for traditional Blue Ridge crafts increased, several of these organizations began to sponsor formal training programs aimed at regulating production. In 1930, for example, Penland Weavers and Potters introduced the summer Penland Weaving Institute to provide formal training for native as well as nonnative participants. However well intentioned, these craft schools often offered instruction by nonnative teachers; for instance, the principal instructor during the early years of the Penland summer program was from Chicago. Some of these teachers freely incorporated Scandinavian designs and technology into their lessons, which increased production and encouraged experimentation, but also compromised traditional craftsmanship.

Foodways

The foods and drinks of the Blue Ridge are here categorized as material culture, though recipes have a customary aspect in that, historically, they were passed from one generation to another by demonstration and by word of mouth (only in later years were they usually written down); also, foods and drinks were often an integral part of regional rituals, ceremonies, and celebrations.

Early settlers flourished in the rugged Blue Ridge wilderness precisely because they complemented their native European foodways with some adopted from the Cherokee. Pioneers were largely dependent upon the hunting of game and the gathering of wild vegetation in season, combined with the annual harvesting of cultivated plants (especially corn, beans, squash, and pumpkins) originally obtained from Native Americans. The most reliable year-round food source was the meat of livestock, and even that source was tenuous, as disease, harsh weather, and wild predators often afflicted a herd. Given the unreliability of food acquisition in the premodern Blue Ridge, residents of the region rarely obtained balanced nutrition; from a contemporary perspective, their diet contained too much starch, fat, and cholesterol, and offered insufficient quantities of vitamins. In lean winter months, many people attempted to remedy this problem by eating wild greens. Despite nutritional deficiencies in their food, mountain families spent considerable time obtaining, preserving, and preparing it. In addition to being necessary for physical survival, food functioned as a vehicle for social interaction. Otherwise beset with rural isolation and hard work, the region's residents have long appreciated the opportunities for gathering that meals occasioned.

Traditionally, the people of the Blue Ridge maintained a simple diet. Breakfast, frequently prepared and consumed before dawn, consisted of some combination of pork (bacon, ham, or sausage), a breadstuff and spread (biscuits, cornbread, or fritters covered with butter, jam, jelly, honey, or molasses), eggs, grits, and gravy, and fresh or stewed fruits/berries. Midday and evening meals often featured one type of meat (usually pork or chicken), gravy (red-eye or brown gravy), one carbohydrate-rich item (dressing, rice, or potatoes), a vegetable (fried green tomatoes, green beans, greens, turnips, or corn), a breadstuff (cornbread or biscuits), and fruit (served fresh, stewed, or in the form of applesauce or pie). On special occasions—Sundays and holidays—dinners offered a larger sampling of available foods, including at least one type of meat (ham, fried chicken, chicken and dumplings, or turkey), dressing, potatoes (Irish or sweet), a vegetable (generally corn or beans), cornbread, fruit (fresh or stewed), and a dessert (usually pie or cobbler).

COOKING

Some staple foods, including a variety of fruits and vegetables, were eaten raw, while others, particularly meats, necessitated cooking. Many early Blue Ridge settlers cooked in outdoor fire pits, which were established in safe, sheltered, and cleared locations. Generating sparks by striking flint against metal, settlers would ignite dry kindling (chunks of pine, wood chips, and broomstraw), then would add dry hardwood sticks (most often hickories, oaks, and poplar). When a bed of coals had been established, food could be cooked. Eventually, settlers would construct log cabins containing indoor fireplaces, with external chimneys made of stacked stones (in later years, of bricks and concrete) to channel smoke out of the house. A typical fireplace featured a horizontal iron bar, which was fixed into the fireplace walls approximately three feet from the floor. Other fireplaces contained an iron crane attached at one side and hinged so that it could swing out from the fireplace into the cabin's central space. S-shaped iron hooks would be hung from both of these bars to support pot handles, permitting the hanging of iron pots over the coals for the cooking, heating, and stewing of food and the boiling of water. One common type of pot, the Dutch oven, would be placed directly into the coals, with some being shoveled on top of the pot's iron lid. Used for baking bread, cakes, and cornbread and for roasting meat, the Dutch oven required careful monitoring—coals had to be distributed evenly, since unequal concentrations of hot coals might burn the food within. Another cooking container set right on the coals was the iron frying pan.

Until the twentieth century, most utensils and tools used in the region were hand constructed, and some possessed individualized stylistic ornamentation. After a meal, people would clean pots and utensils with sand, rags, or homegrown luffa ("dishrag") gourds.

Not all open-fireplace cooking required pots. Some people would place vegetables like corn, potatoes, and onions, as well as nuts, directly into the hot coals to roast them in their natural coverings. One type of bread was also cooked right in the coals: called ash cakes, these were chunks of dough covered with cloth and put in the fireplace.

Historically, blacksmiths in the region constructed, among their other creations, numerous iron tools for use around fireplaces, including pothooks, pokers (for moving pots and stirring coals), and shovels (for cleaning out old ashes, which would be scattered in gardens to add essential potassium to the soil). By the twentieth century, most Blue Ridge households possessed commercial cast-iron wood stoves. These appliances, despite the advantages they offered, required a considerable cash investment. They were also dangerous: stovepipes would sometimes get clogged with creosote (residual tar left from burning green wood), which would often catch fire, occasionally burning down cabins and houses. Nevertheless, wood stoves cooked foods more efficiently and distributed heat more effectively than fireplaces, and, if properly maintained, were cleaner. The difficulties posed by the burning of wood, though, led many people to invest in

Taken inside the log cabin at Humpback Rocks Pioneer Exhibit near the northern terminus of the Blue Ridge Parkway, this photograph represents a typical nineteenth century Blue Ridge cabin interior; note the skilled craftsmanship evident in the fireplace and the board (puncheon) floor. By World War I, many people in the Blue Ridge had abandoned dank, dark cabins for more comfortable frame houses. (Courtesy of the Blue Ridge Parkway Photo Library)

electric and gas stoves when those appliances became available and afford-able, though that meant being dependent upon costly energy sources.

FRUITS, VEGETABLES, AND WILD PLANTS

From the early days of settlement into the twentieth century, virtually every family in the region maintained a vegetable garden. Usually posi-tioned near the cabin or house for easier surveillance of animal scavengers like groundhogs and rabbits, a Blue Ridge garden would typically yield such vegetables as corn, beans (of several varieties), peas, potatoes, carrots, onions, okra, tomatoes, cucumbers, and squash. Also found on farmsteads were fruit trees, especially apples, crab apples, cherries, and pears. During the summer and early fall, vegetables and fruits were eaten fresh, but, as the first frost neared, people would begin to stock their root cellars (and basements) with numerous sealed containers full of vegetable soups, meat-

Two women prepare a meal for family members in the kitchen area of the Garrett family house, near Montebello, Virginia, in the early 1950s. Shown in this photograph are two improvements found in many rural Blue Ridge houses by the early twentieth century: larger windows and the cast-iron wood stove. (Courtesy of the Blue Ridge Parkway Photo Library)

based vegetable stews, pickled vegetables, sauerkraut, relishes and chutneys, as well as preserves, jams, jellies, and fruit butters.

Although they depended heavily upon cultivated plants, the people of the Blue Ridge also gathered a wide range of wild plant foods: berries (including blackberries, blueberries, elderberries, and serviceberries), fruits (such as black cherries, crab apples, pawpaws, and persimmons), nuts (chinquapins, hickories, and walnuts), roots (Jerusalem artichokes), leaves (dandelions, lamb's-quarters, mustards, and violets), and stems (cattails),

Orchards are common in the Blue Ridge, with apples being the fruit most frequently grown. The Shenandoah Valley is nationally famous for the quality of its apples. (Photo by Hugh Morton)

as well as edible mushrooms and fungi. As with cultivated plants, people canned certain wild plant foods, especially wild fruits and berries, for future consumption.

Until the twentieth century, containers for preserving foods were handmade out of crockery or wood; commercial glass jars (Mason jars) were more easily sealed and more sanitary, and thus eventually replaced the older types of containers. The people of the region preserved beans by canning and also by stringing them up and letting them dry in long chains known as "leather breeches" (so called because of the beans' resemblance to pants hanging on a clothesline). Preserving root vegetables and apples involved piling them carefully in wooden boxes and storing them in a root cellar. Preserved fruits and vegetables improved the diets of Blue Ridge families, providing essential nutrients during the lean winter months.

WILD GAME

From the early years of settlement to the present, the people of the Blue Ridge have combined the hunting of game with the raising of domesticated animals (specifically, fowl and livestock). The wild animals eaten in the region include fish, frogs, birds, small mammals, deer, and bear. Typically, fish (ranging from brook trout caught in high mountain streams to bass raised in farm ponds) would be cleaned, with the fillets then rolled in cornmeal and fried in a greased iron skillet. If they could not be consumed immediately, fish would be stored in a springhouse or, in later years, a freezer. Bullfrogs were prized for their legs, which would be dipped in flour and fried. The turkey was the primary game bird in the Blue Ridge, though hunters also brought home ducks, quails, doves, and, in earlier years, passenger pigeons. Many parts of a turkey were utilized: the breast meat and legs would be fried, the rest of the meat stewed, and some organs also eaten; the wings would be dried and used as fire fans. Small game mammals (including groundhogs, squirrels, possums, rabbits, and raccoons) were common in the Blue Ridge, and some people would regularly hunt them; many others, though, felt that these animals possessed too little meat to merit the tasks of capturing, skinning, and cooking. Deer, on the other hand, were widely prized, being easier to butcher than smaller game mammals and providing far more meat for the effort. After the initial cutting up of a deer, sections of meat would be hung in a cool place so that excess blood could drain out. Not long afterward, the sections would be carved into venison steaks (round, sirloin, or T-bone), roasts, and/or ribs, while scraps of the remaining meat would be added to stews. Some people would eat deer livers and hearts, though other internal organs were usually not consumed. Onions were sometimes added to the venison during cooking to temper the wild game flavor. In recent years, modern pressure cookers have been employed to render venison more tender. Deerskins, of course, were valued for the leather they yielded.

Bear meat was once commonly eaten in the region. After slitting the animal along the underside with a knife, the hunter would carefully remove a bear's hide, then cut the meat into roasts and steaks for immediate cooking, hams and shoulders for salt curing, and less desirable parts for stews. Although bear meat was notoriously tough, many people made it more tender through various techniques such as parboiling the meat before roasting it. In addition to using rifles, Blue Ridge hunters caught bears by setting traps. In more modern times, commercial steel foot traps have been set in areas frequented by bears, but in the old days hunters would build bear pens (traditional baited deadfall traps), which were placed in gaps. Food would lure a bear into a dug-out pit, and the animal's grabbing the bait would trip the logs positioned over the pit. The weight of the logs would trap the bear, holding it in the pit until a hunter's return.

DOMESTICATED ANIMALS

By the early nineteenth century, overhunting had begun to take its toll on wild game populations in the Blue Ridge. Residents grew increasingly dependent upon domesticated animals—fowl and livestock. The most common kind of fowl in the region, the chicken, traditionally served as more than food. Chickens pecking around a farmstead helped to control insect pests and ticks, while roosters acted as surrogate watch dogs, squalling when interlopers approached (in recent years, guinea hens have fulfilled these same functions on some farms). Nonetheless, chickens were primarily raised for eggs and meat. Before prepackaged chicken could be purchased at grocery stores, people would kill a chicken by hand, twisting its neck; it would then be hung on a rope, its neck sliced so that the blood would drain out; finally, the chicken would be placed in hot water to remove the feathers (which were saved to stuff pillows). People in the region have long favored fried chicken, but they have also eaten it broiled, roasted, and stewed, and have often added chicken to pies and mixed it with dumplings.

Historically, the most common kind of livestock in the Blue Ridge was the domesticated hog. Hardy and of voracious appetite, hogs flourished in the region's restrictive mountain environment. People would brand their hogs, then set them free to scavenge in the woods. Retrieving and butchering them was the hardest part of raising the hogs. Virtually all parts of the animal would be consumed as food: head, brain, snout, tongue, many internal organs, feet, and tail. Hog fat would be converted into "cracklins" (eaten with bread) and lard (a staple ingredient in many recipes). A family might butcher half a dozen or more hogs each winter. Some of the pork would be eaten immediately, but most was preserved for future use through one of several procedures: salting the meat and hanging it in a meathouse, smoking it in a smokehouse, or canning it (often as an ingredient in stews). More recently, pork has been stored in freezers.

Cows were widely raised in the Blue Ridge, except in the steepest or roughest terrain. As with a hog, few parts of a butchered cow went unused. Some cow meat would be consumed fresh, with the rest preserved in the aforementioned ways. Cow fat would be used for cooking and also converted into tallow, which served both as a leather preservative and as an ointment against croup. A cow's skin, of course, would be converted into leather, so essential for the making of shoes, saddles, and other material objects.

DAIRY PRODUCTS

Most Blue Ridge families possessed a cow that provided milk and other dairy products. Fresh cow milk would be allowed to stand in a receptacle; after the cream had risen, it would be skimmed off. The milk would be fed to children and the cream converted into butter. Making butter involved

A hog butchering near Vinton, Virginia, 1955. Blue Ridge residents traditionally used most parts of a hog. (Courtesy of the Blue Ridge Parkway Photo Library)

the pouring of cream into a jar which was stored in a cool place; when a couple of gallons had been gathered, the cream would be poured into a ceramic churn, and the churning would commence, with the butter maker using a wooden implement known as a dasher to stir the cream. If a favorable temperature had been achieved—neither too warm nor too cold—the butter would form quickly. In the old days, making cheese was much harder work than it is now, as people had to obtain the necessary rennet from a cow's stomach; recently, commercial rennet has become available. Many people over the years have opted for cottage cheese, which does not require any rennet. Before refrigerators were common in the region, dairy products and other perishables (eggs, meat, and vegetables) would be stored in covered wooden or ceramic (and, in later years, glass) containers, which would be placed in springs or springhouses.

SWEETENERS

Like people everywhere, Blue Ridge residents have been known to have a sweet tooth. Before modern times, cravings for sweet things could not be satisfied with cane sugar, since that product was generally unavailable in most communities. Instead, people in the region would make molasses and harvest honey. The process of making molasses would begin with the springtime planting of sorghum cane seeds in small mounds. Farmers would carefully tend to these plants, thinning some and watering the rest to ensure large fleshy stalks. In the fall, when the seed clusters at the top of the sorghum cane stalks had turned hard and red, farmers would remove the leaves from the stalks, lop off the seeds (saving them for the next year's crop), and then harvest the stalks, carrying them directly to the nearest sorghum mill before they could dry out. If a farmer did not own a mill he would use another's, his "toll" being the surrendering of a sizeable portion of his molasses syrup to the mill owner. Placed in the center of a cleared area, a sorghum mill consisted of three metal rollers; one of these rollers would be turned by the rotation of a log (known as a "sweep") drawn by a horse. The sorghum stalks would be fed through the rollers and crushed, with the green sorghum juice running into a trough which channelled it through a layer of burlap and then into a barrel. Periodically, the contents of this barrel would be strained, then drained into a nearby "boiler box" (a rectangular pan set over a stoked furnace). After being boiled in this pan for a few hours, the sorghum juice would be drastically reduced in volume (ten gallons yielding approximately one gallon of syrup). The foamy residue which appeared on the surface of the juice during the boiling process would be removed by means of a "skimmer" (a wooden strainer). When the juice turned into a thick caramel-colored syrup, the molasses makers would carefully lift the boiler box off the furnace and place it securely on logs; then, the molasses syrup would be removed with a small saucepan, strained, and poured into containers for storage.

Harvesting honey in the Blue Ridge was an imperfect science. A person discovering a hollow tree occupied by a swarm of bees might cut the tree down and open it to see if it was laden with honey, while attempting to avoid potentially dangerous stings by waving smoking torches near the bees to render them sluggish and less aggressive. The person would quickly scoop up any honey into buckets before it spilled out onto the ground. Some residents of the region would increase the likelihood of finding honey on their farmsteads by manually propping up hollowed tree trunks in which bees might build honeycombs; in addition to supplying honey, these "bee gum" stumps ensured the pollination of the crops and the edible wild plants which a family depended upon for survival. As trade with low-landers increased after the Civil War, commercial cane sugar became a popular sweetener in the region. Along with refined white flour, another commercial product introduced during this period, sugar revolutionized food preparation in the Blue Ridge. The two ingredients made possible a wide

One step in the process of making molasses: squeezing juice from sorghum cane with the help of a horse-powered cane mill. (Courtesy of the Blue Ridge Parkway Photo Library)

variety of dishes, especially desserts like cookies, cakes, pies, cobblers, custards, and puddings.

BEVERAGES

Historically, the most popular beverages in the Blue Ridge were, among adults, coffee and tea, and, among children, milk. In the old days, to ensure that hot coffee was on the breakfast table, people would get up well before sunrise, put coffee beans in a pan, roast them over hot coals in the fireplace or wood stove, then grind the beans and boil the ground coffee in a pot of hot water. Teas were primarily valued for their medicinal properties. In an effort to promote good health, people would drink teas derived from parts of native plants—the roots of sassafras, the twigs of spicebush and sweet birch, and the leaves of plants of the mint family (such as catnip). Some teas, it was believed, could cure specific ailments: spicewood tea, for instance, was thought to have the power to rid children of measles.

Seasonally, people in the Blue Ridge also drank cider, made by straining the juice out of apples (either by mashing the fruit with a wooden plank or by using the hand-cranked machine known as a cider press). A portion of the cider would be consumed immediately, and the rest would be stored in containers, some of which would be set aside to ferment into vinegar or apple brandy (applejack). Other liquors produced in the region included beer (made from persimmons and apples), wine (from muscadine grapes, blackberries, and rhubarb), and whiskey (from grains like corn and rye).

LIQUOR MAKING

A notorious (and often misunderstood) example of folk technology in the Blue Ridge was the still, a sophisticated mechanism which manufactured liquor. Since the traditional process of liquor making known as moonshining was usually an illegal activity, the technology with which people produced liquor was not standardized; that is, since people were unable to purchase ready-made components, they built their own stills, improvising with both natural and artificial materials (the term "still" referred both to the entire apparatus used for the distillation of alcoholic beverages and to one specific part of that apparatus). Typically, the mechanism would be constructed in a secluded place not visible from any road or walkway (sometimes under dense plant cover, sometimes in a cave) and near a reliable source of clear, cold water, such as a spring or creek.

A few days before firing up the still, the moonshiner would combine the various ingredients which produced whiskey: mash (ground-up unsprouted corn), malt (ground-up sprouted corn), rye, water, and sometimes cane sugar. After this mixture had fermented for a few days, the moon-

Blue Ridge farmers have long marketed their products and produce in rustic roadside stands. Harve Gragg of Linville, North Carolina, sells homemade cider and honey beside a well-travelled road. He is the second of three generations of Graggs to operate roadside stands. (Photo by Hugh Morton)

shiner would build a fire, usually out of slow-burning hardwoods like ash, oak, and hickory, in the firebox (built out of rock and clay, this was the opening to a still's furnace). On a protective shelf inside the furnace sat a copper barrel—the specific part known as the still; because of the shelf, the fire did not directly touch this barrel, but the barrel nonetheless absorbed the force of the heat. The moonshiner would pour the aforementioned mixture into the barrel to boil it. The resulting steam would rise into the cap (a smaller copper barrel which topped the "still" barrel). The steam would leave the cap and enter a copper pipe known as the cap arm; under great pressure, the steam would pass downward into a tightly spiraling copper tube known as the worm. Positioned inside a large wooden barrel filled with cold water continuously piped in from the water source, the worm was cool in temperature; the steam now would condense and become liquid. After the worm exited the wooden barrel near its base, the just-made alcohol would be filtered through hickory coals, then channelled through a funnel into a waiting container (in the old days a clay jug or small wooden

A demonstration still, Laurel Springs, North Carolina; an actual, working still would, of course, be covered by dense foliage or hidden in a cave. (Courtesy of the Blue Ridge Parkway Photo Library)

barrel, and in later years a glass jar). When full, the container would be sealed and stored in a secret location.

Before the 1920s, moonshiners in the Blue Ridge distributed most of their liquor to others in their immediate localities. However, after the Volstead Act of 1919 prohibited the manufacture and sale of alcoholic beverages throughout the United States, Blue Ridge-produced liquor was much in demand. The region's moonshiners increased their production, and new liquor makers set up operations, leading to conflict between the upholders of the federal law—local sheriffs and federal officers—and those involved in producing and transporting the liquor to markets outside the mountains. Sheriffs were now in the awkward situation of having to enforce a law which many in their communities distrusted; a number of sheriffs refused to arrest local moonshiners (some of whom were kin), believing them to be victims of a discriminatory policy.

Hunting Dogs

The people of the Blue Ridge have long loved to hunt, not only for the procuring of meat and hides but also for adventure and camaraderie. In fact, catching an animal was not always the primary goal of a hunting trip, as in the case of fox hunting. People did not eat foxes unless they were extremely hungry. A group of fox hunters (occasionally made up of members of one family, women sometimes included, but more commonly consisting of several male friends) would go in pursuit simply for the thrill of the chase—or to exercise their dogs. Of the two species of foxes found in the Blue Ridge, the red fox was favored for its habit of running in the presence of dogs, whereas a gray fox would immediately hide.

Trained hunting dogs would not only assist their masters on hunting trips but also help to safeguard farmsteads from animal and human intrusions. Several kinds of hound dogs have been common in the Blue Ridge, including the beagle, the blue tick hound, and the Plott bear hound. Other breeds found in the region were the bulldog and two kinds of terriers—the black-and-tan and the Airedale. Hunters would sometimes train a young dog by taking it on a hunt and letting it join other dogs in following a

This photograph, taken near Crossnore, North Carolina, in the late 1950s, depicts a traditional coon dog training session. A raccoon would be placed on top of a pole in some body of water, whereupon a coon dog would be released to swim out and catch it. Pressure from animal rights activists has led to a discontinuation of this activity. (Photo by Hugh Morton)

game animal's scent; when the game was caught, the hunter would restrain the more experienced dogs, allowing the trainee dog to investigate the object of the excitement, which imprinted the image of the game animal upon the dog. Sometimes a hunter would teach his dogs to respond to a signature horn sound (produced by his blowing into a cow horn), which would enable the hunter to better control his dogs during hunting trips.

Rifles

Of all the tools which enabled settlers to eke out a living in the Blue Ridge, the one most valued by its owner was the rifle. This instrument of destruction was also a machine of complexity and beauty. The most common type of rifle among early settlers was the American muzzle-loading flintlock longrifle, the forerunner of which was first developed during the mid-1700s in eastern Pennsylvania (an amalgamation of the best in German, French, English, and New World gun technologies). Daniel Boone, when embarking for the frontier from Pennsylvania in 1750, carried with him a muzzle-loading flintlock longrifle made by a German gunsmith who lived near Lancaster, Pennsylvania. Before long, variations of the Pennsylvania prototype were being built in the Blue Ridge, with these mountain rifles possessing a slightly smaller caliber. At the time of the American Revolution, gunsmith William Bean was making crude but much-sought-after flintlock longrifles on the western slope of the Blue Ridge (near present-day Jonesborough, Tennessee). By the 1790s, several establishments were producing well-crafted longrifles in the Virginia Blue Ridge, including the Honaker shop (in Pulaski County) and the Simpson shop (in Staunton).

Each gunsmith incorporated individualized design features into his longrifles. William Bean and his family, for instance, would make rifles bearing little or no ornamentation (such as inlay) and would paint the wooden parts with linseed oil and carbon blackening to minimize the reflection of light off the guns. Although their rustic appearance did not appeal to hunters in more settled areas, the Beans' longrifles perfectly suited the needs of early settlers in the Blue Ridge wilderness. A flintlock longrifle was remarkably accurate because of its design: the inside of its barrel was grooved, which meant that a lead ball would spin quickly when it passed through, and would have a steadier flight once it left the barrel.

Major modifications of the longrifle occurred in the early nineteenth century. In the 1820s, the flintlock firing system was abandoned for the percussion-cap lock firing system, and in the 1830s the fullstock handle was altered to the halfstock. Shortly thereafter, advances in gun technology rendered obsolete the muzzle-loading rifle. As people in the Blue Ridge could afford to do so, they bought or traded for the new, more sophisticated breech-loading and repeating rifles. The gun which had helped to settle the Appalachian frontier—the handmade muzzle-loading American flintlock longrifle—was soon forgotten, replaced by more efficient models constructed out of standardized, mass-produced parts.

In the 1920s, interest in the flintlock longrifle was revived, as many Americans began to romanticize the early Appalachian frontiersmen. Gunsmiths across the country made replicas of the flintlock longrifle, and a new generation soon developed respect for pioneer hunters, realizing that the historic rifle was a challenge to operate. Firing off a single shot from an eighteenth century flintlock longrifle involved not only the construction of the rifle, but also the preparation of black powder from self-mined minerals, the making by hand of flints and lead balls, and, finally, the loading, aiming, and firing of the slow, awkward, heavy, and loud gun. Despite the technological shortcomings which had led to its original disappearance, the flintlock longrifle was revived because it was emblematic of a lost American Eden, a preindustrial era when frontiersmen like Daniel Boone, against enormous odds, thrived in the American wilderness.

A flintlock longrifle match on Hi Tye Mountain near Waynesboro, Virginia, 1954. (Courtesy of the Blue Ridge Parkway Photo Library)

Fascination with the flintlock longrifle spread, until thousands of people across the United States owned replica guns. Before long, many one-time and several annual shooting contests, or matches, were being offered nationwide, including several in the Blue Ridge, which tested the accuracy and quickness of longrifle shooters. Encouraged to use their own hand-made rifles and ammunition, contestants in these matches would shoot at a stationary target (often the center of an X drawn on a piece of cardboard posted to a wooden board) positioned a good distance away, usually fifty yards. Everyone would be allowed three shots, with the winner being the shooter who consistently hit closest to the target. Sometimes contestants would be required to shoot while lying down, sometimes while standing up. Matches usually required an entry fee, though some were sponsored by local organizations. Winners might receive a food prize, such as a large cut of beef, or perhaps money and/or a trophy. These matches would provide longrifle aficionados with opportunities to check the effectiveness of equipment, test their shooting abilities, exchange information with other gun enthusiasts, and resurrect some semblance of the pioneer spirit found on the frontier. One organization of longrifle revivalists within the region, the Blue Ridge Mountain Men, has staged shooting matches and hunting trips which have required the exclusive use of flintlock longrifles.

The Blue Ridge Today

Growing up in Washington, D. C., I had visited the Blue Ridge many times during my youth, but my first opportunity to stay there for an extended period came when I worked as a counselor at a summer camp located just over the Virginia border in Hampshire County, West Virginia. That was when I met Jack Schaffenaker, "the earthworm man." As the following first-person account conveys, that summer Jack taught urban and suburban campers and counselors much about rural life in the Blue Ridge region— and much about living, period.

Jack Schaffenaker, "The Earthworm Man"

I sat there on the lodge's back porch, pondering my predicament: the camp's director had just handed me a form which listed my teaching assignment for the summer, and I knew nothing about the subject. He wanted me to teach the kids something about "environmental ethics," and I had no idea what that term meant. Hoping I had misread my instructions, I jumped off the porch to retrieve the form—I had torn it up and scattered the pieces in the thick brush under the porch. Careful not to arouse the poisonous spiders I had been told hid out in that brush, I recovered all the pieces and reconstructed the form; sure enough, it said what I feared it said. I returned to my perch to brood.

It was my first day at my first real job, and already I regretted signing up. The camp's director had claimed he wanted high school graduates interested in the environment, but he had mentioned nothing about "environmental ethics." I assumed that at most I would be required to work in the darkroom, lead a bird walk or two, and perform some of the banjo tunes

Jack Schaffenaker teaching the author a new tune.

I had learned from records; instead, I had been assigned a great responsibility—I had to tell some children about something so complex and important
that I myself didn't understand it.

Then I realized that if the camp's director found me pouting on the back
porch, he might put me on the next Greyhound headed back to Washington ("the city built on a swamp" was my name for that place). Recalling
that I had accepted this job mainly to escape the hot air of another Washington summer, I decided I would be better off staying at camp, despite the
burden of responsibility I now faced—who knows, I thought, I might even
learn something. Since I didn't want to spend another long sultry summer
mowing down weeds and mopping up swimming pools, I jumped off the
porch again—this time to join the other counselors for the afternoon
picnic.

So that the counselors could get to know one another, the camp's director had organized a picnic to be held on top of the ridge which loomed
over the camp's lodge. The path up the ridge was actually an old rutted
logging road overgrown with nettles. Apparently oblivious to the stinging
in their legs, the other counselors raced up the path. They were talking so

loudly that they scared away the wildlife—angry, I let them get far ahead of me. I had come to these mountains to get away from such people. Walking alone, I took my time, enjoying the early summer wildflowers.

When I finally got to the top, I saw that the other counselors were already playing capture the flag on the grassy crest of the ridge. I sat on a rotting stump and began to eat my lunch. At first I watched the two teams run around wildly, shouting their battle cries at each other, but I soon grew tired of peering at them, and closed my eyes. Mountains—the Blue Ridge Mountains—were blocking my vision, reminding me of my school's concrete walls. Opening my eyes, I turned around, looked the other way. In that direction, off at the edge of the crest, I noticed a lichen-scarred oak—it was quite gnarled, and seemed to spread further horizontally than vertically. That tree had not only endured blizzards, thaws, droughts, and pesky insects, it had somehow escaped the teeth of the saw. I walked over to climb it.

From thirty feet up, I looked westward, into the hollow where the camp's lodge stood. I couldn't locate the lodge—its architects had built it at the edge of the hollow near the spring, in dense forest—but in the center of the hollow was a huge field, and in the center of the field was a mound of stones, the remains of a cabin's chimney. I had never before seen a human structure so humble, so accepting of its own mortality. The logs had long since rotted, and a black locust was growing where perhaps the bedroom used to be.

Looking westward from up in that oak tree, I thought that I had discovered a place where suburban houses and golf courses weren't yet the rule. I thought that, here in Hampshire County, West Virginia, on this isolated mountain farm, I might forget about Washington, at least for a while. Then I looked the other way. Just beyond the closest ridge to the east crept the shadows of wealth. In that direction I saw that several subdivisions were under construction. The earth-moving machines seemed massive to me, even from my distant perspective. These mountains, I thought, were being invaded by an infantry of legal aliens, who appeared to be better equipped than the natives for this territorial struggle. Developers were destroying farms, fields, and forests, replacing them with colonial brick houses—that made me really angry, for I had grown up in such an environment, and knew how hollow that world could be. Descending from the tree, I ran back to camp to unpack my bags.

Now I was determined to take my teaching assignment seriously, though the meaning of "environmental ethics" still eluded me. It occurred to me, though, that, because the camp's emphasis on nature study most appealed to well-endowed Washingtonians, the campers I'd be teaching might well be the children of such people as senators, lawyers, and developers. Since they wouldn't necessarily learn about "environmental ethics" at home, I decided that my greatest responsibility was to show the campers concrete examples of the impact of our civilization on the mountains. Initially, this was my plan: I would transport the boys and girls with me in the camp's van (the director approved of this, as long as I also picked up the camp's mail, supplies, and groceries) so that we might assess the extent of the region's environmental damage. We would obtain pH readings on several creeks below subdivision developments to determine if those waters were still okay for fish; we would survey the sites of future subdivisions to determine if any endangered species lived there; and we would sketch and photograph buildings on nearby farmsteads to document the culture of the mountain people.

But as I thought more about it, I began to decide that it would be irresponsible to study the region's culture passively or to talk pompously about "environmental ethics." I hadn't yet met a soul from the Blue Ridge, but I sensed how threatened the mountain way of life was. I didn't need an expert to inform me that deserted cabins, wasted fields, and woodlots condemned by "for sale" signs don't make for a healthy community.

I now realize that I was then associating the fate of this place with my own smaller fate. Like the people of the Blue Ridge, I had personally experienced environmental exploitation and the loss of a sense of human community: when I was a teenager, developers cut down the trees I had climbed as a child and constructed a high-rise building where my boyhood house used to be. Since I had noticed that the other counselors didn't show much interest in the local culture, I decided that my main role at camp was not to pontificate about "environmental ethics" but to introduce the campers and the local people to each other, so that we all might better understand each other's plights.

But in truth, I knew very little about the local people. To learn more, I visited a local library, but none of the books I found there spoke to me. The following day, I mustered up the courage to introduce myself to two nearby farmers and to ask them about the recent surge of land buying by outside companies. These farmers were respectful toward me (perhaps they detected my naive sincerity), but I couldn't understand them. They talked with an accent that was unfamiliar to me, and they communicated their bitterness in what amounted to a foreign language, using terms like "middleman" and "eminent domain"—words I hadn't learned in high school civics class. Land rich (they owned many, many acres) but cash poor, these farmers were directly threatened by rapidly changing national, state, and local economies. They described how, with each year, they were paying more in taxes and earning less for crops. That being the case, their anger at the intrusions of outsiders was justified—of all the people in Hampshire

County, they had the most to lose, economically, from all the "progress." However, after talking with them, I foresaw difficulty in interesting the campers—if they were as easily distracted as I had been at their age—in the farmers' rather abstract predicament. Because of their specialized knowledge of farm-management techniques and their relative wealth (one of them drove a Cadillac, a status symbol I had seen all too much of in Washington), the two farmers' lives had been more changed, culturally, than those of their less-prosperous neighbors. Although I would try to take the children to visit these farmers, I decided that the campers would benefit more from meeting less-compromised local people.

I planned to locate an Appalachian character who by the grace of time had remembered how to live in these mountains, simply yet successfully, without taking too much; someone who could view his or her mountain culture not as an embarrassment but as a blessing. Surely somewhere, in some dark hollow, there survived an authentic mountain person—someone who could teach us all the real meaning of "environmental ethics." And if I did locate such a person, I vowed never to spook him or her with that phrase.

The next day, I called all the state and county agencies in the phone book, hoping that somebody could recommend a person who might be willing to meet with the campers. Strangely, when I called the three or four people recommended to me, the television was always blaring in the background (once, I believe I heard the theme song to *The Beverly Hillbillies*). I discovered that all of these people had lived at least part of their lives in Washington or some other big city, and that none of them lived in a traditional way.

The following day, frustrated by my lack of good leads, I decided to scrap the scientific method and randomly travel the county's back roads. For the next three days, I drove down dirt and gravel roads, sure that in the next "holler" I'd find a real mountain person. I only found myself . . . lost. On the morning of the third day—the day the campers were to arrive—I, in my haste to follow up on a lead, forgot to fill the tank at Whitacre's Grocery while passing through Capon Bridge; later that afternoon, on a dirt road, the van gasped and stopped, exhausted. I walked a mile or so, then stumbled upon a Washingtonian's estate, where someone sold me a gallon of gas (and gave me some water free of charge). Driving back to camp, I stopped in Capon Bridge to pick up the camp's supplies and to fill up the van with gas.

When I walked in the store, Mrs. Whitacre looked up from her cash register and said, "There's a guitar picker named Jack living down toward Cold Stream. I'm sure he'd be happy to have the kids by." The day before,

I had pleaded for her help in locating somebody who could teach the campers what I couldn't teach them; she had said that she would think about it.

I told Mrs. Whitacre that I'd like to meet Jack as soon as possible—preferably the next morning, since the campers would have arrived by then. Mrs. Whitacre called his cousin, since Jack didn't own a phone; this cousin, who lived close to Jack, said that she would drive over to his house and ask him if I might stop by with some campers the following morning, around nine. Fifteen minutes later, the cousin called with the news that Jack would be expecting us. After getting directions to his house from Mrs. Whitacre, I sped toward camp.

When I got back, the campers had arrived and dinner was being served. During dinner, I learned that it was easier to talk with the children than I had thought it would be. Yet, when several campers began telling jokes about the people they had met that day on their way to camp (one boy, for example, mocked Mrs. Whitacre's mountain accent), I realized how important my job really was.

That night, I couldn't sleep. Relieved that I would finally meet an authentic mountain man, I was also apprehensive—I didn't know quite what to expect. I had seen *Deliverance*, and I had already discounted the stereotyped image that the movie projected, the craggy face of that inbred mountain youth scowling like a rattlesnake at the city slicker tourists. Instead, I had accepted a kinder but romanticized image of the Appalachian people, developed from my reading of the *Foxfire* books: the next day, I imagined, I would meet a backwoods philosopher who would freely share his wisdom and his jug of moonshine.

Neither of these images accurately described Jack, as I discovered the next morning. He didn't dwell in some far-off hollow, in a ramshackle log cabin; rather, he lived a five-minute drive from Capon Bridge, just off a paved two-lane road, in a cinder-block house which resembled a garage. But before those eight campers and I saw Jack's house, we located his tattered handmade sign by the roadside. It advertised his trade: "earthwurms for sail. 1 cent each." I parked the van by the road, and the children bounced out onto Jack's grassy driveway; Jack strolled out to meet us, waving at us strangers. "How you folks doin'?" he said. His was a spontaneous, nearly toothless grin.

I was planning to invite Jack to go fishing with us that morning, but before I could even introduce myself, he offered to show us his favorite fishing spot in the Cacapon River, which flowed across the road from his house. Perhaps Jack had spied the fishing rods in the back of the van. I offered to buy some worms from him. So Jack filled the children's Dixie cups with dirt, then dropped several earthworms in each one. One camper, a girl, stared at him in disbelief. "A penny a worm? Jack, you'll never get rich that way." He replied, "Why, when peoples live like me they jest don't need no money." Jack wouldn't accept even a penny from us.

We all got back into the van, with Jack choosing to sit in the back with the campers, where they talked about fishing. The road wound along the Cacapon; I negotiated a tight turn, after which Jack pointed to the right, toward a weed-choked bank beside the river. I parked beside the road, and the children scattered on the riverbank to cast their lines where he had pointed. Meanwhile, I sat by Jack on a fallen sycamore and listened as he finished a fish story he had begun telling in the van. He was the slowest speaker I had ever heard, but, because of his accent and his pattern of thinking elliptically, I could understand only about half of what he was saying.

When Jack was done with his story, I asked him about his house. I was curious to know why he had built it out of cinder blocks and not out of logs. Jack told me that, upon learning he had been drafted into the military in the 1940s, he built it for his mother. She was alone—his father had divorced her. Apparently, the people of that region, for all their flamboyant fundamentalism, were quite forgiving: neither Jack nor his mother was ostracized because of the divorce. After all, Jack's German ancestors had been some of the earliest Europeans to settle near Capon Bridge. Schaffenaker Mountain, one of the most impressive hills around, was named after his great-grandfather.

Jack was suddenly interrupted by a camper screaming, "I got one! I got one!" We ran upstream to join the boy, who was already reeling in a pan-size fish. He was bent over, ready to grasp it, when Jack stepped forward, advising him to wet his hands first, lest the fish's slimy coat be removed, which would endanger the fish when it was back in the water. Obeying Jack, the boy dipped his hands in the river, then proceeded to unshackle the fish. Just before tossing it back in the river, the boy suddenly looked at Jack and offered him the fish. Jack laughed, then shook his head, stating, "You can't eat him an' his granchildern both: I'll probly be lots hungrier then than now. Jest set him free."

We walked back to the sycamore. Jack continued reminiscing. He said that, upon his return from the Philippines, he had bought, with his military recompense, a small farmstead on an isolated side of a mountain; there he raised what vegetables he needed and hunted for meat. The war was haunting his dreams, he said, so he started stalking through the deep woods by moonlight, hunting possum. Then, his mother died. In his grief, Jack sold his farm and joined the Coast Guard, which stationed him in Algeria. The house he had built for his mother remained unused for four years, unoccupied but not abandoned. When his sorrow was spent, Jack returned to West Virginia and moved into the cinder-block house. He was now the only surviving Schaffenaker, other than his family's namesake mountain.

Soon, I summoned the campers back to the van—we had to return to camp in time for lunch. When we stopped by Jack's house to drop him off, several children asked me if we could invite him to join us the next morning on our hike along Slonaker's Creek. Without consulting the camp's director, I said, "Sure!" Jack immediately accepted the offer. Promising him I would return early the next morning, around eight, I opened the passenger door, but Jack would not get out of the van; he clearly did not want us to leave—he wanted to show us something. Not wishing to hurt his feelings, I motioned for all the campers to climb out of the van. While Jack walked up his driveway and into his house, the campers and I gathered on the bank of his hand-dug fish pond and watched dragonflies dive bombing mosquitoes. So that we could sit down, we overturned some of the metal buckets Jack used in his earthworm business. Soon he rejoined us, cradling a guitar. It was, he was proud to declare, a vintage Gibson hollowbody—he had traded his old truck for it. After allowing each of the children to strum a chord or two, Jack announced that he would now play us some "good ol' tunes." I was quite excited, thinking that I would hear some traditional Appalachian folk music played the way it should be played, by a genuine mountain musician. While in high school, I had checked out books and records on folk music from the library, all in an effort to teach myself how to sound like a real folk musician; now I would finally hear this music come to life. Jack fiddled with the tuning pegs to find the right pitch, then began picking. What came out of that guitar, though, was not folk music—by my definition anyway; instead, Jack impressed the children with his rendition of "Johnny B. Goode." They responded by banging on the buckets with fallen sticks. This music making was cacophonous, but all were enjoying themselves, especially Jack.

The next morning, I arrived at his house just after eight. Jack was ready, with a canteen in one hand and a corduroy jacket in the other. Out by the road, he turned his hand-painted sign over; it now informed passersby that there were "no more wurms for sail."

This was to be a "nature" hike; that is, we would walk along Slonaker's Creek through an unspoiled limestone canyon, with, as I justified the hike to the camp's director, the ultimate intention of locating a specimen of the rare walking fern, which supposedly grew there. The campers greeted Jack at the trailhead, and we started down the muddy trail. The forest was like a symphony that morning, with flute-like thrushes answering the kettle drumming of ruffed grouse. Soon, four boys fell behind the rest of the group; seemingly oblivious to the harmonious sounds around them, they began yelling at each other. I ran back to see what was bothering them.

Perhaps because it was their first time in the woods, or perhaps because of the primeval setting, a commercialized fantasy world had possessed them, derived from a popular board game called "Dungeons and Dragons." Behind every tree, in their shadowy imaginations, warlocks were lurking.

Jack had waited ahead by the ford with the remaining children; when he observed the temporary victory of the supernatural over the natural, he proceeded, as we crossed the creek, to tell those boys a "haint" story he'd been told by a relative when he was their age: "We're comin' up upon a house, just a bit further down, where a real 'haint' lives. And, by crackies, it's a mean ol' 'haint' . . ."

Suddenly aroused, the boys asked him, "What's a 'haint'?"

"Why, you-uns call them 'ghosts,' but 'haints' is scarier 'cause you-uns 'haint' never seen one. Anyways, no peoples been livin' thar for years. I member hearin' 'bout ol' man Slonaker gettin' spooked and leavin' like a flash . . ."

"What happened?"

"Well, peoples say that he was plumb fool to live thar, what with the thangs that done happened thar before."

"Like what!"

"Well, they say that, a long time back, a man who was visitin' heered some chains rattlin' in the attic. He climbed the starrcase, step by step, the chains bangin' louder and louder . . ."

By now, the boys were interested only in Jack's story. They listened intently as he described in his mesmerizing cadence the truly neck-wrenching plight of a man trapped by his own fear. That was the way I interpreted the story, anyway. One of the boys retold it to the rest of the campers, leaving out most of the details, and nobody at camp slept much that night.

That summer, I took more than a hundred campers to visit Jack at his cinder-block house—or, as he affectionately called it, his "fall-out shelter" (his ten years in the military had left him with a large vocabulary of useful jargon). Many of the campers wanted to assist him in his summer tasks. While the boys would help Jack tend to his earthworms, the girls would observe from a secure distance, wanting to be far enough away should the boys try to play pranks with the worms. Often the girls would avoid the boys by working in Jack's vegetable garden. Amused by this division of labor, Jack also encouraged the children to overcome it. Some of the boys willingly harvested tomatoes alongside the girls, and a few of the girls developed a fascination for the life cycle of the earthworm. Boys and girls alike teased Jack for his habit of talking to worms, and, upon learning that he fed his worms shredded newspaper, the children often reminded him that "these are the best-read worms in the world."

The last time I saw Jack was in late August, my last day at camp. The campers had been gone for a couple of days, but I had stayed to help clean up the lodge. I was to board a bus the next day—college loomed ahead of me like an iceberg. I was thinking that I would rather spend the fall canoeing with Jack down the Cacapon, fishing by day and listening to his legendary guitar at night.

That day, driving over Schaffenaker Mountain to visit Jack, I saw that the whole county was tinged by drought. His crops were withering in the August heat and his fish pond had all but disappeared—only a puddle of muddy water remained in the middle. And I'm sure he was sorry to watch the apples perish on the trees in his yard. Yet he was cheerful as ever; after all, his house was cool and his well still drew. To Jack, drought was an abstraction like "environmental ethics," and he wouldn't allow abstractions to pester him like horseflies—he'd swat them out of his life. He liked things plain and simple.

He was not plain and simple, though. He had met too many people from too many different backgrounds. He had witnessed too much death and destitution and experienced too much pain. I doubt that Jack even thought of himself as "Appalachian" anymore, just human. Yet he knew his place on earth as few people do. And he freely shared his heritage: following his example, children became, if only for a part of a day, skilled fishermen, worm farmers, and storytellers. Also, Jack was instrumental in showing me how to play the banjo with feeling, how to change the tuning to fit the particular song, how to bend notes without breaking the string.

As I walked up the freshly mowed driveway, I noticed a hand-built wheelbarrow wobbling toward me on bent bicycle wheels. Jack had been digging mud out from his fish pond, to insulate his worm cans with mounds of earth before the first frost. Yet, as soon as he saw me, he waved, laid his burden down, ambled into his house, and returned with his guitar.

"Let me help you with that," I said to Jack, pointing at the wheelbarrow.

"Later," he replied. After placing two small Wheeling steel cans upside down in the grass, he said, "Hey, haven't heard from 'Old Joe Clark' for awhile!" Understanding his hint, I began plunking the melody of this traditional mountain tune, one of many he had taught me how to play. Jack had scarcely begun strumming his accompaniment when a man wandered up the driveway, clapping his hands out of time. He was from Washington, he said, "gambling" his weekend fishing on the Cacapon; he was stopping by to purchase some worms—and to see if Jack would recommend possible hot spots. However much he depended on a healthy population of fish in the river, Jack freely disclosed a couple of his favorite sites. The man, anxious to try his luck, thanked Jack, handing him "ten bucks for the tip and a dozen worms." Jack explained to the man that his price was a penny a worm and that visiting a spell was a pleasure that "don't cost even a penny." The man—after insisting, even arguing, that Jack should keep the money—strutted back down the driveway toward his Volvo, as if he'd just donated to the charity of his choice.

Jack just laughed. "We-ell, it'll always come in handy come tax time."

We proceeded to play "Soldier's Joy" and "Over the Waterfall" and a few folk songs, including "John Henry" and "John Hardy." Then I had to leave. Since I had borrowed the van, I had to make it to Whitacre's Grocery before it closed, to pick up the camp's supplies.

Jack followed me out to the van. I climbed in, closed the door, and started the engine, then rolled down the window to thank him for teaching me all those tunes. I told him I looked forward to making more music the next summer.

He didn't live that long.

Conclusion

In the nineteenth century, after the displacement of the Cherokee from the region, the principal residents of the Blue Ridge were the descendants of eighteenth century settlers. From diverse European (and, in some cases, African) cultural backgrounds, yet united by their common experience of eking out a living in a restrictive rural mountain environment, these people continued to utilize the regional folklife which their ancestors had forged by borrowing from many (including Native American) cultural sources when the Blue Ridge was still wilderness. This group's tenacious commitment to place and tradition assured the survival of aspects of Blue Ridge folk culture well into the twentieth century.

At least three other distinct social groups have called the Blue Ridge home. By the end of the nineteenth century, the building of railroads into the region—and subsequent industrial development—spawned populations of urban dwellers in hub cities like Asheville, North Carolina, and Roanoke, Virginia. Many members of this group felt caught between traditional and modern worlds, between a difficult and limiting yet psychologically familiar rural past and an alienating yet dynamic urban present (Thomas Wolfe's writings give expression to these ambivalent feelings).

Two groups of outsiders have emerged within the Blue Ridge in the last third of the twentieth century, and both have been making a significant impact on cultural life in the region. One group is made up of retirees who have relocated to the region's urban/suburban areas (e. g., the Asheville-Hendersonville, North Carolina, area) and resort towns (e. g., in the vicinity of Linville, North Carolina), citing reasons ranging from the Blue Ridge's rural scenery to its relaxed pace of living (ironically, the various developments intended to serve this group have had the effect of altering the region's natural landscape, while the influx of new residents has sped up the pace of life in some areas, bringing, among other changes, congestion and higher property taxes). The other group of outsiders is composed of younger individuals, who, dissatisfied with the urban and suburban circumstances into which they were born, went "back to the land," settling in rural sections of the region to live "the simple life." Close and sustained interactions between natives and nonnatives within any given region generally have a compromising effect on that region's folk culture; yet, many of those who have gone "back to the land" in the Blue Ridge have taken interest in the region's traditional life. Some individuals have even made an effort to learn specific regional verbal, customary, or material traditions by apprenticing themselves (informally and in formal settings such as craft schools and workshops) to native-born folk artisans, musicians, and storytellers. This situation, of course, has caused tension between natives and nonnatives, especially when some act of commodification of culture has occurred. At other times, many elder natives—observing that younger natives in pursuit of upward social and economic mobility were leaving the region and/or embracing mainstream American culture—have accepted the efforts of these people from elsewhere to revive aspects of traditional Blue Ridge culture.

What is the future of Blue Ridge folklife? In a word, uncertain. Although lingering in more rural sections of the Blue Ridge, the region's folklife is threatened by numerous pressures, including the construction of new roads and the improvement of existing ones; the harvesting of natural resources (including logging and, in a few locales, mineral mining); ongoing cultural homogenization via mass media and mass communication technologies; tourism; recreation (especially golf courses and ski resorts); the development of second homes; and the in-migration of outsiders. Given the proximity of the Blue Ridge to growing piedmont cities (such as Charlotte, North Carolina) and to the eastern megalopolis (including Washington, D.C.), these pressures will only increase in intensity. The eroding of the last vestiges of rural isolation (psychological as well as geographical) within the Blue Ridge will inevitably render obsolete whatever remains of the regional folklife which that isolation originally fostered.

Of course, it is always possible that unforeseen economic and/or social crises might cause members of forthcoming generations to become so disenchanted with civilization that they, like Daniel Boone and his fellow settlers, go "back to the land" in the Blue Ridge, and in the process attempt to revive useful regional folkways which had been abandoned. Alas, it is more likely that Blue Ridge folklife will play little or no active role in the everyday experience of the region's future residents.

If one day they do disappear from daily life, the region's traditions probably won't be forgotten. Parks, museums, living history exhibits, archives, classrooms, recordings, videos, and books will no doubt serve to remind a wide populace—those who will reside in the region and those who won't—of Blue Ridge folklife, which may well be embraced by some future generation of Americans as being emblematic of a lost America, representing a simpler way of life which once thrived in a saner time and place.

Introduction

Previous general studies of traditional Blue Ridge culture include Alberta Pierson Hannum, *Look Back With Love: A Recollection of the Blue Ridge* (New York: Vanguard Press, 1969); Jean Thomas, *Blue Ridge Country* (New York: Duell, Sloan & Pearce, 1942); Eugene Joseph Wilhelm, *Folk Geography of the Blue Ridge Mountains* (Ann Arbor: University Microfilms International, 1972); Roy Edwin Thomas, *Southern Appalachia, 1885–1915: Oral Histories from Residents of the State Corner Area of North Carolina, Tennessee and Virginia* (Jefferson, N. C.: McFarland & Co., 1991); Lyntha Scott Eiler, Terry Eiler, and Carl Fleischhauer, *Blue Ridge Harvest: A Region's Folklife in Photographs* (Washington, D. C.: Library of Congress, 1981); and the popular *Foxfire* publications: *Foxfire* magazine and the ten principal *Foxfire* books (Garden City, N. Y.: Anchor Press, 1972–93). Two books which portray traditional life within individual Blue Ridge communities are Mandel Sherman and Thomas R. Henry, *Hollow Folk* (New York: Thomas Y. Crowell Co., 1933) and Muriel Earley Sheppard, *Cabins in the Laurel* (Chapel Hill: University of North Carolina Press, [1935] 1991).

David T. Catlin explains the significance of the word "blue" in the name Blue Ridge in *A Naturalist's Blue Ridge Parkway* (Knoxville: University of Tennessee Press, 1984), 67. The quotation characterizing the Blue Ridge as a "biological archipelago" is in Marcus B. Simpson, Jr., *Birds of the Blue Ridge Mountains* (Chapel Hill: University of North Carolina Press, 1992), 6. The assertion that overhunting was a major factor in the abandonment of the Blue Ridge is from Harry M. Caudill, *Night Comes to the Cumberlands: A Biography of a Depressed Area* (Boston: Atlantic Monthly—Little, Brown and Co., 1962), 10. The concept of "folklife" is discussed by Don Yoder and others in *American Folklife* (Austin: University of Texas Press, 1976).

Chapter One

Two books which discuss early Native American presence near and within the Blue Ridge region are Charles Hudson, *The Southeastern Indians* (Knoxville: University of Tennessee Press, 1976) and Lynda Norene Shaffer, *Native Americans Before 1492: The Moundbuilding Centers of the Eastern Woodlands* (Armonk, N. Y.: M. E. Sharpe, Inc., 1992). The quotation explaining the preference of Woodland people for settling along floodplains rather than in mountainous areas comes from Hudson, 62. Descriptions of eighteenth century Cherokee life can be found in *Travels of William Bartram*, edited by Mark Van Doren (New York: Dover Publications, [1791] 1955), part 3, chapters 3 and 4.

The quotation beginning "Inhabitants flock here daily . . ." is in John Mack Faragher, *Daniel Boone: The Life and Legend of an American Pioneer* (New York: Henry Holt and Company, 1992), 30. Eighteenth century settlement within the Blue Ridge region is discussed in depth in Ora Blackmun, *Western North Carolina to 1880* (Boone, N. C.: Appalachian Consortium Press, 1977) and is sketched in the opening chapters of W. D. Weatherford and Earl D. C. Brewer, *Life and Religion in Southern Appalachia* (New York: Friendship Press, 1962). Information regarding the political and social conditions in adjacent lowland regions of Virginia, North Carolina, and South Carolina before the Revolutionary War is in Rhys Isaac, *The Transformation of Virginia, 1740–1790* (New York: W. W. Norton & Co., 1982) and Charles Woodmason, *The Carolina Backcountry on the Eve of the Revolution*, edited by Richard J. Hooker (Chapel Hill: University of North Carolina Press, 1953).

The Watauga Association is discussed in Blackmun. The quotation beginning "Aspects of the reorganization . . ." is from Isaac, 311. An excellent biography of Daniel Boone, with an assessment of his historical/cultural significance, is John Mack Faragher, *Daniel Boone: The Life and Legend of an American Pioneer* (New York: Henry Holt and Co., 1992). Another study of Boone is Lawrence Elliott, *The Long Hunter: A New Life of Daniel Boone* (New York: Reader's Digest Press [Thomas Y. Crowell Co.], 1976). William Peden recently edited Thomas Jefferson's *Notes on the State of Virginia* (Chapel Hill: University of North Carolina Press, [1787] 1996).

An engaging if rambling and disorganized account of the Battle of Kings Mountain is in Shepherd Monroe Dugger, *The War Trails of the Blue Ridge, Containing an Authentic Description of the Battle of Kings Mountain, the Incidents Leading up to and the Echoes of the Aftermath of this Epochal Engagement, and Other Stories Whose Scenes are Laid in the Blue Ridge* (Banner Elk, N.C.: Puddingstone Press, [1932] 1974). The quotation about the bivouac at Cowpens, its source unattributed, appears in Dugger, 33, while the verse about marching from Cowpens, likewise unattributed, is in Dugger, 35. Also unattributed is the quoted reference to Ferguson's legendary skill with a pistol, which appears in Dugger, 103. A later quotation beginning "Stones are not too hard . . ." is attributed to Dugger, 104, while the inscription from Ferguson's grave marker is from a photograph in Dugger,

105. Two final quotations assessing the impact of the Battle of Kings Mountain are in Dugger, 8 and 84–85. A concise summary of the Battle of Kings Mountain is in Mark Mayo Boatner III, *Encyclopedia of the American Revolution*, Bicentennial Edition (New York: David McKay Co., 1974), 575–83. The military feats of the Overmountain Men are discussed in Pat Alderman, *The Overmountain Men: Early Tennessee History, 1760–1795* (Johnson City, Tenn.: The Overmountain Press, 1970), 62–144. In *Great Valley Patriots: Western Virginia in the Struggle for Liberty* (Verona, Va.: McClure Press, 1976), Howard McKnight Wilson underscores the fact that the residents of the Virginia Blue Ridge and the Shenandoah Valley were also active in the struggle for independence from the British. The aborted State of Franklin is discussed in Alderman, 181–251, and in Mary French Caldwell, *Tennessee: The Dangerous Example—Watauga to 1849* (Nashville: Aurora Publishers, 1974), 149–83.

Chapter Two

Information on the Blue Ridge gold rush, nineteenth century border disputes, economic struggles, and political representation within the North Carolina Blue Ridge can be found in Ora Blackmun, *Western North Carolina to 1880* (Boone, N. C.: Appalachian Consortium Press, 1977). A definitive history of slavery in the Blue Ridge is in John C. Inscoe, *Mountain Masters, Slavery, and the Sectional Crisis in Western North Carolina* (Knoxville: University of Tennessee Press, 1989).

Many have written about the final displacement of the majority of the Cherokee tribe from ancestral lands, since the forced march to Oklahoma known as the Trail of Tears ranks with Wounded Knee as one of the most tragic consequences of U.S. governmental policy toward Native American peoples. John Ehle's *Trail of Tears: The Rise and Fall of the Cherokee Nation* (New York: Anchor Press, 1988) sets the stage for the incident, while John G. Burnett's eyewitness account, "The Cherokee Removal through the Eyes of a Private Soldier" in *Journal of Cherokee Studies* 3, no. 3 (1978): 180–85, provides details of the march and suggests that some of the soldiers who led the march felt considerable ambivalence regarding their official duties. The quotation from President Andrew Jackson is in Charles Hudson, *The Southeastern Indians* (Knoxville: University of Tennessee Press, 1976), 463.

Tourism, transportation, and public education in the nineteenth century Blue Ridge are addressed in Blackmun. Information on transportation and public education can also be found in John C. Campbell, *The Southern Highlander & His Homeland* (Lexington: University Press of Kentucky, [1921]

1969). The 1935 quotation from historian Arnold J. Toynbee comes from
Robert J. Higgs and Ambrose N. Manning, editors, *Voices from the Hills:
Selected Readings of Southern Appalachia* (New York: Frederick Ungar Publishing Co., 1975), 387. The quoted population figures are in Blackmun,
288.

Numerous books discuss the Blue Ridge region's pivotal role in the Civil
War. Concise descriptions of the various campaigns, battles, and skirmishes
which occurred in the Blue Ridge are in James M. Mcpherson, *Battle Cry
of Freedom: The Civil War Era* (New York: Ballantine Books, 1988) and John
G. Barrett, *The Civil War in North Carolina* (Chapel Hill: University of
North Carolina Press, 1963). The John Brown quotation appears in Mc-
Pherson, 208. McPherson's comment regarding "Stonewall" Jackson's
Shenandoah Valley Campaign (May–June 1862) is on 460. Information on
Unionist raider George W. Kirk is in Dugger's *The War Trails of the Blue
Ridge* (Banner Elk, N. C.: Puddingstone Press, [1932] 1974), chapter 4.
The excerpt of a letter from Lieutenant J. C. Wills to North Carolina Gov-
ernor Z. B. Vance appears in Barrett, 241.

A discussion of the effects of postwar industrialization, both within the
Blue Ridge region and throughout the southern mountains, is in Ronald
D. Eller, *Miners, Millhands, and Mountaineers: Industrialization of the Appala-
chian South, 1880–1930* (Knoxville: University of Tennessee Press, 1982).
Wilma A. Dunaway, *The First American Frontier: Transition to Capitalism in
Southern Appalachia, 1700–1860* (Chapel Hill: University of North Carolina
Press, 1996), calling into question the long-held belief that southern moun-
tain people were largely self-sufficient until the postwar period, asserts that
small-scale market economies developed in the Southern Appalachians (including in the Blue Ridge) well before the Civil War. A history of railroads
in the region can be found in Neal Brian Westveer, *Railroad Crossings of the
Blue Ridge* (Little Switzerland, N. C.: Memories Press, 1990).

Information about logging in the Blue Ridge, including the Biltmore
Estate forestry school, is in Ina Woestemeyer Van Noppen and John J. Van
Noppen, *Western North Carolina Since the Civil War* (Boone, N. C.: Appalachian Consortium Press, 1973), chapter 14. The quotation from Gifford
Pinchot regarding the Biltmore Forest is in Van Noppen and Van Noppen,
303. The various government-sponsored conservation projects in the region are discussed in Charlton Ogburn, *The Southern Appalachians: A Wil-
derness Quest* (New York: William Morrow & Co., 1975); Harley E. Jolley,
The Blue Ridge Parkway (Knoxville: University of Tennessee Press, 1969);
"The CCC: The Road to Recovery" and "The WPA" in George P. Reynolds, editor, *Foxfire 10* (New York: Anchor Books, 1993), 240–302; and
Jules Loh, "Back Then We Had the WPA," *Asheville Citizen-Times*, June
23, 1991, features section: 1D, 6D. The claim that no paved road existed in
Floyd County, Virginia, before the parkway is from Jolley, 11. An assess-

ment of the environmental impact of suburban development in the Virginia Blue Ridge is in William E. Shands, *The Subdivision of Virginia's Mountains: The Environmental Impact of Recreational Subdivisions in the Massanutten Mountain—Blue Ridge Area, Virginia: A Survey and Report*, rev. 2d. printing (Washington, D. C.: Central Atlantic Environment Center, 1974).

Many people, from eighteenth century naturalists like Andre Michaux and William Bartram to present-day tourists, have journeyed to the Blue Ridge to study its geographical features and diverse flora and fauna. The region's natural history is explored in Charlton Ogburn, *The Southern Appalachians: A Wilderness Quest* (New York: William Morrow & Co., 1975); Maurice Brooks, *The Appalachians* (Boston: Houghton Mifflin Co., 1965); Roderick Peattie, *The Great Smokies and the Blue Ridge: The Story of the Southern Appalachians* (New York: Vanguard Press, 1943); David T. Catlin, *A Naturalist's Blue Ridge Parkway* (Knoxville: University of Tennessee Press, 1984); Marcus B. Simpson, *Birds of the Blue Ridge Mountains* (Chapel Hill: University of North Carolina Press, 1992); Annie Dillard, *Pilgrim at Tinker Creek* (New York: Harper's Magazine Press, 1974); and various authors, *The Distributional History of the Biota of the Southern Mountains* (Blacksburg, Va.: Virginia Polytechnic Institute and State University, 1969–71).

My descriptions of the Joyce Kilmer Memorial Forest stem from visits in the late 1980s, at which time I interviewed Oleta Nelms. Additional information and the Roosevelt quotation came from the files of the U. S. Forest Service station in Robbinsville, North Carolina.

Studies which address the stereotyping of Southern Appalachian people include W. K. McNeil, editor, *Appalachian Images in Folk and Popular Culture*, 2d ed. (Knoxville: University of Tennessee Press, 1995); David E. Whisnant, *All That Is Native & Fine: The Politics of Culture in an American Region* (Chapel Hill: University of North Carolina Press, 1983); J. W. Williamson, *Hillbillyland: What the Movies Did to the Mountains and What the Mountains Did to the Movies* (Chapel Hill: University of North Carolina Press, 1995); and David C. Hsiung, *Two Worlds in the Tennessee Mountains: Exploring the Origins of Appalachian Stereotypes* (Lexington: University Press of Kentucky, 1997). One such study which focusses exclusively on the Blue Ridge is Stephen Foster, *The Past Is Another Country: Representation, Historical Consciousness, and Resistance in the Blue Ridge* (Berkeley: University of California Press, 1988). The William James quotation, originally from "On a Certain Blindness in Human Beings" in *Essays on Faith and Morals* (1896), appears in Van Noppen and Van Noppen, 59–60. The quotation from John Solomon Otto is from "Plain Folk, Lost Frontiersmen, and Hillbillies: The Southern Mountain Folk in History and Popular Culture," *Southern Studies: An Interdisciplinary Journal of the South* 26, no. 1 (spring 1987): 10.

Chapter Three

The dialect of American English known as Appalachian English is treated in Walt Wolfram and Donna Christian, *Appalachian Speech* (Arlington, Va.: Center for Applied Linguistics, 1976) and in the work of scholar Michael Montgomery.

Shorter forms of traditional verbal folklore collected in the Blue Ridge are featured in Newman Ivey White, general editor, *The Frank C. Brown Collection of North Carolina Folklore* (Durham: Duke University Press, 1962), volume 1 (that volume also features North Carolina tales, legends, and games). The quoted proverb is in volume 1 of the *Brown Collection*, 334; also in that same volume are the two quoted riddles, 294 and 299, and the rhyme, 145.

The regional penchant for spinning stories, particularly among aged people, is explored in Patrick B. Mullen, *Listening to Old Voices: Folklore, Life Stories, and the Elderly* (Urbana: University of Illinois Press, 1992). The definitive collection of translated Cherokee myths is James Mooney, *Myths of the Cherokee and Sacred Formulas of the Cherokees* (Cherokee, N. C.: Cherokee Heritage Books, [1900] 1982). Of related interest is Mary Regina Ulmer Galloway, editor, *Aunt Mary, Tell Me a Story: A Collection of Cherokee Legends and Tales as Told by Mary Ulmer Chiltoskey* (Cherokee, N. C.: Cherokee Communications, 1990). Two collections of non-Native American legendary folktales are David Clark, editor, *Blue Ridge Facts and Legends* (Charlotte, N. C.: Clark Publications, 1955), and John Alexander Mull, *Mountain Yarns, Legends, and Lore* (Banner Elk, N. C.: Puddingstone Press, circa 1970s). Numerous Daniel Boone legends (some of which stem from the Blue Ridge) are in John Mack Faragher, *Daniel Boone: The Life and Legend of an American Pioneer* (New York: Henry Holt and Co., 1992). Information on regional stories of the supernatural can be found in Eliot Wigginton, editor, *Foxfire 2* (Garden City, N. Y.: Anchor Press, 1973), 324–61, and in Eliot Wigginton and Margie Bennett, editors, *Foxfire 9* (Garden City, N. Y.: Anchor Press, 1986), 370–90. Appalachian humorous folktales and jokes (some of which were collected in the Blue Ridge) are in two books by Loyal Jones and Billy Edd Wheeler, *Laughter in Appalachia: A Festival of Southern Mountain Humor* (Little Rock: August House, Inc., 1987) and *Curing the Cross-eyed Mule: Appalachian Mountain Humor* (Little Rock: August House, Inc., 1989). The "Preacher and the Bear Tale" as told by Stanley Hicks is from *Stanley Hicks Live* (Dallas: Moonshine Records, 1983). Donald Davis's description of his family's fondness for storytelling is from Radio Smithsonian Cassette #993, the 100 Years of Folklife Series (Washington, D. C.: Smithsonian Institution, n. d.). A history of the Hicks family and the Jack tales is in Robert Isbell, *The Last Chivaree: The Hicks*

Family of Beech Mountain (Chapel Hill: University of North Carolina Press, 1996). Richard Chase's compilations of Blue Ridge tales include *The Jack Tales* (Boston: Houghton Mifflin Co., 1943), *The Grandfather Tales* (Boston: Houghton Mifflin Co., 1948), and *American Folk Tales and Songs, and Other Examples of English-American Tradition as Preserved in the Appalachian Mountains and Elsewhere in the United States* (New York: Dover Publications, [1956] 1971). One recent scholarly study of the Jack tale tradition is Joseph Daniel Sobol, "Jack of a Thousand Faces: The Jack Tales as Appalachian Hero Cycle," in *North Carolina Folklore Journal* 39, no. 2 (summer–fall 1992): 77–108.

Several Blue Ridge musicians are featured in the video *Appalachian Journey*, Alan Lomax, producer (American Patchwork Series, Public Broadcasting Service Home Video, 1990). Information on folksinger Frank Proffitt and the ballad "Tom Dula"/"Tom Dooley" is in Sandy Paton, lyric brochure for *Frank Proffitt of Reese, North Carolina* (Sharon, Conn.: Folk-Legacy Records, 1962); Anne Warner, *Traditional American Folk Songs from the Anne and Frank Warner Collection* (Syracuse: Syracuse University Press, 1984); and Newman Ivey White, general editor, *The Frank C. Brown Collection of North Carolina Folklore* (Durham: Duke University Press, 1962), volume 2, 703–14. The Frank Warner/Alan Lomax version of "Tom Dula"— essentially the "Tom Dooley" of Kingston Trio fame—appears in John A. and Alan Lomax, *Folksong, U.S.A.* (New York: Duell, Sloan and Pearce, 1947).

Blue Ridge folk songs are featured in W. K. McNeil, *Southern Folk Ballads, Volume One* (Little Rock: August House, Inc., 1987); W. K. McNeil, *Southern Mountain Folk Songs* (Little Rock: August House, Inc., 1993); and Herbert Shellans, *Folk Songs of the Blue Ridge Mountains* (New York: Oak Press, 1968). One recording which specifically focusses on traditional Blue Ridge music is *Ballads and Songs of the Blue Ridge Mountains: Persistence and Change* (New York: Asch Recordings, 1968). An excellent study of religious music traditions in one Virginia Blue Ridge community is Jeff Todd Titon, *Powerhouse for God: Speech, Chant, and Song in an Appalachian Baptist Church* (Austin: University of Texas Press, 1988). Of related interest is the recording/booklet set entitled *Children of the Heav'nly King: Religious Expression in the Central Blue Ridge*, Charles K. Wolfe, editor (Washington, D.C.: Library of Congress, American Folklife Center, 1980).

The transference of the banjo from its origins among slaves in the lowland South to its favored status among Anglo-American musicians in the Blue Ridge (and other areas in the southern mountains) is discussed in Cecilia Conway, *African Banjo Echoes in Appalachia: A Study of Folk Traditions* (Knoxville: University of Tennessee Press, 1995). Singer, song collector, and music promoter Bascom Lamar Lunsford is the subject of a full-length biography by Loyal Jones, *Minstrel of the Appalachians: The Story of Bascom Lamar Lunsford* (Boone, N. C.: Appalachian Consortium Press, 1984), and a documentary film, *The Ballad of a Mountain Man: The Story of Bascom Lamar Lunsford*, David Hoffman, director (the American Experience Series, Public Broadcasting Service Video, 1989).

The quoted lyrics of the traditional ballad "As I went over London's bridge . . ." (version B of "Geordie") is from Cecil J. Sharp and Maud Karpeles, *English Folk Songs from the Southern Appalachians*, volume 1, 2d., enlarged ed. (London: Oxford University Press, 1932), 241. Volume 1 of this edition features ballads, while volume 2 includes songs, a few hymns, and nursery songs and frolics. Sharp's "Introduction to the First Edition, 1917," incorporated into the second edition, presents his expression of the significance of his and Karpeles's collecting trips to the southern mountains. In the order of their appearance, the first, fifth, and eighth quotations attributed directly to Sharp come from this "Introduction" (on pages xxv, xxiii, and xxv); the second quotation attributed directly to Sharp is from David E. Whisnant, *All That Is Native & Fine: The Politics of Culture in an American Region* (Chapel Hill: University of North Carolina Press, 1983), 113; the third, fourth, sixth, seventh, ninth, tenth, and eleventh quotations attributed directly to Sharp are in Maud Karpeles, *Cecil Sharp: His Life and Work* (Chicago: University of Chicago Press, 1967), on pages 144–45, 147, 145, 150, 145, 145, and 145–46. The Olive Dame Campbell quotation is in Whisnant, 113; the five quotations attributed to Maud Karpeles appear in her book (144, 144, 145, 147, and 169–70); while the quotation from the unidentified woman who liked Sharp's conversation is also in Karpeles, 149. The two comments by David Whisnant appear in Whisnant, 119 and 124, as does the assertion from Bertrand Bronson (124). The quotations from Jim Trantham are taken from my interview with Trantham, which was conducted in Canton, North Carolina, in June 1990.

The commentary by Ralph Peer appears in Charles Wolfe, brochure for *The Bristol Sessions* (Nashville: Country Music Foundation Records, 1991), 2. A comprehensive introduction to the historical background and the various subgenres of country music (including a chapter on bluegrass) is in Bill C. Malone, *Country Music, U.S.A.*, rev. ed. (Austin: University of Texas Press, 1985). One study devoted entirely to bluegrass is Neil V. Rosenberg, *Bluegrass: A History* (Urbana: University of Illinois Press, 1985). Richard K. Spottswood's observation that the first outdoor bluegrass festival was staged by Bill Clifton in the Blue Ridge appeared in *Bluegrass Unlimited* 31, no.1 (July 1996): 9.

Etta Baker's guitar playing can be heard on *One-Dime Blues* (Cambridge, Mass.: Rounder Records, 1991); *Music from the Hills of Caldwell County* ([place of origin unknown]: Physical Records, 1975); *Instrumental Music of the Southern Appalachians* (Tradition Records, circa late 1950s); and *The Fingerpicking Blues of Etta Baker* (Woodstock, N. Y.: Homespun Video, 1996).

Michael Kline's article about Walker Calhoun appeared in *The Old-Time Herald*, Aug.–Oct. 1990, 24–28. The full title of Calhoun's award-winning cassette is *Where the Ravens Roost: Cherokee Traditional Songs of Walker Calhoun*; copies may be ordered from the Mountain Heritage Center, Western Carolina University, Cullowhee, NC 28723.

Chapter Four

Information on religious life within the Blue Ridge region can be found in Paul F. Gillespie, editor, *Foxfire 7* (Garden City, N. Y.: Anchor Press, 1982); James L. Peacock and Ruel W. Tyson, Jr., *Pilgrims of Paradox: Calvinism and Experience among the Primitive Baptists of the Blue Ridge* (Washington, D. C.: Smithsonian Institution Press, 1989); Richard C. Davids, *The Man Who Moved a Mountain* (Philadelphia: Fortress Press, 1970); and W. D. Weatherford and Earl D. C. Brewer, *Life and Religion in Southern Appalachia* (New York: Friendship Press, 1962). Footwashing is addressed in Deborah Vansau McCauley, *Appalachian Mountain Religion: A History* (Urbana: University of Illinois Press, 1995), 87 and 223–24, while full-immersion baptism is discussed in Howard Dorgan, "Liquid Graves and Dripping Saints," *Now & Then: The Appalachian Magazine* 11, no. 3 (fall 1994): 10–12. The rituals associated with Southern Appalachian Pentecostal-Holiness sects are discussed in Thomas Burton, *Serpent-Handling Believers* (Knoxville: University of Tennessee Press, 1993). All scriptural quotations are from the Authorized King James Version of the Bible (Cleveland: World Publishing Company, 1913).

Many Blue Ridge folk beliefs (referred to as "superstitions") are included in Newman Ivey White, general editor, *The Frank C. Brown Collection of North Carolina Folklore* (Durham: Duke University Press, 1962), volumes 6 and 7. The quoted beliefs, all collected in the region, were listed in volume 6 of *Brown* (in order of appearance, on 10, 107, 348, 308, 614, 411, 442, 652, 516, and 604). These, of course, are only a handful of the countless folk beliefs which have circulated in the Blue Ridge; they were chosen simply because they are characteristic of the general types of beliefs found in the region.

Information on planting by the signs is in Eliot Wigginton, editor, *The Foxfire Book* (Garden City, N. Y.: Anchor Press, 1972), 212–27. Faith healing is also covered in *The Foxfire Book*, 346–68. Folk beliefs regarding bees and human births are mentioned in Eliot Wigginton, editor, *Foxfire 2* (Garden City, N. Y.: Anchor Press, 1973), 293. Also in *Foxfire 2*, 274–303, is information on midwifery. Regional home remedies employing medicinal plants and various other ingredients are in *The Foxfire Book*, 230–48; in Eliot Wigginton and Margie Bennett, editors, *Foxfire 9* (New York: Anchor Press, 1986), 12–82; and in Ferne Shelton, *Pioneer Comforts and Kitchen Remedies: Old-timey Highland Secrets from the Blue Ridge and Great Smoky Mountains* (High Point, N. C.: Hutcraft Publications, 1965).

Courtship and marriage in the Blue Ridge are discussed in Muriel Earley Sheppard, *Cabins in the Laurel* (Chapel Hill: University of North Carolina Press, [1935] 1991), chapters 11 and 12. Regional burial customs are explained in James K. Crissman, "Body Snatchers, Predators, and Premature Burials: Intriguing Facts about Mountain Wakes," *Now & Then: The Appalachian Magazine* 11, no. 3 (fall 1994): 14–15; in Crissman, *Death and Dying in Central Appalachia: Changing Attitudes and Practices* (Urbana: University of Illinois Press, 1994); and in *Foxfire 2*, 304–23.

The history of Decoration Day/Memorial Day in the Blue Ridge is addressed in Crissman, *Death and Dying in Central Appalachia*, 151–55. Traditional regional observations of Easter and Christmas are sketched in Linda Garland Page and Hilton Smith, editors, *The Foxfire Book of Appalachian Toys & Games* (Chapel Hill: University of North Carolina Press, 1993), 65–67. That book also describes some ceremonial activities associated with the harvest season, 67–70. More information on regional harvest-time activities can be found in a chapter entitled "Corn Shuckin's, House Raisin's, Quiltin's, Pea Thrashin's, Singin's, Log Rollin's, Candy Pullin's, and . . ." in *Foxfire 2*, 362–77.

The list of regional festivals and celebratory events is only a sampling—there are many others. An attempt has been made to mention the best known and the most representative. My information stems from telephone conversations with associates of sponsoring organizations and local chambers of commerce, from brochures produced by festival sponsors and by local and state tourism offices, and from magazine and newspaper articles. Given the possibility of scheduling changes and budget crises, persons wishing to visit a listed festival or celebratory event are strongly advised to consult organizers/sponsors for its current status.

Much of my information regarding traditional Blue Ridge dances came from the documentary film *Ballad of a Mountain Man: The Story of Bascom Lamar Lunsford*, David Hoffman, director (the American Experience Series, Public Broadcasting Service Video, 1989); Jane A. Harris, et al., *Dance a While*, 5th ed. (Minneapolis, Minn.: Burgess Publishing Co., 1978); Betty Casey, *International Folk Dancing U.S.A.* (Garden City, N. Y.: Doubleday & Co., 1981), 304–6; Benjamin Albert Botkin, *The American Play-Party Song* (New York: Frederick Ungar Publishing Co., 1963): and a brochure entitled "Folk Music in the Roosevelt White House: An Evening of Song, Recollections and Dance" (n. p.: 1982).

My primary source regarding Blue Ridge games was the aforementioned *Foxfire Book of Appalachian Toys & Games.* Volume 1 of *The Frank C. Brown Collection of North Carolina Folklore* also contains descriptions of regional games, as does Eliot Wigginton, editor, *Foxfire 6* (Garden City, N. Y.: Anchor Press, 1980), 140–310. The section about Cherokee stickball incorporates observations and quotations recorded by the author at an October 1988 exhibition stickball game which coincided with that year's Cherokee Fall Festival (held annually in Cherokee, North Carolina). The quotation from John R. Finger appears in *Cherokee Americans: The Eastern Band of the Cherokees in the Twentieth Century* (Lincoln: University of Nebraska Press, 1991), 58. Background information on the game was obtained from Charles Lanman, "Indian Ball 1848 Version," *The State* 22 (1955): 16, 36; James Mooney, "The Cherokee Ball Play," *The American Anthropologist* [Old Series] 3 (1890): 104–32; John Gulick, *Cherokees at the Crossroads*, rev. ed. (Chapel Hill: University of North Carolina Press, 1973); and from the author's interview with Cherokee historian Mary Ulmer Chiltosky in October 1988. "The Ball Game of the Birds and Animals" is included in James Mooney, *Myths of the Cherokee and Sacred Formulas of the Cherokees* (Cherokee: Cherokee Heritage Books, [1900] 1982).

Chapter Five

The quotation from Henry Glassie is taken from *Pattern in the Material Folk Culture of the Eastern United States* (Philadelphia: University of Pennsylvania Press, 1968), 17–19.

The woodworking techniques of the Blue Ridge are elucidated in Eliot Wigginton, editor, *The Foxfire Book* (Garden City, N. Y.: Anchor Press, 1972), 31–37 ("Wood") and 38–52 ("Tools and Skills"). Information about regional log structures—cabins, frame houses, barns, and outbuildings—can be found in Henry Glassie's "The Types of the Southern Mountain Cabin," in Jan Harold Brunvand, *The Study of American Folklore*, 3rd. ed. (New York: W. W. Norton & Co., 1986), 529–62; Terry G. Jordan, *American Log Buildings: An Old World Heritage* (Chapel Hill: University of North Carolina Press, 1985); and C. A. Weslager, *The Log Cabin in America: From Pioneer Days to the Present* (New Brunswick, N. J.: Rutgers University Press, 1969). The quotation from Jordan is on 14. A section on log cabin construction (including information on building chimneys) is in *The Foxfire Book*, 53–114, with a follow-up report in Eliot Wigginton and Margie Bennett, editors, *Foxfire 9* (Garden City, N. Y.: Anchor Press, 1986), 391–437. A chapter on smokehouses appears in Eliot Wigginton, editor, *Foxfire 3* (Garden City, N. Y.: Anchor Press, 1975), 354–60.

Information on tub wheel mills is in Eliot Wigginton, editor, *Foxfire 2* (Garden City, N. Y.: Anchor Press, 1973), 142–63, while traditional water-powered sawmills are discussed in Eliot Wigginton, editor, *Foxfire 6* (Garden City, N. Y.: Anchor Press, 1980), 321–96. Traditional (tub wheel and waterwheel) and modern (turbine) waterpower systems are compared in Norman Mack, editor, *Back to Basics: How to Learn and Enjoy Traditional American Skills* (Pleasantville, N. Y.: Reader's Digest Association, 1981), 94–95.

Information on traditional fence designs is in William G. Lord, *Blue Ridge Parkway Guide: Roanoke to Grandfather Mountain* ([Asheville, N. C.]: Eastern Acorn Press, 1982), no pagination, and in Will Orr, "Traditional Farm Fences: A Cherished Symbol in the Parkway Scene," *Parkway Milepost* (fall–winter 1996–97): 7. Wagon making is explored in *Foxfire 2*, 118–41, and in *Foxfire 9*, 267–320.

Regional furniture traditions are treated in Allen H. Eaton, *Handicrafts of the Southern Highlands* (New York: Dover Publications, [1937] 1973); *The Foxfire Book*, 128–38; and George P. Reynolds, editor, *Foxfire 10* (New York: Anchor Books, 1993), 377–93. The anecdote about Jim Gosnell is from Eaton, 156. Eaton also offers information on various smaller utilitarian objects made out of wood, 163–65, and on whittling, 179–83.

Descriptions of fiddle making can be found in Eliot Wigginton, editor, *Foxfire 4* (Garden City, N. Y.: Anchor Press, 1977), 106–25, while information on the making of mountain dulcimers is in *Foxfire 3*, 185–207. Banjo making is also addressed in the latter volume, 120–85, and in *Foxfire 6*, 54–83. Kyle Creed's Formica-fingerboard banjo is mentioned in Cecilia Conway, *African Banjo Echoes in Appalachia: A Study of Folk Traditions* (Knoxville: University of Tennessee Press, 1995), 185.

The folk toys of the Blue Ridge are discussed in Linda Garland Page and Hilton Smith, editors, *The Foxfire Book of Appalachian Toys & Games* (Chapel Hill: University of North Carolina Press, 1993), and in *Foxfire 6*, 140–310. The latter book devotes a separate section, 84–92, to songbows.

Shoemaking is addressed in *Foxfire 6*, 109–39, and hide tanning in *Foxfire 3*, 55–78. The process of producing cloth—from raising sheep to spinning and weaving with wool—is explained in *Foxfire 2*, 172-255; that same volume includes a description of hand washing clothes in iron pots, 256–65. Information about quilting can be found in *The Foxfire Book*, 142–50, and in *Foxfire 9*, 207–37. The assertion that the Blue Ridge was historically not fertile ground for pottery making comes from John A. Burrison's preface to a long section exploring pottery traditions throughout the South, in

Eliot Wigginton and Margie Bennett, editors, *Foxfire 8* (New York: Anchor Books, 1984), 71–80.

The quotation from the mission statement of Penland Weavers and Potters is from the aforementioned *Handicrafts of the Southern Highlands*, 80. That book, a classic study of Southern Appalachian craft traditions, discusses various efforts to market traditional material objects for economic and social empowerment.

Blue Ridge foodways are surveyed in Linda Garland Page and Eliot Wigginton, editors, *The Foxfire Book of Appalachian Cookery* (Chapel Hill: University of North Carolina Press, 1992). In addition to featuring invaluable information on beverages, dairy products, domesticated animal and wild game preparation, condiments, vegetable dishes, breadstuffs, desserts, and typical menus in the region, that book prints many favored recipes collected from Blue Ridge cooks. Fireplaces, fireplace utensils, stoves, and pots and pans are also discussed in *The Foxfire Book of Appalachian Cookery*, chapter 1.

Traditional knowledge about gardening is featured in *Foxfire 4*, 150–93. Information about springtime edible wild plants is presented in *Foxfire 2*, 47–94, while *Foxfire 3* includes information about wild plants traditionally eaten in the summer and fall (274–353).

The Foxfire Book contains material on the hunting of various wild animals, 249–63, and on the preparation of wild game, 264–73, in the Blue Ridge. Material on regional bear hunting (including information about bear pens and hunting dogs) is featured in Eliot Wigginton, editor, *Foxfire 5* (Garden City, N. Y.: Anchor Press, 1979), 437–94. Preparing domesticated hogs for the dinner table is discussed in *The Foxfire Book*, 189–207, while *Foxfire 3* offers regional perspectives on the raising of cattle, 79–94, and on the stewardship of various domesticated animals, 95–119. Cheese making is addressed in *Foxfire 4*, 385–93.

The process of making molasses out of sorghum cane is described in *Foxfire 3*, 424–36, and information on regional approaches to beekeeping is in *Foxfire 2*, 28–46.

The history of moonshining and the building of stills are examined in *The Foxfire Book*, 301–45; *Foxfire 4*, 471–77; Joseph Earl Dabney, *Mountain Spirits* (Asheville, N. C.: Bright Mountain Books, 1974); and Wilbur R. Miller, *Revenuers & Moonshiners: Enforcing Federal Liquor Law in the Mountain South, 1865–1900* (Chapel Hill: University of North Carolina Press, 1991).

Blue Ridge foxhunting traditions are explained in the aforementioned *Blue Ridge Parkway Guide* (no pagination). Flintlock longrifles—their history, technological design, and modern revival—are discussed in depth in

Foxfire 5, 208–436. Of related interest in that same volume is a section on ironmaking and blacksmithing, 77–207.

Two museums dedicated to showcasing Appalachian material culture traditions are the Museum of Appalachia in Norris, Tennessee, and the Museum of American Frontier Culture, located in the Blue Ridge near Staunton, Virginia. In an effort to represent the folklife of the three European groups most prevalent in settling the Blue Ridge/Appalachian/American frontier, the Museum of American Frontier Culture features three reconstructed European farmsteads—one German, one English, and one Irish. This museum also maintains a model Shenandoah Valley farmstead to illustrate the fact that the region's early settlers forged a folklife suitable for the frontier by borrowing usable folkways from several different cultural traditions.